Striking Beauties

Striking Beauties

WOMEN APPAREL WORKERS IN THE U.S. SOUTH, 1930–2000

MICHELLE HABERLAND

THE UNIVERSITY OF GEORGIA PRESS   ATHENS AND LONDON

© 2015 by the University of Georgia Press
Athens, Georgia 30602
www.ugapress.org
All rights reserved
Designed and set in 10.5/13.5 Kepler Std Regular
by Kaelin Chappell Broaddus
Printed and bound by Thomson-Shore, Inc.
The paper in this book meets the guidelines for
permanence and durability of the Committee on
Production Guidelines for Book Longevity of
the Council on Library Resources.

Most University of Georgia Press titles are
available from popular e-book vendors.

Printed in the United States of America
15 16 17 18 19 P 5 4 3 2 1

Library of Congress Control Number: 2014956536

ISBN 978-0-8203-2584-2 hardcover
ISBN 978-0-8203-4742-4 paperback
ISBN 978-0-8203-4754-7 e-book

British Library Cataloging-in-Publication Data available

Contents

Illustrations

TABLES

Acknowledgments

A project that takes as long as this one to complete results in a long list of acknowledgments. It is my particular pleasure, after all these years, to finally have an opportunity to thank all of those who supported me on the long journey to this point.

The Graduate School Fellowship at Tulane University provided me with five years of funding that helped me to research and write the dissertation on which this book is based. In addition, a Women's Studies Grant from the Newcomb Center for Research on Women provided financing for an additional research trip.

Clarence Mohr, my advisor at Tulane University, guided me and the project from the very beginning. His vision for this book and his unparalleled knowledge of southern history inspired me to recognize the importance of the apparel industry to the field of southern history. Moreover, he never lost faith in me, or the project, even when I moved several states away.

Without the mentorship and advice of Robert Zieger, I would surely never have completed this project. Many years ago, Bob inspired me to think of workers in new ways, and in many ways his own work is reflected in the pages that follow. Bob taught me the meaning of the role of mentor in every way. I treasure his counsel and guidance, even more now that he has gone.

Without the kind and helpful folks at the Southern Labor Archives I would undoubtedly have floundered among stacks of boxes. Archivists Annie Tilden, Bob Dinwiddie, Julia Young, and Traci JoLeigh Drummond were especially helpful, as they drew my attention to relevant collections and shared their extensive knowledge of southern labor history. I have begun the process of sending the recordings of the oral histories I conducted to the Southern Labor Archives, for I can imagine no better place to safeguard and respect these accounts of the lives of southern workers.

Emily Clark and Jeffrey Turner deserve a special mention, for it was in our classes at Tulane that this project was first conceived. I will always treasure their good humor and the lasting friendships that developed out of our shared passion for southern history. They are the truest of colleagues.

Since my arrival at Georgia Southern University, I have been fortunate to join a group of colleagues who helped me to persevere and see this project to its conclusion. From the moment I stepped on campus, Annette Laing, Sandy Peacock, and Cathy Skidmore-Hess demonstrated an interest in this project and offered support in a myriad of ways, from reading drafts to invitations to tea at just the right moment. I thank them for making me feel so welcome in the community of scholars and bright minds that they have created down here in southeast Georgia. Special thanks to my dear friends and colleagues Laura Shelton and Jon Bryant for reading drafts and patiently enduring yet another discussion about garment workers. But mostly I want to thank them for helping me to realize that compassion is the historian's strongest analytical tool.

At different stages, this book has benefited from careful critiques by Bruce Clayton, Janet Davidson, Mary Frederickson, Kenneth Fones-Wolf, Rebecca Sharpless, John Salmond, Melissa Walker, Jonathan Daniel Wells, Sheila R. Phipps, and an anonymous reader for the University of Georgia Press. Their comments strengthened the manuscript tremendously and I am especially grateful for their insights.

My friendships outside of academe provided me with necessary diversions, reminding me that life continued outside of libraries and apparel factories. The evening assemblages of friends at neighborhood dog parks in New Orleans and Atlanta were particularly welcome respites from the academic world. Andrea Goetze Wilkes is one of those people you come across only rarely in a single lifetime. An attorney for the National Labor Relations Board, Andrea has reminded me of the real-life struggles of workers today and, in so doing, has made the story of the workers in these pages all the more meaningful and compelling. Chris and Jennifer Higgins and Lori Blank and Eric Braun learned long ago to stop asking me about the-project-that-cannot-be-named. Instead, they offered patient support and wonderful distractions in long talks about the South, politics, and the joys and trials of parenting. The friends we've embraced along the way have enriched this project by making it seem so relevant, while at the same time providing a space away from it.

As I traveled through Alabama, it was my great fortune to meet Paula McLendon. Her commitment to social justice for workers rivals that of anyone I have ever met. Paula introduced me to a diverse network of clothing workers in Alabama and provided the necessary contacts for the oral histories that are the backbone of this project. Many thanks are owed to Bobbie and Bill Malone, for they introduced me to Gussie Woodest and thus the first oral history of this project was born. A special word of appreciation is owed to all of the apparel workers and unionists whom I interviewed over the years. Together they helped this historian understand not only the nature of work and life in a southern apparel town but also the true dimensions of southern hospitality.

And finally, I thank my family for being so supportive of my academic and professional pursuits. My father, mother, and sister knew, probably long before I did, that eventually I would finish this book. My sister and mother spent many long hours encouraging me to forge ahead and for that and so many other things, I will be forever grateful. My father has always been a passionate teacher and an academic at heart. He knows, better than anyone, that without his inspiration I would never have attempted a life in academe.

There are no words to adequately express my gratitude for Glen Hamilton. He wisely refrained from reading drafts of the book, despite my repeated requests, but his keen mind and clever wit are evidenced on virtually every page.

Finally, I dedicate this book to my daughter, Norah Maureen Hamilton, in the hopes that she will come to understand that *"all labor has dignity."*

Introduction

THE PLACE OF APPAREL IN THE HISTORY
OF SOUTHERN INDUSTRIALIZATION

Facing Weak Sales, Levi Strauss Plans Factory Shutdowns.

Small Town, Hard Times: Overseas Competition
Shutting Linden's 40-Year-Old Factory.

Van Heusen Closing Three Alabama Plants; 1,050 Will Lose Jobs.

A Bleak Future: Thousands of Alabamians Have Lost
Their Jobs as Apparel Plants Have Closed.

Textiles Head South; Imports Unravel Apparel Industry.

The headlines are old news now.[1] All across rural America, manufacturing interests have closed their doors forever, making ghost towns of the
communities that thrived there. The once-bustling factories have become
eerily quiet plants, marked by empty parking lots with For Sale signs in the
front. Beginning in the 1970s and gaining steam throughout the 1980s and
1990s, the long, slow decline of manufacturing industries hurt American
workers as they struggled to find jobs in company towns that no longer
had a company. Few got rich from their work in America's manufacturing
industries, but there was a respectable wage to be made in the nation's
automobile, electronics, textile, and apparel factories. Southern communities were hit especially hard by the closings of textile and apparel facto-

ries. In recent years a handful of southern historians have begun to consider this final chapter in the history of southern industrialization, but the majority of this scholarship has focused on the rise and, only occasionally, the fall of the textile industry.

By turning our attention to the apparel industry, this book considers the history of a neglected area of southern industrialization. In 1972 the southern apparel industry employed more than half a million southerners, and eight out of ten of those workers were women. The apparel industry's eventual decline conforms to a familiar pattern of deindustrialization in post–World War II America. Free trade brought an end to manufacturing jobs as corporations sought to increase profits by lowering labor costs and moving operations overseas.

The history of the southern garment industry is best viewed from the shop floor, from the perspective of women workers themselves. The struggles of women workers in the South to provide for their families and to achieve dignity through their work is central to the rise and fall of industry in the South. The title of this volume was inspired by a newspaper clipping in the Amalgamated Clothing Workers of America (ACWA) Red Book, a scrapbook collected by the largest union in the men's clothing industry. In coverage of a 1937 strike in Kentucky, the *Princeton (Ind.) Daily Clarion* featured a photograph of a woman worker styling another woman's hair while on strike at Louisville Textiles, Inc. The caption to the photo read, "Striker Beautifies Striker: Girls will be girls wherever they are and whatever they are doing." This book aspires to tell the stories of these striking beauties of the twentieth-century South, the women who worked on the sewing lines, making clothes and making a living for their families.

Above all else, this book seeks to preserve the voices of the women who sewed clothes and claimed a distinctly feminine space in the history of America's working classes. The Southern Labor Archives at Georgia State University contain a treasure trove of interviews with southern workers and organizers. The staff and archival collections are an invaluable resource for those interested in the lives of southern women workers. It gives me great satisfaction to know that the oral histories I collected for this book will join the Southern Labor Archives' impressive collection. Each woman interviewed for this project expressed disbelief at the idea that someone would be interested in her ordinary life. Yet in their daily struggles to put food on the table and earn a living as sewing machine operators, southern women engaged a much larger, near-constant movement of American workers proving true Martin Luther King's 1968 declaration in support of striking sanitation workers in Memphis that "all labor has dignity." This is a story worth telling and understanding.[2]

Throughout the nineteenth century, whether rich or poor, most women knew how to sew. All of the needlecrafts, including basic sewing and embroidery, were considered essential skills for young women to master. Mothers taught their daughters to sew, as they knew that the girls would someday marry and assume the task of creating basic clothes for themselves and children of their own. Initial attempts to mechanize sewing in the mid-eighteenth century were problematic, and the earliest sewing machines garnered few supporters. Most clothing was homespun, designed and constructed at home. But with the advent of the first satisfactory sewing machine in the 1830s, along with the standardization of measurements and sizes, interest in mechanized sewing grew. By the turn of the twentieth century, the sewing machine was commonplace. In major cities across the country, ready-made clothing became a hallmark of newly opened department stores. Clothing production moved from the home to the sweatshop and eventually to the factory, but throughout this transformation, its dependence on women's labor remained the same. With its traditional and long-standing preference for women workers, the apparel industry has always been among the most feminine of industries. Seamstresses and sewing machine operators became the archetypal feminine industrial laborers of the twentieth century.

The association of women's labor with the manufacturing of clothing was scarcely a twentieth-century development. As far back as the colonial period, women sewed and spun cloth for their families; some contributed significantly to household earnings by selling the products of their domestic labor. It is not surprising, then, that the textile and apparel industries that developed in the centuries that followed would seek to hire women workers.[3] Sewing and spinning were essentially domestic crafts that evolved into women's outside work.[4] The fact that sewing and garment manufacturing came from crafts that symbolized domesticity throughout the eighteenth and nineteenth centuries is not without significance. The industrialization of the South, following patterns of industrialization in earlier decades in the North and West, further extended these once-domestic crafts onto the shop floor. As the industrial revolution transformed spinning and sewing from domestic tasks into factory work, the processes became known as textile and apparel manufacturing. Of the two related

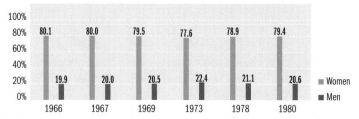

FIGURE 1. Employment in the U.S. apparel industry by sex, 1966–80.
U.S. Equal Employment Opportunity Commission, *Equal Employment
Opportunity Report: Job Patterns for Minorities and Women in Private Industry,*
1966–80.

industries, apparel manufacturing hired a larger percentage of women
workers. Throughout most of the post–World War II era, women made up
approximately 80 percent of the workers in the American apparel industry,
while the textile industry consistently employed more men than women
workers. Moreover, from 1960 to 1990 the apparel industry employed
nearly twice as many women as the textile industry did.[5] Clothing workers
were women workers, building on a long-standing traditional reliance on
women's skilled labor for clothing construction.

From the very beginning, notoriously low wages were an essential feature of the apparel industry. Perhaps because of its origins as a nonwaged
domestic craft, sewing was always a poorly paid occupation. As Mary Anderson, director of the U.S. Department of Labor's Women's Bureau, argued in a 1931 report, low wages in the textile industry were the "direct result of the low money value usually attached to the services of the woman
in the home."[6] In addition, the structure of the apparel industry facilitated
a perpetual search for the lowest possible wage. Speaking about the apparel industry in 2005, the executive director of the National Labor Committee in New York, Charles Kernaghan, remarked, "It's a race to the bottom. The idea is to find those workers who will accept the lowest wages,
the fewest benefits and the most miserable working conditions."[7] His ob-
servation would have been just as true a century earlier.

Unlike many industries, most notably the textile industry, the apparel
industry developed with decentralized production. Subject as the industry was to the variances of fashion and seasonal demand, the production
of one particular garment or style often occurred in many places, with different aspects of production contracted out to the least expensive shops.

Apparel firms would design the garment and then sign contracts with different subcontractors to assemble and sew the garments. These independent subcontractors competed fiercely with each other, as they were dependent on the firms they contracted with for their very survival. The pressure for production led to terrible working conditions in these subcontractors' shops, or as they were more aptly known, sweatshops. The complicated, decentralized structure of clothing production has largely endured to this day, even in the face of globalization.

The structure of the garment industry and its reliance on low wages facilitated its eventual movement to the South. Northern apparel companies were accustomed to contracting work out; it was an essential part of their business model. As the possibilities presented by advances in transportation became clearer in the first two decades of the twentieth century, apparel firms looked to the South. At first they looked to the immediate south, relocating to places like Reading, Pennsylvania, Baltimore, Maryland, and Cleveland, Ohio. But as the unions followed, wages increased and firms began to look even farther south. The gradual relocation of apparel producers to the South took place over an extended period. In 1920 approximately 9.5 percent of women workers in the South worked in the clothing industry. That figure lagged the national average of 10.7 percent.[8] In their perpetual search for lower wages, apparel firms found southern workers in Tennessee, Alabama, Georgia, and the Carolinas willing to work for lower wages than their northern counterparts. When boosters and politicians from the South promised a favorable business climate free from the hassles implied by organized labor, they garnered substantial interest from northern clothing companies. Promises of a desperate and pliant workforce sealed the deals.

Small towns and rural counties across the South engaged in their own regional race to the bottom as they competed with one another to lure companies with promises of new factories built to the companies' specifications. The new factories were most often paid for by local communities, typically through the issuance of municipal bonds. In 1955 industry newspapers reported that over the course of just three years, more than eight rural communities in Mississippi had won their bids to build factories for garment manufacturers. In each of these cases, local residents raised the money needed to build the factories through bonds.[9]

The apparel industry's proclivity for employing women workers meant that manufacturing in rural southern counties was a significantly femi-

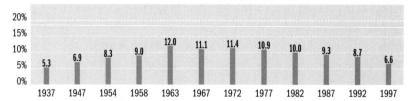

FIGURE 2. Region-wide percentage of manufacturing employment in the southern apparel industry, 1937–97. U.S. Bureau of the Census, *Economic Census of Manufactures*, 1937–97.

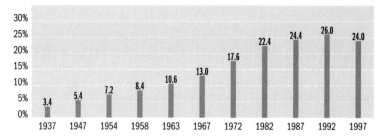

FIGURE 3. Percentage of U.S. apparel establishments located in southern states, 1937–97. U.S. Bureau of the Census, *Economic Census of Manufactures*, 1937–97.

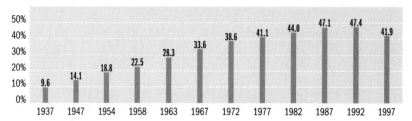

FIGURE 4. Percentage of U.S. apparel industry employees located in southern states, 1937–97. U.S. Bureau of the Census, *Economic Census of Manufactures*, 1937–97.

nine vocation. On the basis of numbers alone, women clothing workers should occupy a central place in the history of southern labor. Even after the number of apparel workers in the nation declined in the 1970s, the industry still accounted for nearly 9 percent of all manufacturing jobs in the South, making it one of the largest manufacturing industries in the region and an important source of women's employment. Since 1950 the number of clothing workers in southern states has exceeded the numbers employed in the traditional clothing-industry centers of New York, New Jersey, and Pennsylvania.[10]

Figures compiled from the *Economic Census of Manufactures* reveal that the number of apparel factories in the South grew steadily throughout most of the twentieth century. In 1937 best estimates indicate that only 3.4 percent of the nation's apparel manufacturing establishments were located in the South.[11] By 1963 that figure had nearly tripled and 10.6 percent of the industry's factories were located in southern states. A few decades later, the South accounted for over a quarter of the nation's apparel factories. Moreover, the factories that situated themselves in the South tended to be larger and hire more employees than those in other regions. As a result, the percentage of the nation's apparel workers located in southern states exceeded the percentage of apparel factories in the South. In 1937, 9.6 percent of the national apparel workforce was composed of southern workers. A quarter century later, as new factories proliferated, the South grew to account for just over 28 percent of the nation's apparel workforce. By 1992, as the impact of free trade reached its height, the figure for apparel workers in the South had nearly doubled, reaching 47.4 percent.[12]

Despite the apparel industry's tremendous economic importance in the region, remarkably little is understood about the industry itself or the southern women, black and white, who labored in garment shops across the South. These stories are important, for they provide a window into the effects of industrial relocation and the development of a working-class identity among southern women. The southern apparel industry reached its peak just as the nation was struggling to define the accomplishments of the civil rights movement. Many histories of this period focus on the contours and meanings of the civil rights movement, leaving the lived experience of working-class southerners sometimes obscured. But it is at this ground level that the accomplishments of the civil rights movement were challenged and defined. Race-, gender-, and class-based identities intermingled in the sewing rooms of the South. In this way, the apparel industry offers a shop-floor perspective of the larger processes of segregation and desegregation. When protectionist trade barriers were lifted, southern women workers created consumer-oriented strategies to respond to the challenges wrought by free trade and the influx of cheaper, imported clothing. Despite the popularity of Buy American movements in the 1980s and 1990s, clothing factories closed their doors and familiar

American brands like Vanity Fair and Levi's became the property of transnational corporations. Garment workers were left scrambling in the face of an inexorable global shift toward free trade. The factories that had once provided much-needed jobs for women in the rural South shuttered their doors forever.

Scholars interested in the working lives of southerners have written volumes of impressive work on the textile industry. One of the earliest studies, appearing just as the southern industry matured in the 1920s, stressed the importance of the social dynamic of the mill village and suggested that textile workers benefited from the noblesse oblige of mill owners.[13] Subsequent scholars challenged this view of the southern textile industry and emphasized the victimization of rural southerners at the hands of ruthless mill owners. In recent years, historians have perceived textile workers as both the heroes and victims of industrialization, often simultaneously.[14] The themes uncovered by southern labor historians in their examinations of the textile industry resonate loudly throughout the larger field of southern history and, more particularly, in the history of the southern apparel industry. Studies of textile workers and their communities provide especially fertile ground for considering such important historiographical issues as southern exceptionalism. The much-studied northern textile workers and their communities provide a sort of foil for the southern textile experience. Southern labor historians who focused their studies on textile workers also repeatedly found themselves reflecting on the failure of textile labor unions to attract and maintain the loyalty of these industrial laborers.[15] In the process, these historians uncovered a variety of distinct cultures among southern workers who exhibited hostility or suspicion toward efforts at unionization. Recent studies have shown that mill villages were sometimes, ironically, the location of both horrendous exploitation and extraordinarily tight cultural bonds. The culture that textile mill workers hammered out of their miserable surroundings was, in and of itself, an important form of resistance to the domination of mill owners. Historians of the southern textile industry created studies with implications far beyond the scope of the industry itself and its workers. The scholarship on southern textile mill workers has made important contributions to our understanding of race, class, and gender dynamics in the modern South.[16]

Recent scholarship on southern textiles also revealed some of the less appealing aspects of the industry, and perhaps of working-class culture in the South, especially with respect to the bitter racial antagonisms that divided workers throughout much of the twentieth century.[17] Some historians have argued that the failure of organized labor to overcome these racial divisions helps to explain the failure of organized labor among southern workers as a whole. Often placing the Congress of Industrial Organizations' (CIO's) Operation Dixie at the center of their studies, historians have examined the racial exclusivity of the early textile mill labor force, the ambiguous attitude of union officials toward black equality, and the eventual desegregation of the textile industry.[18] The textile industry has thus provided scholars with an important window on the history of southern workers, their responses to organized labor, and their culture. The issues uncovered by the studies of textile workers have important implications for the southern apparel industry as well.

And yet the dominance of the textile industry in southern labor historiography has been a mixed blessing. Placing textile mill labor at the heart of the southern industrial experience has had the effect of obscuring the significance of its related enterprise, the apparel industry.[19] The scholarship on southern textiles has subsumed the story of the southern apparel industry and, by implication, suggested that there was little difference between the two industries. The apparel and textile industries are distinct from one another, however. Furthermore, they are industries with separate pasts. Since the government began accumulating national data on manufacturing, the apparel and textile industries have had different industrial classifications and labor forces. Moreover, until recently, apparel and clothing workers were represented by different labor unions.[20] While the majority of the scholarship on southern textiles restricts discussion to those factories that manufactured cloth, the sublimation of apparel under the label of textiles has occasionally resulted in a misunderstanding of the two distinct southern industries, presenting them as if they were the same.[21] In fact, textile workers and apparel workers have qualitatively distinct sets of skills, and the nature of textile factory work is quite different from the work that occurs in apparel factories. The history of the southern clothing industry and its workers merits individual attention, for it yields its own distinctive story. The histories of the two related southern industries are intertwined, but they are also distinct from one another.

Since the 1940s the apparel industry has been a close rival of the textile industry in the South by a number of measures. In 1947 textile workers outnumbered apparel workers in the region nearly four to one. Over time,

however, the apparel industry's southern employment grew. In the late
1970s the industries employed nearly equal numbers of southerners. By
1982 apparel employment in the South exceeded that of the textile industry.
The apparel industry has always been more labor intensive than the textile
industry because of its relatively low level of mechanization. Over the last
century, the basic process of manufacturing clothes has remained virtually
the same. The image of an individual woman guiding two pieces of cloth
underneath a sewing machine needle is still accurate. The industry continues to have a relatively low level of mechanization and technological innovation, and this serves as a partial explanation for the large numbers of immigrant women within the industry's labor force. In 1975, during an era of
significant technological innovation in other American industries, the *New
York Times* ran an article emphasizing the continuing reliance on human
hands to manufacture clothes. "A robot with the manipulative ability of a
human being is the dream of the apparel engineer," the article explained.
"One day, the dream may be realized, but in the meantime sewing of garments still remains very much as it has been for the last 100 years—a piece
of cloth is laid over another and both are guided by human hands through
a sewing machine."[22] And those human hands have typically belonged to a
woman. Twenty years later, the story was much the same. An economist
from the American Apparel Manufacturers Association explained, "You

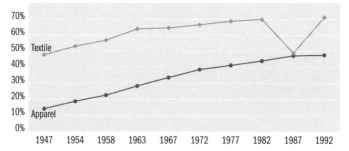

FIGURE 5. Percentage of U.S. apparel and textile employees located in
southern states, 1947–92. The Census Bureau did not report data on the
textile industry for several states in 1987, in accordance with federal law
that prohibits the disclosure of information on individual companies.
The states for which textile employment data was withheld were Florida,
Georgia, Kentucky, Louisiana, Maryland, Mississippi, Texas, Virginia, and
West Virginia. For this reason, the sharp decline in the share of southern
textile workers in 1987 is believed to be inaccurate. U.S. Bureau of the Census,
Economic Census of Manufactures, 1947–92.

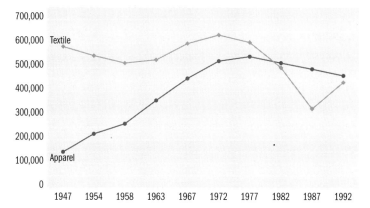

FIGURE 6. Number of southern apparel and textile workers, 1947–92. The Census Bureau did not report data on the textile industry for several states in 1987, in accordance with federal law that prohibits the disclosure of information on individual companies. The states for which textile employment data was withheld were Florida, Georgia, Kentucky, Louisiana, Maryland, Mississippi, Texas, Virginia, and West Virginia. For this reason, the sharp decline in the number of southern textile workers in 1987 is believed to be inaccurate. U.S. Bureau of the Census, *Economic Census of Manufactures*, 1947–92.

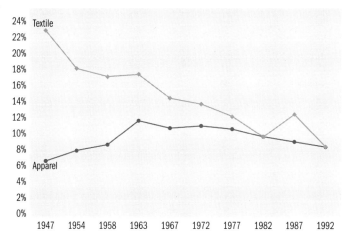

FIGURE 7. Textile and apparel employees as a percentage of all manufacturing employees in the South, 1947–92. U.S. Bureau of the Census, *Economic Census of Manufactures*, 1947–92.

can automate design, you can automate pattern setting and cutting, but sooner or later you have to push fabric through a sewing machine."[23]

On a national level, the number of clothing workers has always exceeded the number of textile workers. In contrast to the apparel industry, the textile industry benefited from a myriad of labor-reducing innovations, and thus the overall number of textile workers declined at a faster rate than that of the apparel industry. In addition, both industries suffered serious declines beginning in the late 1970s, as imported clothing competed with more expensive domestically produced clothing and textiles. In 1992 the textile industry accounted for only 616,400 of the nation's manufacturing workers, while the apparel industry employed 985,000 workers. Restricting the figures to production workers only, the difference between the two industries is still substantial. The apparel industry employed nearly 300,000 production workers, or 35.9 percent more than the textile industry in 1992.[24]

While the textile industry tended to concentrate in the Piedmont South, where it dominated the economies of several Atlantic seaboard states, the apparel industry was more widely dispersed. Textiles may have been the most important industry for states like North Carolina, South Carolina, and Georgia, but in 1977 the apparel industry was the number-one manufacturing employer in Alabama, Mississippi, Tennessee, and Virginia. In Georgia and South Carolina, where textile mills led state manufacturing economies, apparel was the second-largest industrial employer, as it was for the region as a whole.[25] Although textiles certainly dominated much of the South, especially early in the twentieth century, the apparel industry clearly played an important role in the economic and cultural history of the South as well.

By virtue of its size, its reliance on female labor, and its broad geographic scope, the southern apparel industry provides an opportunity to connect the often disparate concerns of southern cultural history, labor history, and women's history. This study examines the essential features of the apparel industry in the South and the varied experiences of clothing workers during the industry's great expansion from the late 1930s until the demise of the southern branch of the industry at the turn of the twenty-first century. Telling the story of the women who operated the sewing machines and gave the clothing industry a southern dimension provides an opportunity to consider the role of organized labor in the South, the changing demographics of the region's industrial workforce, the creation of a southern and feminine work culture, and its impact on race relations and labor relations.

The history of the southern apparel industry also illuminates the larger trajectory of industrialization across the region and throughout the twentieth century. For all of the southern apparel industry's distinctive qualities, its origins are closely related to those of the textile sector. Although there is little evidence that clothing factories were drawn to the South solely because of the presence of textile mills, the ability of textile mills to hire poor white southerners at wages far below those found in the North served as an advertisement of sorts for the related apparel industry.[26]

Southern historians have long been fascinated with the South's resistance to unionization, and the apparel industry provides ample opportunity for examining antiunion strategies from a new perspective. By the time apparel companies reached significant numbers in the South in the 1930s, southern employers had developed an arsenal of time-tested strategies to defeat organized labor. Historians generally agree that the South resisted unionization because it threatened white supremacy, because collective action ran counter to the fierce individualism of white workers, and because the cotton economy rested on control of low-wage agricultural labor.[27] But the substantially feminine composition of the apparel workforce also shaped employers' responses to unionization efforts. Media, law enforcement, and local government combined forces to defeat organized labor at the shop level, where class, race, and gender identities were intertwined. Employers' antiunion strategies utilized gender- and race-based stereotypes to undermine the solidarity of working-class women in the South.

The apparel unions were key players in the history of organized labor in America. The International Ladies' Garment Workers' Union (ILGWU) gained national standing as a result of its efforts to combat exploitation and the proliferation of sweatshops after the infamous 1911 Triangle Shirtwaist Factory fire that took the lives of 146 young women workers in New York City. The ACWA organized workers in the men's clothing industry and created industry-wide standards of production that shortened the workweek and improved working conditions. Together these two unions were among the most progressive and successful unions in American labor history. The ILGWU and ACWA used their substantial resources and mobilized quickly as the industry headed south. Both unions fought mightily to improve southern workers' wages and working conditions, organizing factories one by one across the region. Both unions supported progressive labor reforms, and southern garment workers benefited from the labor protections of the New Deal era. Reflecting the achievements of the apparel unions in the North, the newer southern factories were generally less like sweatshops and more modern in both industrial structure and architecture. In addition to wage protections, apparel union contracts routinely included an array of improvements over nonunion shops, including better wage structures, paid holidays, grievance procedures, and sometimes an option to purchase health insurance through the union. On other points, the garment unions were less progressive. In their efforts to organize the South, both unions sometimes reinforced gender inequality and accommodated southern patterns of racial segregation. While women outnumbered men in the rank and file of both unions, the leadership positions of the two unions were most often held by men. Very few women rose beyond the position of organizer, and neither union ever achieved a woman president. Unionization offered the best possible structure for achieving solidarity in the southern apparel industry, but the unions themselves suffered from a stubborn patriarchy that proved difficult to dislodge.

The New South that dawned in the decades after Reconstruction saw the development of a class of industrial workers that was larger, more isolated, and less socially assimilable than the small, urban workforces of antebellum days. Although some of the habits of agricultural production continued in the new industries of the South, many were left behind as newly industrialized workers created their own culture.[28] Working women in the New South brought a new set of concerns to the workplace, concerns that addressed their role in southern society as well as concerns of the family. Employers also created a new work culture, defining new work habits, creating mill villages, and forming new, industry-wide regional associations.

Southern women had always been divided according to class and race. But industrialization brought those differences into the foreground, as poor white women came to dominate the textile and garment industries and poor black women were relegated, much as they always had been in the South, to domestic service and agricultural labor. In addition to the often-cited southern advantage of cheap labor, civic boosters frequently advertised the whiteness and nonethnic status of their labor pools.[29] Industrialists recruited white family labor, thereby including women and children in wage labor and shutting out black families from the same opportunities. Occupational segregation by both race and gender, it was thought at the time, would minimize any potential competition for labor with agriculture. Industry in the New South would be white and significantly feminine, while agriculture would remain black.[30]

In the years surrounding World War II, a great number of clothing factories responded to these initiatives by opening all over the South. As they did, they capitulated to the southern system of racial segregation. After the passage of the Civil Rights Act of 1964 the whiteness of occupations within the apparel industry would be successfully challenged, and the racial and ethnic diversity of the industry would increase. With the achievements of the civil rights movement, African American and Latina women workers came to account for a large percentage of what was once a predominantly white industry. As the ethnic and racial diversity of the southern clothing industry increased, organizing efforts were more successful. The influential union label and boycott strategies of the clothing industry provide an important perspective on the place of women workers in southern culture and the labor movement. The role of women as the primary consumers of the family placed them in a critical position to influence the success or failure of boycotts, union label programs, and, ultimately, solidarity. But as the U.S. apparel industry's protracted collapse began in the 1970s, apparel unions chose to rely on "Buy American" boycott campaigns that pitted them against the very workers they had once hoped to organize.

The history of the U.S. apparel industry is a play in three parts, a trilogy of sorts. The first part is the oft-told tale of immigrant women working in close, fetid sweatshops in the Northeast to make fashions that they themselves could never afford to wear. The second part in the series, however, is much less well known and understood. It is a story of local women trying to make their way in an industry that always seemed on the run and in decline but ironically offered them unprecedented economic opportunities. But it is at this local level in the apparel communities of the South that the effects of national and international labor policies were experienced most directly. It is in this context that the history of the southern apparel industry and its workers must be understood. For as geographically isolated as the clothing factories often appeared to be, the truth is that southern women workers were engaged in a constant negotiation with global forces. The final part of the trilogy is still being written, as multinational apparel manufacturers close their doors in the U.S. South and flee to the Global South for its lower wages and minimal industrial regulation.

This study begins with a discussion of the industry's move to the U.S. South. Alabama emerged in the 1980s as the state most heavily dependent on the apparel industry. Within Alabama, Vanity Fair was the state's largest manufacturing employer as early as the 1970s. At its peak, Vanity Fair owned seven factories across the state and employed thousands of women in Alabama. As a company that relocated from the North to the South seeking lower production costs and to avoid unionization, Vanity Fair is emblematic of the larger southern apparel industry. The next chapter examines southern women workers' experiences on the shop floors and strike lines of the apparel industry. Employers joined forces with local police and media to portray women strikers and unionists as a threat to traditional gender roles. The third chapter considers the patterns of occupational segregation by race and gender and argues that both employers and organized labor accommodated these patterns. Chapter 4 examines the role of unions in challenging occupational segregation. The successes of the civil rights movement resulted in significant demographic changes in the southern apparel workforce as African Americans found once-closed doors open to them. Chapter 5 discusses the history of the union label, reflecting its history as a tool of both exclusion and inclusion in the industry. While early label campaigns overlooked women workers' role as consumers, later campaigns reflected the advances of second-wave feminism and featured strong images of women workers. The final chapter examines the southern apparel industry's move to Mexico and considers the role that the garment unions have played in the decline of the U.S. apparel industry.

This is the first book-length study of the middle part of that larger trilogy of the apparel industry. Coming first is difficult, for there are surely many important stones left unturned. What follows is intended as an introduction of voices that need to be included in the history of working-class southerners. The story I have sought to tell focuses on the workers themselves. The histories of fashion and the business of apparel manufacturing are better told elsewhere. My intention is to reveal the lived experiences of the working women of the South who found community and exploitation, livelihoods and hard times inside southern garment factories.

Chapter One

"THERE WASN'T ANY JOBS FOR WOMEN"

THE APPAREL INDUSTRY'S
MOVE TO THE SOUTH

In 1947 Arcola "Cola" McLean went to work for Vanity Fair as a sewing machine operator. She was thirty-nine years old then, born and raised in a small town "off the highway" in rural Alabama. Like many other southern women of her generation and economic situation, McLean achieved only a limited education. Looking back on her life when she was ninety years old, McLean fought back tears as she remembered her biggest sorrow, her inability to have children. With her husband and career long passed, McLean was alone and vulnerable in the last years of her life. Seven decades earlier, as a young woman, she married and worked alongside her husband in the fields. Agriculture was hot and difficult work in southern Alabama, and she hated it. But in 1947, soon after a modern clothing factory opened its doors in nearby Jackson, she saw a new opportunity for her life. The factory was clean and cool and paid wages that could improve her and her husband's standard of living. Surrounded by the desperate poverty of Clarke County, Alabama, she and hundreds of other women saw Vanity Fair as a way to escape the fate of the fields.[1]

Years later, when the International Ladies' Garment Workers' Union distributed leaflets at the factory where McLean worked, she and her fellow women stitchers walked right on by the organizers. Earlier that day, before the sewing room operators finished their shift, the managers at Vanity Fair had called a meeting. The message of that meeting was clear: the company would close its doors before it went union. McLean recalled that the union organizers "tried to get in, but the Vanity Fair people, they told us, they made a speech and they told us that they wouldn't operate under a union. So we all voted against it."[2] In a poor, rural county like Clarke County there were few other occupations. This was especially true for white women, who really had only two options for employment, the fields or Vanity Fair. Besides, everyone understood what the factory had meant to Jackson and the surrounding towns in Clarke County. Some saw the company as a savior of sorts for an area that, at the time, was trapped by its dependence on a dying livelihood.[3] Prices for cotton had hit rock bottom in the latter years of the Great Depression and the market showed no signs of improvement. Even before the Depression hit, cotton's profitability had been declining steadily. In 1923 one pound of cotton yielded a market price of 28.69 cents; in 1931 the price had fallen to 5.66 cents. The average price for the period 1925–29 was just over 9 cents per pound. Some observers noted that cotton yields were so high in 1930 that prices for the South's principal commodity were expected to fall below the cost of production.[4] In Monroe and Clarke Counties families lived for generations in ramshackle structures that had never been painted. There was little electricity or reason for getting it, since few could afford the utility bill that would come with it. As one longtime resident of Jackson put it, "We had nothing."[5]

Vanity Fair, and the money the company brought into the local economy, transformed the poor county into a series of small towns that seemed to have a bright future. But it was a future that depended, almost exclusively, on Vanity Fair. Jackson and Monroeville, the two medium-sized towns in southern Alabama where Vanity Fair opened plants in the late 1930s, were not quite company towns, but they relied heavily on the income brought by Vanity Fair and a few other small clothing manufacturers. There were sawmills and a few public utility projects, but they employed mostly male workers. McLean explained rural women's transition from farm to factory, noting the desirability of jobs at Vanity Fair: "When I first started working there I got fifty cents an hour. But that was good, I just thought that was great because there wasn't any jobs for women. You could farm, but you couldn't make any money. You couldn't sell what you made. Nobody didn't have no money." The desperation in McLean's description echoes the toll the Great Depression and rural poverty took on families in Jackson and elsewhere in the South.

The rise in female employment had a significant impact on the household economies of Jackson and Monroeville. Dot Guy worked at Vanity Fair for more than thirty-seven years. On the occasion of her retirement in 1984, her daughter wrote a poem in her honor.

> The Total Woman is nothing new
>   for 37 years—just look at you
> You brought home the bacon
>   and cut out the fat
> To you Dear Mom
>   we take off our hat
> Your Husband, your children: Betty, Don & Ray
>   are proud of what you've done
>   at Vanity Fair Lingerie
> So Welcome home Mom from Vanity Fair
>   to days of rest with nary a care
> We'll all be happy to have you there
>   and no longer out making
>   Ladies Underwear.[6]

In the sixty years that Vanity Fair operated factories in southern Alabama, tens of thousands of women contributed unprecedented monies to their household budgets, often making them the primary earners for their families.

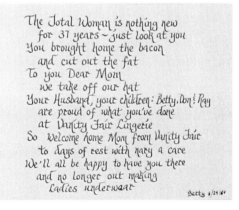

FIGURE 8. Dot Guy shares the framed poem that her daughter wrote for her on the occasion of her retirement from Vanity Fair. Michelle Haberland.

FIGURE 9. A close-up of the poem. Michelle Haberland.

By 1986 Vanity Fair was the largest employer in the state, underscoring the importance of the clothing industry to Alabama's economy.[7] But at the local level, the dominance of the apparel industry was particularly striking. The garment plants in Monroeville and Jackson had a tremendous influence on the economies of Monroe and Clarke Counties, respectively. As recently as 1997, the manufacturing sector of Monroe County included a large textile factory, three apparel factories, a few paper mills, and a handful of wood product manufacturers. The apparel industry was one of the largest manufacturing sectors in Monroe County. In the same year there were fewer occupational options in Clarke County, where Vanity Fair's Jackson plant accounted for a substantial percentage of manufacturing employment. In 1997 only three industrial sectors were represented in Clarke County: apparel, wood products, and paper manufacturing.[8]

The development of the southern apparel industry took place over several decades in the mid-twentieth century. The consolidation of the power of organized labor and rising labor costs pushed garment manufacturers out of their traditional centers in the Northeast. At the same time, southern communities devised strategies to attract the companies to their towns. In the process of moving south, the industry's overall structure and workforce changed substantially. In these ways Vanity Fair's move from Reading, Pennsylvania, to southern Alabama was prototypical and provides an opportunity to understand these changes from a local perspective.

The U.S. apparel industry began in the Northeast more than a century ago. In New York, the first American city with a substantial ready-made clothing industry, the work of producing men's clothing tended to be carried out in many different shops. A single suit could involve the work of tailors, cutters, and seamstresses, most of whom did not labor under the same roof. The women's clothing industry generally relied on more of the processes being completed in one place, but by an ever-changing labor force of recently arrived immigrants.[9] In both the men's and women's clothing industries, sewing was "put out" through a complicated system of jobbers and contractors. Jobbers designed the garment and marketed it to retail outlets, but the majority of production processes, including obtaining the fabric and cutting, sewing, and pressing the garment were completed in independently owned contract shops. Confronted with the tiny profit margins offered by the jobbers, contract shops engaged in cutthroat competition with one another, each seeking to pay the lowest wages possible. Because the profit margins in the apparel industry were so small, even small reductions in labor costs could prove beneficial to a company's bottom line. Today, multinational companies have replaced the jobbers in the search for the lowest production costs, but the basic processes and structures of the industry remain the same.[10]

Beginning in the 1930s and continuing through the 1960s, much of the industry looked to relocate to the South. By the time of World War II the clothing industry employed over 150,000 southerners, totaling 14 percent of the nation's apparel industrial workforce. Like Vanity Fair, many of these southern apparel employers were actually runaways, companies that closed their operations in the Northeast and reopened their factories in the South.[11] A much smaller number of apparel firms were indigenous to the South, some dating from the turn of the century in states like Texas and Louisiana. The movement of apparel companies to the South was part of a larger pattern of industrialization that reached its height in the two decades after World War II. Labor-intensive industries were particularly likely to relocate, as the savings achieved by paying lower wages would have a more significant impact on profit margins. So, along with the apparel firms, labor-intensive manufacturers of textiles, furniture, paper, and electronics moved south in search of greater profits.

In traditional industrial location studies, economic and business historians have typically identified labor and transportation costs as key factors. More recently scholars have contended that manufacturers often moved in search of lower labor costs while also making desired changes to the demographic composition of the workforce. Industrial relocation results in significant and lasting changes in community and labor organization. The workers themselves, at the new locations and the old, were central factors in the decision to move a factory. As workers in older factories gained a greater voice in determining their working conditions, companies looked to communities that promised a malleable labor force. A recent study of the textile industry's move to the South found that workers were most effective in influencing capital mobility and plant relocation when they banded together and worked collectively. Textile managers and company owners shared a widespread understanding of southern workers as "docile," and this figured centrally in decisions to move factories to the South. In an effort to bring jobs to their communities, local boosters often echoed this characterization of southern workers. Economic geographers have contributed much to the debates over the relative importance of human factors in industrial location theory. From their studies a model emerged in which the spatial divisions of labor and management create a geography of uneven development in capitalist economies. The pursuit of the perfect combination of factors is ceaseless and does not result in stability. Instead, industries and factories are continually on the move across a geography of human and spatial factors. Labor is similarly in a constant state of flux, changing and adapting to human and spatial factors. In this way, location has the effect of shaping the relationship between employer and employee.[12]

The movement of the apparel industry to the South was the result of a combination of factors, some of which pushed the industry out of the North and others that pulled the industry to the South. In the years before World War II, wage increases in the Northeast, especially those brought about by union contracts, were cited as a reason to shut down factories and move south.[13] In addition, in order to attract sewing machine operators in tight labor markets in the North, employers were compelled to advertise and offer inducements to prospective applicants. In 1920 Vanity Fair's Reading, Pennsylvania, factory recruited women workers with promises of "congenial work" and solid wages through advertisements in the local newspaper, the *Reading Eagle*. Vanity Fair also enticed potential workers with access to a library, an on-site cafeteria, and medical services.[14] Higher wages and perks such as these ate into the already-slim profit margins of apparel employers. In the years after World War II, garment manufacturers continued to stream out of cities as urban renewal plans reshaped the garment districts of New York, Baltimore, and Chicago. The buildings that once housed contract shops were often torn down to make way for commercial office space or high-rise apartments. The post–World War II demographic shift away from urban centers into suburban areas resulted in a smaller pool of potential employees for the inner-city clothing factories. Increased crime was also cited as a reason for leaving garment districts in the Northeast.[15]

The most significant factor behind a company's decision to leave the Northeast was typically an increased level of solidarity and union militancy among workers in the area. As workers gained greater control through union membership, companies began to seek new locations. In 1921 a wave of strikes hit the apparel industry. More organized than ever before, seventy-five thousand workers in Chicago, Philadelphia, and New

York struck to oppose the demands by several apparel manufacturers' associations that workers accept a return to piecework wages and an extension of the workweek to forty-eight hours.[16] The two primary clothing industrial unions behind this wave of activism were the Amalgamated Clothing Workers of America, which restricted its activities to the menswear industry, and the International Ladies' Garment Workers' Union, which organized workers in women's wear. By the end of the 1920s, the apparel industry was significantly organized.

The clothing unions offered some structure and security to employers in the complicated industry, often operating cooperatively within individual garment shops and moving beyond the usual focus of industrial unions on wages and working conditions. The ILGWU and the ACWA helped define the relationship between contractors and assisted companies in marketing their products. That cooperation led to increased solidarity among workers and some important gains in wages and working conditions.[17] By the 1940s, an observer noted that "a type of co-operation began in which little account was taken of customary lines of demarcation between managerial and union functions." The clothing unions had helped to define the organizational structure of the industry. Through their unions, apparel workers altered the structure of the industry to benefit their situations. That companies would seek to flout that control conforms to the models established by economic geographers in which the pursuit of a perfect combination of factors is unending.[18]

As was the case for most manufacturing industries, the apparel industry suffered terribly during the Great Depression. Vanity Fair reported a record loss of just under $100,000 in 1932 and continued operating losses for most of the 1930s. From the perspective of apparel company executives, President Roosevelt's New Deal emboldened workers with its guaranteed right to organize labor unions. In the apparel center of Reading, workers organized nearly all of the hosiery factories and staged a walkout in 1933. Shortly after the walkout, the owner of Vanity Fair began to look into relocating his factory in the South. As a result of these kinds of factors, the overall level of industrialization in the South grew and the number of apparel manufacturing establishments in the region increased by 435 percent between 1937 and 1954.

Northern clothing manufacturers were not only pushed out of the North but also drawn to the South. In an effort to attract industry, promoters from southern cities and towns advertised that they could pro-

TABLE 1. Growth of the Apparel Industry in the U.S. South, 1937–54

	1937	1947	1954	Percentage change
Employees	67,632	152,095	224,195	231.5
Establishments	419	1,667	2,241	434.8

Source: U.S. Bureau of the Census, *Economic Census of Manufactures*, 1937–54.

vide a pliant labor force and ample natural resources for manufacturing companies wishing to relocate. The years after World War II witnessed a particularly large expansion of the southern branch of the U.S. apparel industry as new factories opened their doors to southern workers throughout the region. Some of the earliest southern factories were in cities like Dallas and Atlanta, but apparel manufacturers were quickly caught up in programs like Mississippi's Balance Agriculture with Industry (BAWI) program that led factories to the countryside.

Southern states and local governments attempted to attract businesses with programs that featured municipal investment and government subsidies as a way to finance plant construction and tax breaks for runaway industries. Conceived as a plan to lift Mississippi out of the Great Depression, BAWI was the first successful state-sponsored industrial relocation incentive program. Shortly after its inception in 1936, it became a model for other southern states and communities. At the outset of the program, the BAWI board required all local communities to submit plans and gain approval before offering bonds to attract companies. Echoing the words of Henry Grady, the South's first prominent advocate of industrialization from half a century earlier, the BAWI program made frequent mention of the abundance of "native Anglo Saxons" in Mississippi and the willingness of its workers to accept low wages.[19] Garment manufacturing concerns were especially receptive to the incentives offered under the auspices of the BAWI program.[20] One early example of Mississippi's success in attracting low-wage, labor-intensive industries can be found in the history of the Reliance Manufacturing Company. In the late 1930s Reliance, a shirt and pajama factory, established a plant in Jackson, Mississippi. Residents welcomed the company with job applications and a community-financed factory.[21] Some companies continued to benefit from BAWI. According to one report, in 1954 city officials in Hattiesburg, Mississippi, planned to "sell another $425,000 in BAWI bonds to finance the construction of an addition" to the Reliance plant constructed years earlier. Owing to the success of the much-copied BAWI program, by the time of World War II, southern states were already leading the nation in the manufacture of men's work clothes.

Ralph McGill, the famous southern social commentator and columnist for the *Atlanta Constitution*, noted that apparel companies were often the first "shysters" to take advantage of southern states' earliest efforts to attract industry to the South. With particular displeasure, he described the learner system, in which prospective employees would train, or "learn" their jobs, for starkly reduced wages or no wages at all. He wrote, "Sometimes the learner's period was dragged on and on—only to have the factory close. Often, when their standard hours began to mount as their skill increased, they would be fired and replaced by another 'learner.'" McGill also cited a case in which prospective garment workers were willing to sign contracts to authorize regular deductions from their wages to repay the cost of building the factory.[22] Even in the face of these conditions, the apparel industry was the largest recipient of factory facilities offered by local governments all across the South.[23]

In addition to formal programs such as BAWI, chambers of commerce from a number of states and communities advertised for potential runaway industries in business journals and initiated reams of correspondence highlighting the particular reasons businesses would find it profitable to relocate to a given locale. A 1957 letter from a commercial real estate company listed a plant for sale in Pickins, South Carolina, and boasted that the surrounding community contained six other sewing plants, "all of which are non-union [like] the Pickins plant."[24] Shortly after Georgia passed a right-to-work law of its own, a "Committee of 100" in Augusta, Georgia, succeeded in attracting new industry to the area and listed the relocation of the Wilson Shirt Company as one of its achievements for 1958.[25] The Louisiana Department of Commerce and Industry ran an advertisement in a 1968 issue of *Business Week* stressing the state's desire to attract industry from northern states. Featuring a new twist on right-to-work laws adopted throughout the country, but especially in southern states in the decade after World War II, the state of Louisiana advertised its newly passed "Right-to-Profit" laws. These laws "removed government restraints from private industry" as "part of Louisiana's capitalist plot."[26] States and communities offered incentives ranging from tax relief to pro-business legislative programs, as well as nonunion labor pools, all in an effort to attract runaway industries, apparel among them.[27]

The efforts of southern municipalities to attract industry worked, at least for the apparel industry. In Tennessee, for example, small communities were successful in their appeals to clothing manufacturers when other efforts at industrial recruiting proved fruitless. Of all the industries that relocated to Tennessee after the Great Depression, apparel factories were the most numerous and the largest beneficiaries of community-subsidized incentives. In Morehead, North Carolina, the Pennsylvania-based Regal Shirt Manufacturing firm enjoyed a built-to-specifications factory that was leased from a group of local businessmen, Morehead City Builders, for the sum of one dollar per annum for a period of five years, with an option to renew for an additional five years with the same terms. According to testimony before the National Labor Relations Board (NLRB), "City Builders contributed the use of the factory building in return for the increased business which would flow to its members through the operation of the factory." As a result of hundreds of stories like these across the South, from 1919 to 1939 the clothing industry was the fastest-growing industry in the region.[28]

Vanity Fair's experience in Jackson, Alabama, followed the usual pattern. In the late 1930s local businessmen got together to sell municipal bonds in order to attract an industrial employer to their community in central Alabama. As a result of the opening of the apparel factory, female manufacturing employment increased in the region. One woman, remembering the impact of Vanity Fair on Clarke County, joked that the men worked to sell bonds to attract Vanity Fair and then "Vanity Fair put the ladies to work and the men stayed home and kept house."[29]

The famous Oneita Knitting Mills, which operated plants in both Andrews, South Carolina, and Cullman, Alabama, was also a runaway firm, seeking to avoid unionization by operating in the South. A company official stated that the "Right-to-Work laws in both Alabama and South Carolina" protected the Andrews plant from unionization after the Cullman plant was organized.[30] In 1952 Oneita Knitting Mills of Utica, New York, shut down its operations and reopened its doors in a community-sponsored factory in Andrews. Earlier that same year, residents of Andrews bought fifty-dollar bonds to finance the conversion of an abandoned tobacco warehouse into a suitable facility for sewing operations. A longtime resident recalled that "anyone in town who could afford it" bought bonds to bring Oneita to Andrews.[31] The Oneita factory in Andrews, South Carolina, began manufacturing underwear for department stores such as J. C. Penney, Sears, and K-Mart, but over the years the factory abandoned its underwear lines and diversified its operations to include T-shirts, sweatshirts, and children's clothing. In these later years, Oneita opened additional plants in Lane, Cades, Florence, and Fingerville, South Carolina. Oneita also expanded to North Carolina and Alabama. Until its closure in 1999, Oneita was the leading employer in Andrews, and at its height the company employed over three thousand employees throughout the South.[32]

Soon after the factory opened its doors, the ILGWU recognized the new Andrews plant as a runaway branch of a New York company with which the union had held a contract.[33] In the years after World War II, the ILGWU sought to identify runaway factories and reveal their connections to northern, unionized firms. By doing so, the union could successfully argue in cases before the NLRB that the new factory was in fact a union shop. In July 1965 the ILGWU won an important victory on this point. The NLRB ruled that runaway companies had to negotiate a new contract with the union that would remain in effect for a period of one year, even if the union did not represent over half the employees in the new shop. An article in the *New York Times* reported, "Needle trade unions have been urging the N.L.R.B. to take a tougher line against companies that move to the South and reopen with new workers." In the 1965 case, the Garwin Corporation (also known as S'Agaro, Inc.) of Miami, Florida, was deemed to be a runaway and was forced to agree to a new contract with the union, skipping the usual step of having the union prove it represented a majority of workers. The Garwin Company originally opened its doors in Queens, New York, in the early 1950s and then closed its operations and moved to Florida two years after signing a contract with the ILGWU in 1961. The U.S. Court of Appeals denied the company's request for an appeal, and the NLRB issued a supplemental ruling in 1968 that upheld the earlier decision of the board.[34] The ILGWU used this strategy to successfully organize Oneita's workers in Andrews and in other runaway factories throughout the South.[35]

The ILGWU represented workers at the Andrews Oneita plant for a little more than ten years. During that time, the union and company maintained at least a semblance of close relations. In 1958 union officials and Oneita management exchanged invitations to company and union social functions. The letters reveal a sort of rapport between the union and management.[36] But eventually the relationship deteriorated. The union ran into trouble in the early 1960s when the company refused to grant a new contract with the same basic provisions as the earlier contract. In July 1963, as a result of the company's refusal to agree to a satisfactory contract with the ILGWU, the Andrews employees went out on strike. Worker solidarity, which initially supported the strike, eventually collapsed, and within six months the strikers had nothing to show for their job action. After the strike and failed negotiations, many Oneita workers began to return to work. The company rewarded those who led the return to work with promotions and plush positions in the company's office. The president of the ILGWU local in Andrews, for instance, went back to work as the personnel manager of the Andrews plant. Eventually the employees of Oneita grew to resent the ILGWU and withdrew from the union en masse. In the year after the failed strike, the union's regional office received a blizzard of letters from individual employees resigning their membership in the union.[37] The close relationship between company and union officials left workers wondering about the union's commitment to their concerns. Even during the strike the close relationship between the company and the union was evident. When a member of Oneita president Robert D. Devereux's family passed away during the strike, the union promised to suspend picketing "during the interment [sic]."[38]

In marked contrast to the rapport between union and management officials, relations between union supporters and antiunionists in the Andrews community were far from amiable. The strike tore apart the community that had worked so hard to attract Oneita. Official complaints about violence and harassment on the picket lines resulted in the issuance of restraining orders against the union and company. During a court hearing about a potential violation of the restraining orders, workers testified that antiunionists in the community harassed them while they picketed Oneita.[39] The community was so divided over the strike that two sisters came to blows on the picket line. One of the sisters, deemed in court documents to be "the aggressor," was arrested and eventually convicted of assault.[40] The conflict took on an important southern quality in the small South Carolina town. This was particularly evident in Judge James Morrison's comments on the two sisters' dispute: "I can easily understand how brothers and sisters can start fighting because one is going to work and the other is on strike. They killed each other in the Civil War. It is my opinion now that that war started one hundred and fifty years too early." For Judge Morrison, the conflict evoked a particularly southern experience, the Civil War. This was a strike in a southern community that had used its own money to finance the construction of the apparel factory. Judge Morrison's loyalty to that endeavor was evident as he oversaw the resolution of the dispute between the union and the company in his courtroom. He said, "I don't mind telling you that I helped bring that organization [Oneita] to the county."[41] In the end, the strike was defeated, workers defected from the union, and the Andrews plant remained unorganized for nearly ten years.[42]

City councils and state governments were not the only proponents of southern apparel factories. In the mid-1950s the ILGWU itself also worked to attract clothing factories to southern locations. Officials of the union often covertly inquired about commercial property without disclosing their union connections. In 1957 Robert Cohn, an attorney for the ILGWU's Southeast Regional Office, responded to a real estate advertisement and inquired about the Pickins, South Carolina, garment factory available for lease.[43] Later that year Cohn received a letter of inquiry from Judy Thomas Manufacturing in Asheville, North Carolina. The union itself had placed an advertisement announcing possible garment contracts available to clothing manufacturers. Although the representative from Judy Thomas stated, "I would be willing to become union if necessary," it was also clear that a union contract was not the most desirable option. Moreover, the head of Judy Thomas boasted of his own connections to New York's garment industry, revealing that his was a runaway company. He wrote, "I am an old-timer, was production man for I. Ginsberg Company of New York [and] I had a plant of two-hundred machines."[44]

Nicholas Bonanno, who would later become the director of the ILGWU's Southeast Regional Office, inquired about the purchase of an apparel plant in Mississippi in the late 1950s. In a letter to the firm handling the sale of the plant, Bonanno listed five northern apparel manufacturers that were "quite interested in negotiating . . . the purchase of the Lucedale, Mississippi plant."[45] In cases like these the ILGWU acted as an intermediary between northern and southern entrepreneurs. It is unclear whether the northern firms listed in Bonanno's letter were organized or not. However, it is clear that by the 1950s the ILGWU's southern officials sought to join hands and help industry move south. This would, of course, potentially add to their membership rolls. But it could also facilitate the drift of the clothing industry away from its traditional power base in the Northeast to a region famed for its resistance to unionization and its low wages.

E. T. "Al" Kehrer served as director of the ILGWU's Southeast Regional

Office from 1953 until 1964. As director, Kehrer personally reached out to a prounion shop in New York, Gerson & Gerson, to gauge the company's interest in purchasing a plant in Walterboro, South Carolina. Jules Honig, a children's dress manufacturer with several locations, including the plant in Walterboro, was facing a financial crisis and was considering closing the Walterboro shop. Kehrer explained the details of the deal in a letter to Gerson & Gerson: "[The] local manager is anxious to continue the operation there as a contractor. The only requirement for the purchase would be to provide payroll money and take over the payments on a number of machines. The latter amount would come to approximately $10,000." Kehrer represented the purchase of Honig's Walterboro operations as a bargain, saying, "This plant has the makings of one of the best children's dress outfits in the entire South and is an excellent opportunity for someone wishing to expand in this field."[46] The records are unclear as to whether Gerson & Gerson responded positively to this offer. But the offer itself is significant, for it speaks to the role that the ILGWU played in trying to keep rank-and-file members employed. If Honig did close its doors in Walterboro, the ILGWU would lose an important local and many members as well.

Cooperation between labor and management was a hallmark of the ILGWU's history in the North. Since the 1920s, apparel unions had often taken on managerial functions, not the least of which were organizing production and creating wage standards.[47] After the industry moved south, the ILGWU seemed to rely on a strategy focused on the strike as the principal tool of labor in the region. Kehrer recalled that when he became director in 1953, the tendency seemed to be to strike when conflicts arose in the southern garment industry. ILGWU president David Dubinsky rarely nixed a strike. In a 1995 interview Kehrer remembered how he came to question the wisdom of a strategy that was so focused on strikes: "Toward the end of my time with the ILG, it began to dawn on me. Why are we striking?" Paying strike benefits to workers cost the Southeast Regional Office a significant amount of money. Under Kehrer's direction, the ILGWU's Southeast Region sought to focus on developing a cooperative relationship with management by helping to connect buyers with sellers and keeping workers employed. Of course, this strategy had an additional financial benefit for the ILGWU as well, for laid-off workers do not pay union dues.[48]

The ILGWU's decision to play a supportive role in the relocation of women's clothing manufacturers to the South was intended to maintain its membership rolls in the North wherever possible, while ensuring that the South did not become the antiunion, low-wage haven of its northern members' fears. In the early years, both the ILGWU and the ACWA had committed themselves to an organizing strategy that focused on the South in an effort to combat the establishment of a southern sanctuary for nonunion, runaway firms. The decision to take this southern organizing strategy a step further and actually assist in the relocation was, in effect, a capitulation to the reality of the restructuring of the American apparel industry. By the 1950s, when the ILGWU began to make its covert overtures to northern firms, most of the relocation of the apparel industry had already taken place. Despite a dramatic increase in the percentage of union members in the southern apparel industry, by 1958 the overall level of unionization for southern garment workers, at 30 percent, still lagged far behind the national average of 60 percent.[49]

The early unionization efforts in the South were clearly focused on the goal of eliminating the region as a runaway territory by minimizing regional wage differentials. Ideally, organized labor could simultaneously protect the jobs of northern workers and improve the lives of working-class southerners by elevating wages and working conditions to a point at which the South would cease to be attractive to northern industry for relocation. Still, southern developers and civic boosters demonstrated considerable audacity when they touted the region's low-wage workforce and then boasted to locals that the new industry would bring great economic development.[50] Cynics might argue that the unions, with their leadership and membership ranks concentrated in the Northeast, were less concerned with improving the lives of working-class southerners than they were interested in protecting northern workers' jobs. While that might have been true in some of the formally organized drives by the national offices of the textile and apparel unions, it was less true of the many occasions in which southern garment workers initiated the organizing efforts themselves. From the Works Progress Administration sewing rooms of Tampa, Florida, in 1937 to the modern Vanity Fair factory in Jackson, Alabama, in 1975, the women workers themselves frequently defined the particular goals of their protests for dignity in the sewing rooms of the South.

Chapter Two

"WHEN YOU CEASE TO BE LADIES, WE WILL ARREST YOU"

WORKING AND STRIKING IN SOUTHERN SEWING ROOMS, 1934–1970

As garment companies moved south during the Great Depression, the region had already experienced significant organizing activity. Although the Congress of Industrial Organizations' Textile Workers Organizing Committee, the heart of the massive organizing campaign Operation Dixie, ran into considerable difficulties organizing textile workers across the Piedmont South, both of the CIO's garment unions, the International Ladies' Garment Workers' Union and the Amalgamated Clothing Workers of America, made important headway in certain parts of the region, organizing white women stitchers plant by plant.[1] In response, factory owners, police, and local newspapers created an atmosphere of intimidation that hinged on gendered perceptions of power and class in southern communities. The organizational successes were sometimes fleeting, and the eventual demise of the southern apparel industry that began in the 1970s as trade barriers were lowered brought an end to many union locals across the region. In the four decades before that decline, southern women garment workers struggled mightily to achieve a measure of dignity through solidarity and work. Southern working-class women's efforts to achieve better wages and working conditions, shorter hours, and union representation appear all the more remarkable when viewed in the context of often-brutal local opposition and the pressures of domestic obligations. The street-level perspective reveals a contest that centered on a gendered and classed understanding of respectability and dignity in southern communities.

Throughout the 1930s and 1940s, employers, local governments, and law enforcement developed tactics to defeat southern garment workers' efforts to attain improvements in wages and working conditions. Patterns of intimidation that were established in the early years of the southern garment industry continued to resonate well into the 1970s. Routine threats to close a company or to eliminate a sewing machine operator's job escalated to violence and gender-based physical and verbal abuse that was at once both political and personal. These patterns shaped how southern women workers saw themselves and the strategies they employed to achieve dignity in their work. After World War II clothing workers and their unions looked beyond strikes to the courts and the National Labor Relations Board for support, while manufacturers and civic boosters continued to utilize government and media to fashion an antiunion business climate.

As was the case in other areas of the South, in its early years the garment industry in Texas provided much-needed jobs for white families at the bottom of the economic ladder. In 1932 agents from the Women's Bureau reported that "practically twice as many women as men were employed" in the Texas garment manufacturing plants agents visited in February of that year. Of the fifty-three clothing factories visited across the state, most were located in North Texas, an area that included the cities of Dallas, Fort Worth, and Plano. Women accounted for over 90 percent of the workers in the Texas clothing factories studied. Of the women working in these factories, more than 75 percent were white, while just under 25 percent were described as "Mexican" women. African American women accounted for less than half of 1 percent of the workers in the Texas factories examined by the Women's Bureau. Working in the clothing industry provided relatively good wages compared with other industries that employed women. The laundries of Texas paid the best wages. White women could expect to earn $7.15 a week sewing men's work clothing. The women's clothing industry paid less, coming in at $5.20 a week for white women. No matter what the industry, however, the Women's Bureau report noted that "Mexican women were receiving very much lower wages than white women, even when working side by side in the same occupation and establishment." In the men's clothing factories, the agents reported that Mexican women earned 21 percent less than their white counterparts. Most women worked nine hours a day, with some regularly working six days a week. The Women's Bureau also noted that older workers, those over forty, were disproportionately concentrated in sewing work, and there were noticeably fewer older workers in the clothing industry than in other industries in Texas. In addition, the clothing industry had the lowest percentage of single white women compared to other industries, with only 23.7 percent of the white women workers unmarried. These early apparel factories of Texas were small plants, with most employing less than forty-one workers. But the report also listed five garment plants that employed more than two hundred workers each.[2]

The conditions in which these women workers toiled were terrible. In one Dallas factory, a sewing machine operator explained, there were no fans and no ice water to combat the grueling summer heat, and workers were forced to use inadequate restroom facilities. The 1932 study of Texas garment factories by the Women's Bureau found widespread problems with lighting, seating, and restrooms. The dangling lightbulb, a symbol of the deplorable working conditions found in apparel sweatshops, underscored the fact that modern conveniences like electricity had failed to ease women garment workers' burdens. In one factory agents noted that women workers had to wear eyeshades as a result of "unfrosted and unshaded drop lights placed at almost eye level." In most cases, though, the lights were too far away from the work desks of women garment workers, making the detailed work required of sewing machine operators more difficult. Women worked long hours sitting on hard, unadjustable, "ordinary kitchen-chair[s]." Most of the factories supplied unsafe drinking water that did not meet the standards for sanitation established by the Women's Bureau. Several factories compelled workers to share cups for water, while others provided no cups at all. Most workers had no access to a lunchroom and were forced to eat at their work desks. The restrooms were particularly lacking. Only a handful of apparel factories provided hot water for washing up, and several forced workers to either share towels or bring their own. Women's Bureau agents labeled one factory "a veritable firetrap," where workers toiled in cramped conditions on the third floor of a building that could be accessed only by wooden stairs.[3]

The industry's low wages and undesirable and frequently unsafe working conditions fueled union organizing in the early years of the southern apparel industry. The slow and steady accomplishment of the CIO's Operation Dixie in the southern garment industry was somewhat surprising given the role that the region played in the unprecedented, worker-initiated General Textile Strike of 1934. Just as the Great Depression seemed to achieve a stranglehold on the South, textile employers initiated "stretch-outs" in an effort to stave off declining profits. Although the "stretch-out" took many forms, the goal was always the same: to maximize production and efficiency by compelling workers to do more work in less time without increasing their wages. The inauguration of President Franklin Roosevelt and the passage of the National Industrial Recovery Act in 1933 bolstered workers' efforts to combat exploitative employer practices like the stretch-outs. Section 7a of the act guaranteed that employees would have "the right to organize and bargain collectively through representatives of their own choosing, and shall be free from the interference, restraint, or coercion of employers of labor, or their agents . . . for the purpose of collective bargaining or other mutual aid and protection." Union organizers seized on the historic provision and proclaimed, "The President wants you to join a union." United Mine Workers of America president John L. Lewis insisted that Section 7a was nothing less than labor's own "Emancipation Proclamation."[4] The National Industrial Recovery Act led to the creation of the National Recovery Administration (NRA) to develop specific codes for each industry. To combat overproduction and underconsumption, the NRA industrial codes limited production and regulated wages and marketing practices for the nation's principal industries. Companies that agreed to work within these parameters were permitted to display a Blue Eagle, indicating their compliance with government-sanctioned business practices.

In September 1934, emboldened by the unprecedented government-guaranteed right to organize, nearly four hundred thousand millhands walked off their jobs to protest a wave of stretch-outs in the nation's textile factories. Today the General Textile Strike of 1934 stands as one of the most impressive displays of worker solidarity in American history. Organized by the United Textile Workers, groups of workers known as Flying Squadrons moved from mill town to mill town in the South, encouraging workers to abandon their machines. As the walkout proceeded into its third day, the violence escalated. At Chiquola Mills in Honea Path, South Carolina, company-supported thugs killed seven striking workers and left more than twenty workers wounded. All of the slain workers were shot in the back while fleeing the picket lines.

In Georgia, Governor Eugene Talmadge declared martial law as nearly

thirty thousand textile workers walked out of the state's factories. Although Talmadge explained to members of the press that National Guard
troops would protect "strikers, union members, non-union members, laborers [and] executives," his actions revealed that such was not the case.
The governor ordered picketers across the state to be arrested. More than
two hundred workers were rounded up and held in what the *New York
Times* described as an "internment camp" that once held German prison-
ers of war during World War I. The effort in Georgia targeted strike leaders and effectively undermined the strike effort across the state. In other
areas of the South, the use of company-hired thugs and National Guard
troops dealt a devastating blow to the solidarity that had given rise to the
historic labor action.

The strike lasted twenty-two days, and at its end workers had little
to show for their great courage and sacrifice. Although Roosevelt urged
companies to rehire workers without discrimination, thousands of textile workers in the South found themselves blacklisted from the textile
industry for the rest of their lives. The United Textile Workers reported
that 339 companies refused to rehire workers who had participated in or
supported the strike. Working conditions did not improve after the strike,
and the Great Depression grew even more entrenched.[5]

In the years following this great defeat, there were indications that labor was on the rise again. In 1935, as the minimum wage and maximum
hours provisions of the NRA's Blue Eagle program expired, garment workers in Texas suffered significant wage cuts, with many earning only half of
the NRA-mandated twelve dollars per week. In addition to the wage cuts,
after the NRA protections expired, workers no longer received time and a
half for overtime work. Dependable and continuous employment was in
great demand in the Depression-era South. Women sewing machine operators often went to their place of employment in the morning, sometimes
traveling significant distances, only to be told that there was no work that
day. Charlotte Duncan Graham began working in the Dallas garment industry in 1929, shortly after finishing high school. Recalling the circum-
stances of her employment, she contended that the factory owners "didn't
care as much about the people that worked for them as they did [for] the
machines because when a machine broke down, they had to have it fixed,
but [when] you broke down, they'd just put somebody else in your place."[6]

Workplace injuries were commonplace. Graham remembered that
she once had a needle break off in her finger and recalled that the thread

was "hanging out of top side and bottom side." It took more than an hour and a half for her to see a doctor. That time was off the clock and entirely uncompensated. Employers treated workers like "you were less than human," she remembered. Experiences like this one led Graham to support the unionization of the Dallas garment industry.[7]

In its effort to follow the runaway industry to the lower-waged South, the ILGWU supported a few strikes in Texas in the 1930s. Plans for a strike in Dallas were discussed by ILGWU officers at a conference in January 1935. Because the strike was coordinated at the national level, union representatives from several different locations were involved, including Dallas, St. Paul, Minnesota, and Kansas City, Missouri. ILGWU regional director Meyer Perlstein sent letters to each of the major women's apparel manufacturers in Dallas, making specific demands for improvements in wages and working conditions. The letters also expressed concern that employers were discriminating against and even firing prounion workers in an effort to prevent unionization. In fact, the dismissal of four ILGWU members at the Morten-Davis Company, a wholesaler owned by John B. Donovan, led to the first walkout of what soon became known as the Dallas Dressmakers' War. According to reports in the *Dallas Morning News*, the first days of the strike at Morten-Davis were "calm." The women strikers "flashed smiles" as they "chat[ted] good naturedly as if they were on an outing." However, the calm did not last long.[8]

The ILGWU's demands for improved wages and working conditions went unanswered, and by the beginning of March 1935 a full-fledged, multifactory strike was underway in Dallas. Workers at thirteen of the fifteen plants in Dallas eventually walked off their jobs, repeating the demands for increased wages and better working conditions, as well as union recognition. Charlotte Duncan Graham explained that the strike was planned at secret meetings in workers' homes: "We'd make housecalls—we'd go to see people—and talk to them at night in their homes." House to house, worker by worker, Graham and her colleagues built solidarity among the garment workers in Dallas.[9]

After Morten-Davis, the next plant to be struck was Lorch Manufacturing. Owned by Lester Lorch, the president of the Texas Dress Manufacturers Association, the factory was a high-profile target. Lorch was the public face of the Texas Dress Manufacturers Association and represented the interests of the fifteen garment plants in Dallas in negotiations with the union and its striking workers. The Lorch strike was notable for reports of violence and repeated scuffles between striking workers, police, and the nonstriking workers and strikebreakers brought in by Lorch. The *Dallas Morning News* repeatedly asserted that the violence was initiated by prounion forces. The newspaper's coverage of the strike described events in terms that made it sound like a so-called catfight among women workers. In the first line of the first article about the Lorch strike, the newspaper reported that women strikers "pulled hair, clawed and slugged each other in lusty abandon" in an effort to prevent workers from entering the sewing factory.[10] It is rather doubtful that the combating workers were feeling "lusty" at the time of the fracas, but the reporter's use of such sexually charged language is significant. The southern press's frequent use of sexual imagery to describe the activity on southern garment workers' strike lines underscores the relationship between prescribed roles of feminine obedience and the punishments for stepping outside of those roles.

At the end of the first day of the strike at Lorch Manufacturing, the *Dallas Morning News* took particular notice of one incident. "One fuzzy-haired, pretty lass of firm physical proportions" opted not to take one of the company-hired taxis and headed toward the bus station to begin her journey home. Two strikers attacked the woman worker, knocking her down. She "got up with fists flying and planted [Jack] Dempsey-like wallops to the jaws of her adversaries." After policemen arrived and diffused the situation, an officer escorted the nonstriking worker to the bus station, where "she calmly took out her vanity [mirror], adjusted signs of the scrap[e] with rouge and powder and climbed in her bus." The gendered gaze of the reporting on the Dallas Dressmaker's War reveals much about the nature of women's work and expected behavior in the South. The righteous defiance of the nonstriking worker, the physicality of the attack, and the strength of her response conformed to a distinctly gendered conception of honor in the South. The indignation of the "battling miss" at the hands of the attacking strikers resulted in behavior that was decidedly unladylike and fell outside prescribed gendered behavior for southern women of any class. But the *Dallas Morning News* assured its readers that all was made right in the end. With the application of a little makeup, the southern woman worker's virtue was restored.[11]

The veracity of these and other reports of strike activity at southern plants is, of course, largely unknowable. On the whole the reporters from the *Dallas Morning News* and other southern newspapers seemed far more inclined to support the position of plant owners than that of the striking women workers. Frequently the police functioned as an arm of the state, defending the positions and interests of wealthy factory owners while limiting the free speech and unionization rights of women workers on the strike lines. The frequent discussion of police officers and their physical confrontations with striking workers suggests that the southern media's sympathies lay most often with the city officials, plant owners, and those workers who refused to join in strikes. Where available, the perspectives of striking workers did not frequently conform to the images portrayed in the press. For instance, during the Dallas Dressmakers' War one unionist complained that off-duty policemen provoked disturbances on the strike lines and that nonstriking workers sometimes carried knives to help protect them as they made their way to work. From her perspective, the police and women workers who crossed the strike lines at Lorch initiated the violence. While reporting on a court hearing in which several ILGWU members were accused of violating a restraining order by attacking nonstriking workers at Lorch Manufacturing, the *Dallas Morning News* noted that the company's attorney accused the women strikers of lying. These accusations were made despite the apparent consistency of the women unionists' accounts of peaceful picketing and contentions that the trouble was prompted by "workers who refused to join [in] the walkout."[12] The perspectives of the striking workers are more difficult to ascertain, but where they do exist, they reveal a counternarrative to the perspectives offered in the southern press. Unfortunately, the viewpoint of the striking workers in the southern apparel industry is often the most difficult to ascertain because southern newspapers so frequently endorsed the perspective of the business community.

Accounts of the efficacy of the ILGWU-led strike in Dallas and the solidarity of the striking workers reflect contrasting allegiances. While the union announced in March 1935 that more than five hundred workers had walked off their jobs, Lorch told the *Dallas Morning News* that "not more than 25 employees out of a total of 915" had participated in the strike and heeded the ILGWU's call for a walkout. The union claimed that 150 women received strike pay, and other records make clear that at least 86 union women were arrested during the strike. Although the ILGWU had spent considerable money trying to drum up support for a citywide strike against the apparel industry in the spring and summer of 1935, union workers suffered during the strike. In most weeks, strikers received only six dollars from the union, exactly half of what they made under the NRA mandate, and subsisted on "day-old doughnuts, cottage cheese and tuna fish."[13]

The strike continued through the spring and summer, with the morning and afternoon editions of the *Dallas Morning News* providing near-daily coverage of the effort. In August 1935 tensions escalated sharply. During one confrontation in front of Lorch Manufacturing, "women workers were disrobed by strikers in a wild melee of scratching, kicking, and cursing." The *Dallas Morning News* ran a front-page headline that screamed, "Strikers Strip Ten Women on Dallas Street."[14] The scintillating details of the incident brought national media attention to the strike. The *New York Times* headline read salaciously, "Women Stripped and 'Spanked' in Strike." The article continued, "Striking women garment workers stripped four women naked, partly disrobed six others and chased them through the streets [of Dallas], spanking and scratching them in wild rioting today." Although the report noted the goals of the strike, "higher wages, shorter hours and union recognition," the article concluded dramatically with the words of a bystander who said she was mistakenly identified as a scab and attacked. Valera McCormick described what happened: "Before I knew it, they grabbed me and tore my clothes to pieces. They threw them in the street, and I had to run three-quarters of a block before I reached the Lorch plant."[15] The imagery offered here was intended to shock. Out-of-control unionists forced a proper southern white woman to run naked down a public street.

By the end of the Dallas Dressmakers' War in October, the police had arrested unionist Charlotte Graham fifty-four times on the strike lines in front of Dallas garment factories. Recalling the events of the spring and summer of 1935, she noted that policemen frequently drank alcohol while on duty at the strike lines and used their billy clubs against striking women workers. In contrast with other, more well-known reports of the stripping incident at the Lorch factory, Graham argued that the police were at the very least complicit in the removal of nonstriking workers' clothing. "Once things got started on both sides, there were a lot of people left without clothes that morning, and the police were having so much fun that when they grabbed us, they'd take us around the corner and tell us to get another [strikebreaker]."[16]

Both the newspaper and Graham noted that Lester Lorch responded to the melee by grabbing stacks of white uniforms from the second floor of his factory and covering women as they made their way into the plant. The forced removal of clothing evoked an underlying narrative of rape. According to the *Dallas Morning News* and the chief of police, good, hard-working, and obedient white southern women were attacked by masculinized strikers and the removal of clothing was an attack on their honor. The perspective offered in the press perpetuated the idea that good, dutiful southern women were in need of masculine protection, even if it was protection from other southern women. Even the whiteness of the uniforms is significant, for the color suggests innocence and purity, while the uniform stands for order and obedience. Graham noted with substantial irony that it was common knowledge that Lorch made the women pay for those uniforms.[17]

As a result of the confrontation in front of Lorch Manufacturing, twenty-seven workers were arrested and charged with "inciting a riot." Dallas police chief Robert L. Jones admonished the twenty-seven workers, saying, "You can carry on your strike and we won't bother you, but when you cease to be ladies we will arrest you."[18] His comments revealed an alternative reason for their arrest. In Dallas the failure of working-class women "to be ladies" was reason enough for police action. The stripped procompany workers' vulnerability served as justification for the police chief's reminder about class and gender norms. The imprisoned women understood the gendered dynamic and played along. The *New York Times* reported, "The women smiled [at the police chief]. They promised to cause no further disturbance." A quick and distinctly feminine smile assured the chief of their acceptance of sanctioned gender roles, and they were released from prison. In the fall, community leaders called for negotiations to end the strike, but Lorch and the Texas Dress Manufacturers Association refused to negotiate. Eventually the striking workers voted to return to work, and the Dallas Dressmakers' War ended with little more than a whimper.[19]

Just two years after the Dallas Dressmakers' War, a strike wave with some familiar features began in the dress shops of the garment industry in Memphis, Tennessee. As spring began to show its colors, Memphis virtually exploded in a spasm of labor activism reminiscent of the General Textile Strike of 1934. In March 150 white women workers at the Tri-State Dress Company factory went on strike for better wages and shorter hours. On the very first afternoon of the strike, unionists clashed with women who sought to keep working. The *Commercial Appeal* reported that by the end of the first day of the strike more than a thousand people had gathered around the factory in support of the workers. Memphis police arrested four women strikers on charges of "disorderly conduct" and "threatening breach of the peace." The press noted that Tri-State's owner's son was attacked by the women strikers, resulting in the destruction of his glasses and coat. By highlighting this one particular attack early on in the reporting, the press effectively masculinized the strikers, rendering these white working-class women as capable of the masculine behavior of assaulting a man and, perhaps more importantly, as capable of standing up for better working conditions, too.[20]

Conventional assumptions about gender meant that women, even more than men, were especially vulnerable to violent attacks from these masculinized women strikers. In its coverage of an attack on an older woman, the *Commercial Appeal* noted with salacious detail that "part of her clothing was torn off." In another instance, "the pretty designer and daughter" of the company owner was "followed down a street" and "almost disrobed by a group of women [strikers]." The image presented in the press of a mob of manly working-class women attacking a chaste middle-class woman in the middle of a street and stripping her of her clothes was salacious enough, but when the subject of these working-class women's aggression was a "pretty ... daughter," it was evident that the newspaper sought to convey a message that the strike had disrupted the region's class and gender norms.[21]

By the mid-1930s the violent removal of white southern women workers' clothing was commonplace on strike lines. Newspaper accounts often led with descriptions of torn clothing and half-naked women, tapping into the historical echoes of a time when rape was a principal weapon in the arsenal of white supremacy. After the 1866 Memphis Riot, a well-orchestrated attack on freedmen and freedwomen by white southern men eager to reassert white supremacy and masculinity in the aftermath of slavery, four freedwomen testified at a congressional hearing that they had been sexually assaulted, often repeatedly, during the three nights that the riot lasted. The wives of African American Union soldiers in Memphis were disproportionately represented among the rape victims. Thus the violent sexual assault of these freedwomen by white men was simultaneously an act of personal and political violence. With a strategy reminiscent of the Redeemers' efforts to divide poor white and black sharecroppers in the 1890s by portraying themselves as the protectors of white southern womanhood, antiunion forces across the South in the 1930s wanted workers to believe that northern unions provoked irrational, dangerous, and even masculine behavior from women workers.[22] There is much significance behind the imagery offered by the newspapers that covered garment workers' strikes across the region. In most but certainly not all of the incidents, newspaper accounts stressed the vulnerabilities and frailties of antiunion, white women workers in the South. At the same time, striking women were sometimes portrayed as superhuman and decidedly unfeminine "Amazons" capable of great violence.

For all of the gendered meanings to be gleaned from the reporting on the Memphis strike, there were additional real and substantial issues to be negotiated. The white women workers at Tri-State complained of a recent wage cut caused by the expiration of the Blue Eagle program, with its guaranteed maximum hours and minimum wage provisions. Strikers carried banners that read, "We Demand Shorter Hours" and "We Demand a Living Wage." Although he denounced any violence, even the generally antiunion mayor of Memphis, Watkins Overton, had to acknowledge the popular support for the strike among his city's citizens. Overton eventually backed the white women strikers' demands for a wage increase and echoed the language of the strike line. He told the city newspaper, "The City of Memphis has no sympathy with any plant which is not willing to pay its employees a living wage." The three-day strike earned white women unionists much of what they had hoped for. Tri-State agreed to increase minimum wages from seven dollars for a fifty-four-hour workweek to twelve dollars for a forty-hour workweek. These concessions brought working conditions back in line with the provisions established by the NRA. At the same time, white southern working-class women proved themselves more than capable of solidarity and a force to be reckoned with.[23]

The quick victory at Tri-State inspired additional activism in Memphis in the spring of 1937. Just a few weeks later, more than a hundred garment workers in two additional Memphis garment plants voted to strike. Management at both the Nona-Lee Dress Company and Kuhn Manufacturing proved to have more staying power than management at Tri-State. For nearly a month the two companies steadfastly refused to recognize their employees' right to be represented by the ILGWU. Meanwhile, union officials demanded a contract, demonstrating that 95 percent of employees at Kuhn and a majority at Nona-Lee had signed union cards.[24]

Conditions in the garment factories of Memphis were far from ideal and explain why women workers voted to strike. The standard workweek

was fifty hours or more a week, and white women sewing machine operators routinely made less than eight dollars a week, significantly less than
the twelve-dollar minimum demanded by the ILGWU and the provisions
of the defunct Blue Eagle program. The sewing rooms of Memphis were
literally sweatshops, with dim lighting and inadequate ventilation. Sewing
machine operators reported being forced to take meals at their machines
and make coffee in the restroom. Merle Zappone, an ILGWU organizer,
called Nona-Lee "one of the worst little prisons I ever saw."[25]

Once workers at Kuhn and Nona-Lee went on strike, press coverage
of the garment industry in Memphis became even more sensationalized.
There were reports of altercations on the strike lines between strikers
and nonstrikers, and much was made of the arrest of eleven unionists.
The *Commercial Appeal* reported that Zappone and a woman supervisor came to blows, shredding each other's clothing in the process. Soon
women from both sides joined in the fight, until police arrested eleven
of the strikers. The newspaper dubbed the arrested women "CIO Amazons" and published eye-catching photographs alongside its reports. To
amplify the gendered gaze of the incident, the paper described the fracas
as a sort of catfight and alleged that Zappone cultivated long fingernails
precisely for such occasions. The *Memphis Press Scimitar* reported, "Feminine clothing flew in disorders which this morning marked the opening
of a strike against the Nona-Lee Dress Company." Noting that the "all
feminine affrays" were more than "the force of 15 policemen" could han-
dle, the report hinted that there was something amiss in the natural order of male over female on the strike lines. The media also used military
imagery to underscore the unnatural and masculine role of women on
the strike lines. When scab workers sought access to the Nona-Lee factory, the *Press Scimitar* described "a battalion of girl workers" marching
through the lines of striking workers. This, the *Press Scimitar* reported, resulted in "girls roll[ing] on the pavement among hats, blouses, skirts and
undergarments." In the media, women scabs were the victims of "disorderly" women unionists on the strike lines in the Memphis garment industry.[26] By mid-April the women unionists returned, victorious, to their
machines, as both companies agreed to contracts with the ILGWU. But
the victory was relatively short-lived. Nona-Lee Dress Company and Kuhn
Manufacturing closed operations by the end of the year, just as they had
promised to do if the unions won.[27]

Despite its ultimate defeat, the activism of white women in the dress shops of Memphis spread across state lines to Tupelo, Mississippi. The women workers at Tupelo Garment Company tried a different strategy to achieve union recognition and better working conditions. Instead of walking off their jobs, they refused to leave the shop, calling a sit-down strike. Unlike a standard strike in which workers protest in front of the factory to prevent workers from entering and working, in a sit-down strike the workers occupy the shop and prevent managers and owners from entering. The change in strategy was likely encouraged by the victory only a few weeks earlier of workers involved in the unprecedented sit-down strike by the United Auto Workers at the General Motors factory in Flint, Michigan. Twisting the usual employer's threat of closing the shop if the workers voted for a union, the white women strikers in Tupelo threatened to join the CIO's ILGWU if their demands for higher wages and fewer hours were not met. In a written statement, workers explained their defiant actions: "If we cannot receive a living wage for working, there is no logical reason for working anyway." Workers complained that the average wage was only eight dollars per week, about half of what they made while the NRA was in effect. The company responded to the walkout by firing seven women activists. While the campaign was underway, the *Commercial Appeal* repeatedly described the situation in Tupelo as "tense." The Memphis newspaper followed the sit-down strike closely, but the solidarity and drama of the three Memphis strikes never quite materialized in Tupelo. Instead, company officials successfully pressured workers into joining a company-organized union by prophesying bloodshed and the closing of the factory if the union succeeded. A subsequent planned walkout failed because, as one striker put it, the women workers "lost their nerve . . . when the showdown came." A showdown it must have been, with threats not only on workers' livelihoods but on their very lives as well. Courageous prounion workers stood up to the company's opposition, facing dismissals, arrests, and at least one beating, all in an attempt to have the ILGWU defend their right to a living wage.[28]

ILGWU organizer Ida Sledge also demonstrated considerable courage in Tupelo. A gang of antiunionists twice came to her hotel room and threatened her physically and verbally. Additional and repeated threats on her life in the antiunion state of Mississippi eventually cast a shadow over the ILGWU's organizing prospects in Tupelo. Jimmy Cox, a local man who led the women workers to the ILGWU, was beaten so severely that he was admitted to the hospital with serious injuries. Shortly after his discharge from the hospital, Cox left town, and the ILGWU suffered a painful defeat and retreat from Tupelo.[29]

In the summer of 1937 the activism of southern women garment workers continued in a Tampa sewing room established by the New Deal's Works Progress Administration (WPA). Such relief work was particularly necessary for poor women because the majority of New Deal relief jobs went to men. During the Great Depression the WPA sewing rooms provided more women with relief work than any other government initiative. Like workers in commercial garment factories, the relief workers in the WPA sewing rooms tended to be older white women whose family situations required additional income just for survival. In 1937 Vassie Lee Hall, a Westville, Florida, widow, wrote to Governor Fred P. Cone, begging him to help her find work in a WPA sewing room. In her letter she explained that as a widow with a ten-year-old son, her situation was dire. Unable to clothe her son, she was forced to keep him out of school. In addition, Hall and her brother supported their "invalid and nearly blind" father, while their mother suffered from dementia. In another letter to Cone, Lelia Hay from Kissimmee despaired because the sewing room where she had been working for more than a year "laid me off because I was over 70 [years] of age." In an effort to plead her case, Hay noted that she had dutifully raised five children largely on her own after being widowed in her fifties. She explained that she was still responsible for supporting one of her adult daughters, who had been paralyzed at the age of seven. Caring for children or disabled family members added additional pressure to women's lives. Working in the WPA sewing rooms was a necessity. Women needed to work and earn money in order to sustain their families.[30]

New Deal relief work conformed to traditional, gendered conceptualizations of women's work. Married women were generally unable to secure positions in WPA sewing rooms unless they could prove abandonment. Emphasizing the diversity of backgrounds among the sewing machine operators involved in the Tampa strike, historian Elna Green points out that these women shared a view of relief work as an entitlement, not a source of shame. They believed that they were entitled to relief because they paid taxes or because they had performed their roles as wives and mothers dutifully. Green points out that women who worked in Florida's WPA sewing rooms rarely pointed to their rights as workers. Instead, they emphasized that they were good wives and mothers and therefore deserved relief work.[31]

The desperate poverty wrought by the persistent and unprecedented depression and the inconsistent and often temporary benefits of relief work meant that even those who found work in New Deal programs sometimes resorted to strikes to achieve better working conditions, more continuous employment, and better wages. After seeing some positive economic news about the previous year, President Roosevelt began to cut back government spending on relief programs in 1937. As cutbacks of New Deal programs translated into layoffs, WPA relief workers went out on strike in cities across America. Sometimes organized by the Workers Alliance, a relief-workers union, strikers protested the layoffs. In Ybor City, Florida, a city near Tampa with its own distinctive history of labor activism, a group of recently laid-off sewing room workers marched into a WPA sewing room. The laid-off workers launched a sit-down strike, occupying the sewing room and insisting that they be allowed to return to work. The *Tampa Tribune* reported that officials feared that the sewing room sit-down strike would lead to a general strike. Indeed, there seemed to be much sympathy for the striking women. Blankets and food were trucked in by labor unions and private citizens to help sustain the striking women relief workers. The city newspaper carried stories that emphasized the striking women's domestic roles, noting that one woman's baby was hoisted through a factory window so that he might nurse at his striking mother's breast. In another article the *Tampa Tribune* included a large photograph of an "improvised clothing line" along with a caption that explained that the women strikers held a "wash day" after being in the factory for several days. After the city called the strike "a menace to public health," WPA officials threatened to fire any worker who failed to show up for work. The sit-down strike ended without the reinstatement of the laid-off workers. The Tampa WPA sewing room strike was different from the labor actions that took place earlier in Texas, Tennessee, and Mississippi because it involved workers who emphasized their domestic roles, not their rights as workers. Still, the tactics used to defeat any glimmer of solidarity among southern working women were much the same. Like the workers in Dallas, Memphis, and Tupelo, the Ybor City sewing room workers were told that continuing the strike would result in the termination of their employment. Even though they worked in a federal program and were, in effect, government employees, their right to strike was limited by the threat of dismissal.

By the 1940s a pattern of violent suppression of labor activism char-

acterized labor relations in the southern garment industry. While organizing Merit Company, a garment shop in Mayfield, Kentucky, ILGWU organizers were fired on five times by antiunionists as they rode together
along a state highway. The newspaper of the Amalgamated Clothing
Workers of America, the *Advance*, reported that another prounion worker
was "knocked unconscious" and the editor of the local newspaper that accepted union advertisements was "severely beaten and left unconscious."[32]

In 1941 the Workers Defense League, a labor advocacy organization
founded five years prior, reported several incidents of violent efforts to intimidate union organizers and workers in the South. One such incident
included Hooper Sprouse, "a 56-year-old picket who was badly beaten
about the head and body by a [Knoxville, Tennessee] policeman." Sprouse
was engaged in a strike led by the ILGWU against Standard Knitting Mills,
the largest underwear manufacturer in the South at the time. Local power
structures often worked against the interests of prounion citizens, in
deference to large employers like Standard Knitting Mills. The Workers
Defense League reported that the grand jury that heard Sprouse's case
against the Knoxville police officers was persuaded not to indict "on the
advice of the prosecutor." The prosecutor who was supposed to represent
the victim's interests in the case actually recommended against an indict-
ment of the police officers. Later that same year, five women ILGWU organizers were beaten for distributing leaflets at Jackson County Woolen
Mills. The Workers Defense League reported that "the mob was led by
State Representative Claude Bilbo," who was also the personnel director
at the plant. Representative Bilbo was a close relative of Mississippi senator Theodore Bilbo, who twice served as governor of Mississippi and was
notorious for his prominence in the Ku Klux Klan. One woman worker
who distributed union information to fellow workers, Jo Lee Walden, was
stabbed and "beaten about the head and body." Warrants were executed
against the instigators of the attack, including Bilbo. Bilbo responded by
filing charges against the striking women who were victims of his attack.
The Workers Defense League characterized the charges against the striking workers as unsubstantiated and noted that this was an attempt to
intimidate the workers and keep them from pursuing the case. In an exchange that merits particular suspension of disbelief, the state prosecutor
offered to drop the charges against Bilbo and his fellow assailants if they
agreed to drop their fraudulent charges against the striking women. Quid
pro quo, it was settled. The government that was supposed to represent

and defend the citizens of Mississippi actually backed Jackson County Woolen Mills instead.[33]

In rural southern communities, apparel workers who sought to improve their working conditions through solidarity were met with violence and intimidation. After 1947, with the antiunion Taft-Hartley Act firmly in place, southern industrialists began to rely more heavily on propaganda campaigns, although the outright physical intimidation of garment workers remained a feature of the struggle to organize the southern apparel industry. Northern Republicans joined forces with southern Democrats to pass Taft-Hartley, an expansive bill that outlawed the closed shop and added a long list of prohibited labor union actions, including sympathy strikes and secondary boycotts. The law increased federal oversight of labor unions and prohibited union contributions to politicians seeking federal office. The Taft-Hartley Act opened the door for southern states to create antiunion "right-to-work" laws that made unionization in the region much more difficult.[34]

In the 1950s boosterism became the cause célèbre for civic-minded southerners. Newspaper coverage reflected that probusiness and antilabor sentiment. Reporting on the ILGWU's organizing efforts at Athco, Inc., in Athens, Alabama, The *Limestone Democrat*'s front-page headline proclaimed, "Athco Workers Urge Union: Go!" The newspaper quoted a written statement by those who opposed the union at the plant: "[W]e do not want a Union and would like for you to leave Athens and stop bothering us. What does it take to convince you? We are destroying your circulars without even reading them. As far as we are concerned, if you left today, it would not be too soon." Above the fold on the same front page, editors at the *Limestone Democrat* chose to run a "Hi Neighbor" column that heralded the many benefits Athco brought to the small town. Promising a weekly payroll of more than $10,000 and better-than-average wages, a planned expansion of the Athco plant would bring comfortable working conditions and more jobs. Many "fringe benefits" were cited, including paid vacations, accident and life insurance, a Fourth of July picnic, and a Christmas party. The newspaper's coverage of the organizing campaign reflected a central premise of the code of southern honor, in which southern men defend the virtues of a seemingly vulnerable class of southern white women.[35] One worker evoked this image when she promised, "Our husbands and fathers are coming after [the ILGWU organizer] next time." With the virtues of southern white women safely protected from the unwanted advances of union organizers, the ILGWU's effort at Athco met its demise.[36]

In the spring of 1955 a majority of workers at the Glendale Manufacturing plant in Asheville, North Carolina, voted to strike in protest of what a seven-woman strike committee described as "unfair labor practices, low wages, intimidation and poor and unsanitary working conditions" at the factory. In a letter published in the local newspaper, the strike leaders explained their mistreatment on the strike lines: "The non-strikers have thrown dead rats, lit firecrackers and rotten eggs at us [and they have] also used profane and disgusting language." The Asheville workers maintained their dignity as upstanding women, undeserving of such treatment, noting that "in spite of these actions . . . we have at all times conducted ourselves as decent, respectable Christian ladies." In this way, the strikers attempted to recast their struggle. They were not aggressive women but "respectable Christian ladies" seeking an improvement in working conditions through union representation. The issue of respectability was clearly paramount to the striking women at Glendale Manufacturing. These working-class women struggled to maintain their dignity as their demands for union representation and better working conditions were met with physical attacks and slander that proclaimed them to be anything but southern ladies.[37]

A few months after the Glendale strike, the *Birmingham Post-Herald* reported that the car of a superintendent at Winston Manufacturing was "dynamited" and the resulting explosion not only destroyed the car but also damaged the superintendent's house. As if to underscore and possibly increase the outrage at the attack, the newspaper described the superintendent and his wife as "the parents of Marilyn Tate, chosen Miss Alabama in last year's Miss America competition." By mentioning this key fact, the *Post-Herald* sought to convey a message about respectability. The fine upstanding parents of a young woman contestant in the all-white Miss America competition were surely beyond reproach and undeserving victims of an alliance of unruly working-class women and union men from the North. Across the South, local newspaper editors and company officials developed a portrait of unionization that was characterized by violence as a deterrent to labor organization campaigns in the South.[38]

Skirmishes over strike lines and organizing campaigns continued throughout the 1950s. In 1958 Peggy Hudson, a forty-one-year-old white woman unionist, was hit by a car on the strike line in front of the Mountain Top garment factory in Hendersonville, North Carolina. Although her injuries were not life-threatening, the attack made striking employees fearful for their well-being and likely intimidated any workers who were undecided about joining the ILGWU. The Henderson local newspaper called the attack an "accident" but noted that Hudson was on the strike line when she was "hit by an automobile ... driven by a worker entering the plant." The worker behind the wheel of the car was crossing the picket line into the plant when Hudson was struck. She suffered abrasions and cuts on her chest and legs. No charges appear to have been filed against the driver and Sheriff Paul Z. Hill described the incident as an accident. The Asheville, Tennessee, local newspaper ran an article the same day with the headline "Picket Hit by Car in Henderson" and confirmed that no charges were filed against the driver of the car that hit the striker.[39]

With no apparent sense of irony, company officials later issued an antiunion newsletter that featured an entire page dedicated to itemizing violent actions alleged to have been committed by unionists across the country. One item was headlined "Amalgamated and ILGWU in Fist Fight on Picket Line." In another item the newsletter reported that a "union member [was] tortured in an elevator because he opposed National Union officials.... Torture deemed unspeakable and may result in death.... [S]ix strong men beat [a unionist] senseless because he offered a motion ... to let more union members vote." Of course, the list of incidents was rather exclusive and one-sided. The newsletter failed to mention any of the times that union women and their supporters were beaten, abused, or threatened, including the previous attack by an antiunionist that took place directly in front of the factory.[40]

The 1963 Oneita strike in Andrews, South Carolina, was characterized by intense intimidation. After years of difficulty at Oneita, Martha Watford joined the ILGWU's efforts to organize the Andrews plant. In a hearing in Georgetown County Court, Watford testified that she was harassed for supporting the strike and unionization efforts. She explained that when her husband was not at the house, she frequently received death threats from a man on the telephone. On another occasion, an unidentified antiunionist drove onto her property late at night and further harassed her. Watford understood the implied threat when the unidentified man said that "many people before had been killed on strike."[41]

In a near-repeat of the attack at Mountain Top in Hendersonville, North Carolina, antiunion workers at Oneita also used a vehicle to intimidate unionists on strike in Andrews. Thelma Bouchette and two antiunionist passengers charged the strike line and called the striking women workers "Dirty Whores!" as they zoomed into the plant. Ronelle Moore, a striking worker who witnessed the episode, noted that there was "a patrolman present [but] nothing was done to prevent further disturbances caused by the employees of Oneita." Moore concluded her testimony by noting that Bouchette intended to "harass and embarrass . . . members of the Union on strike [who were] walking and picketing Oneita." The harassment had a gendered meaning that had far broader implications than the strike. By using a sexualized epithet, the intimidation took on additional significance, reflecting a loss of feminine respectability. As they struggled to make ends meet for their families and to have union representation, the women on the picket lines at Oneita and other southern garment plants endured humiliation and harassment that focused on their roles as women unionists and wage earners.

In another example of intimidation, a woman striker recalled how an antiunion man taunted her by suggesting that her husband's incompetence forced her to work at Oneita. He shouted, "One more has to work because her husband won't work." In actuality, her husband did work outside the home, but he was restricted from strenuous activity by a medical condition. The antiunion man's comment reflected a traditional and conservative conceptualization of femininity that identified men as sole breadwinners and women as non–wage earners. In this way, the comments also suggest the masculinization of working-class women unionists in southern communities. For antiunionists, working and striking became identified with unseemly behavior for women and a disruption of gender roles.[42]

Proclamations of antiunionism were a central component of the post–World War II competition between southern cities for industry. With its bustling port and active business community, Savannah, Georgia, was a town looking toward the future. State and local business recruiters courted northern firms, while the older paper-pulp and food-processing industries continued to thrive and to dominate Savannah's political life. Cities like Savannah seemed to be in a rush to declare themselves more antiunion than their neighbors farther down the interstate. In a 1969 editorial headlined "Upholding Mediocrity" that slammed a prounion Supreme Court decision, the *Savannah Morning News* made the city's estimation of labor unions clear: "Dictatorial methods by management spawned organized labor, but now the roles have been reversed."[43]

Despite the newspaper's protestations against abuses of union power, organized labor made little more than a dent in the ranks of Georgia's working class, with just 14 percent of workers belonging to any kind of industrial union in 1968.[44] It was in a carefully cultivated antiunion, probusiness environment that the Loray Corporation began operations in Savannah in 1966. By the summer of 1968, Loray employed 110 workers sewing dresses for the popular Charm line. Lee Schwartz, a man with much experience in the New York garment industry, led the Loray plant from its beginning. In January 1969 the ILGWU began an organizing campaign at the garment factory on Savannah's industrial west side. Seven employees, six women and one man, formed the organizing committee at Loray. The organizing committee held its first meeting at the Howard Johnson motel with Walter Leste, an ILGWU regional organizer. Schwartz himself, along with an anonymous driver, surveilled the meeting from a black Cadillac in the motel parking lot. As Leste came out of the motel room to confront Schwartz, the driver took off. Leste jumped in his own car and pursued the black Cadillac. Through a comparison of license plate numbers, he later managed to confirm that the car belonged to an attorney often seen with Schwartz.[45]

A few months after the organizing committee meeting, Leste stationed himself by the plant's driveway and distributed union fliers to workers as they arrived and left the factory. Schwartz quickly hired two off-duty police officers to thwart the ILGWU's informational campaign. A few short hours after they were hired, the uniformed officers arrested Leste for distributing handbills near the plant, saying, "The people who own this shop don't want you here." After being arrested on public property, Leste was forced into the executive offices at Loray to await a patrol car to take him to jail. The following day the *Savannah Morning News* ran a brief article about the incident, headlined "Union Man Is Arrested at Plant." After a few days the case against Leste was dismissed by the court. Not only did the ILGWU's attorney argue that Leste was on public property, and thus perfectly within his rights to distribute union literature, but the arresting officer admitted that he did not know which state statute Leste had violated, although Leste had officially been charged with "failing to move when ordered by police officers."[46] Despite the inadequacies of the charge against the union, the effect of a police presence and Leste's arrest was certain, and it made organizing the workers at Loray even more difficult.

Following NLRB procedures passed in 1959, the initial stage of a unionization effort requires that at least 30 percent of the employees in any given production unit sign union cards. The process of union-card signing provides a way to gauge a group of workers' interest in a labor union. Once 30 percent of the employees sign cards, an NLRB-supervised union election can be called to certify a union as the collective bargaining agent of the workers in a production unit.[47]

As the card-signing phase began at Loray in the spring of 1969, the atmosphere quickly became tense. Schwartz signed and posted a threatening bulletin that cautioned employees, "beware of what you sign!" He claimed that signing union authorization cards might result in "union fines, dues and assessments which you really do not wish to pay." Supervisors and Schwartz himself intimidated individual workers on the floor of the sewing room. Just prior to the ILGWU's first organizational meeting in Savannah, Schwartz held a series of "captive meetings" with Loray employees in which he described the union as a "cancer" and made his opposition to the union plain. In these meetings Schwartz repeatedly threatened the workers' livelihoods. He told the women sewing machine operators that he had informants and knew which workers had signed union cards. He promised to pay special attention to the accuracy and quality of prounionists' work, saying, "I can fire anybody, anytime. Not for [the] union, but for 44 other reasons." Schwartz's frequent rants against the union always included the threat of dismissal and surveillance: "This is a non-union plant and it is going to stay a nonunion plant. I can tell you now that there is to be no union in this plant next Tuesday, Wednesday, Thursday or Friday. . . . I do not intend to have a union in this plant. I cannot do anything about the girls after working hours but, if anything happens during working hours, they will be fired on the spot. No talking in the bathroom [or] on my time."[48]

The atmosphere Schwartz created at the Loray plant worsened as Schwartz made true his threats to fire employees for supporting the union. Rene Clark, the only black woman on the union organizing committee, was the first to go. Schwartz implemented an "at-random procedure" to check Clark's production and found that it was lower than the previous week. Schwartz explained that he fired Clark because he "just happened" to look at the production numbers and then gave an order to "terminate that girl at once." Immediately after Clark's firing, Schwartz once again held a mandatory meeting. He made an example of Clark's dismissal right from the start, saying, "I want you to know that there are less people in here today than was in here yesterday and there is going to be less every day." After being informed that the card-signing process had succeeded and there would be a vote of the production employees to determine whether or not the ILGWU would be their representative, Schwartz told his employees that they were free to vote as they saw fit, "but I still say no damn union will be in here. I will survive as I have done before. I had a plant in Gainsburg, Tennessee which because of the union trying to come is a ghost town today." Schwartz's antiunion tactics went beyond dismissal to outright physical harassment on the shop floor. Two union members remembered how Schwartz rushed over to their machines to chastise them on the plant floor for wearing ILGWU buttons. One worker alleged that Schwartz nearly ripped the button off her blouse. After the confrontations, Schwartz stormed away, saying, "I will expect your work to be checked." By that afternoon, another unionist at Loray had been fired.[49]

By April the ILGWU had enough information to file an unfair labor practices complaint against the Loray Corporation for violations of the National Labor Relations Act. Although the NLRB rejected the trial examiner's initial penalty recommendation to forego an election and simply designate the ILGWU as the official representative of Loray's production employees, the board's decision required Schwartz himself to make it clear to his workers that they would suffer no retribution at his hands if they were to vote in support of the union. Saying that an "atmosphere of fear [was] generated by the [company's] illegal threats, interrogations and discharges [of employees]," the members of the board ensured that Loray was sanctioned for its "outrageous" and "pervasive" violations of employee rights.[50] In explaining its creative approach to sanctions in this case, the board noted that the "usual remedies [of] the posting of a notice and the order for reinstatement and backpay for the discriminatees, are insufficient to dissipate the effects of [Loray's] extensive and flagrant unfair labor practices." Instead, the board ordered Schwartz himself to lead the effort to explain to the workers at Loray that they were entitled to union representation if they so chose. He was ordered to personally sign and read a "Notice to Employees" written by the NLRB in which the Loray Corporation pledged not to discourage membership in the ILGWU. The notice prohibited members of the management at Loray from "falsely [telling] employees that if we become unionized nonunion customers would pull their work out immediately, they would be without work, and the factory would possibly close," a frequent antiunion tactic of apparel companies.[51]

The struggle to have a union election at Loray was both dramatic and difficult. Despite the efforts of the union and its new members to bring about a union contract, it does not appear that a contract was ever negotiated. The ILGWU's records contain no mention of the disposition of the union local after 1969. The *Savannah Morning News* made no report of the NLRB decision mandating an election or of the election results. Business records suggest that Loray continued to limp along, perhaps in name only, into the early 1980s, when it was officially dissolved.

From the 1930s through the 1970s, the four decades in which the apparel industry grew in the South, the resolve in southern communities to keep apparel plants union-free was unwavering. In an effort to achieve a living wage and decent working conditions, southern women garment workers took to the strike lines and the courtrooms in cities across the region. They argued for dignity and union representation in the face of a patriarchal alliance of company owners, police departments, and local newspapers that went to great lengths to defeat unionization efforts in the southern apparel industry. Company owners terminated prounion employees and threatened to close factories that voted for union representation. Police officers defended company interests and property, while newspapers repeatedly drew connections between unions and violence. The press depicted southern women unionists as something less than ladies and described their actions in ways that highlighted their vulnerability as women and suggested their deviance from gender norms. During the apparel industry's strongest years in the region, working-class women garment workers were arrested, beaten, and harassed for their solidarity and for their efforts to achieve a measure of economic justice in the South.

Chapter Three

"ROUGH WOMEN"

RACE, GENDER, AND SEGREGATION IN THE SOUTHERN APPAREL INDUSTRY

Segregation is one of the central themes of southern history. From the years after Reconstruction until the passage of the 1964 Civil Rights Act, southerners lived under a set of laws that dictated the separation of whites and blacks. From "whites only" lunch counters to "colored" drinking fountains, the symbols of segregation dominate the landscape of the post-Reconstruction South.[1] In the 1940s civil rights activists launched a battle against the legal system of segregation known as Jim Crow, advocating for its destruction. The National Association for the Advancement of Colored People (NAACP) targeted segregation as one of the first battles of what eventually became a century-long struggle for African American equality. Led by a young Thurgood Marshall, the legal team assembled by the NAACP initially chose to force states to comply with the equality requirement of the famous 1896 *Plessy v. Ferguson* Supreme Court decision, which maintained the constitutionality of separate facilities for blacks and whites as long as they were equal. African Americans dragged southern states to court, arguing that they had to provide equal educational opportunities for African American students, especially in graduate programs. By 1950 the strategy changed, and the NAACP argued that segregation undermined the possibility of equality for all Americans. The NAACP's legal team pursued case after case, arguing that separate could never, by definition, be equal. And through their efforts, they challenged the constitutionality of *Plessy v. Ferguson*, which had contributed the phrase "separate but equal" to the nation's legal lexicon.[2]

Although southern legislatures codified racial segregation at the turn of the twentieth century, the Jim Crow system was more than a matter of law. Social custom was an important part of the system that defined "white" and "colored" places, behavior, and roles. In fact, some civil rights activists would later argue that it was the social side of segregation that was most insidious, most difficult to overcome. Informal, de facto segregation governed many areas of southern life, including workplaces. African Americans would later use the courts to challenge their exclusion from certain workplaces and occupations on legal grounds, but racial segregation persisted until well after the passage of Title VII of the 1964 Civil Rights Act, which banned racial discrimination in employment.

Occupational segregation by race and ethnicity was not new to the apparel industry when it relocated to the South. Garment shops in the North were often segregated by ethnicity and race. Although the apparel unions were officially open to all, in practice the unions reflected the demographics of the garment shops they represented.[3] Apparel employers did not, then, simply succumb to the segregationist cultural norms of the South. It was more complicated than that. Like employers in other industries, southern apparel employers used race as a tool of management. It was a way to coerce workers and curtail solidarity. Recent research has emphasized the ways in which managers created and used categories of race and ethnicity to rank groups of workers. Using race, managers defined the relative worth of different groups' labor and measured them against each other in terms of their suitability for specific occupations and skill sets.[4]

Southern segregation was never exclusively a matter of race. Gender also functioned as a particularly important line of separation, defining feminine and masculine spaces. Although it was rarely expressed in legal codes, southern men and women, both white and black, understood their lives to be bound by clearly prescribed gender roles.[5] As was the case with racial segregation, southern society defined certain activities as masculine or feminine. Although those definitions were dynamic, changing dramatically throughout the twentieth century, the barriers to gender equality in employment received less attention from activists involved in challenging racial discrimination. Overshadowed by the struggle for black equality, occupational segregation by gender remains a largely unexplored topic in southern history. In southern apparel factories, race and gender functioned together, creating a complex system of segregation in which race and gender simultaneously marked the lines of division.[6] An exclusive focus on race-based occupational segregation and discrimination understates the importance of gender in the southern apparel industry and obscures the ways in which race and gender were interconnected in practice. Manufacturing clothes was women's work, and prior to the mid-1960s the occupations within apparel factories were, by design, white or black. Examining the life of southern women apparel workers without understanding these crucial facts and the way this system came to be is to miss much of the story.

In 1937 J. E. Barbey went south in search of a new location for Vanity Fair, his successful glove and women's lingerie manufacturing company in Reading, Pennsylvania. Barbey made no secret of his reasons for leaving Reading, the place that had made him a wealthy and successful industrialist. By the 1930s Reading had come to challenge New York as the center for the manufacture of ready-to-wear clothing. As the apparel industry gained a foothold in the mid-Atlantic states, the apparel unions soon followed. A wave of strikes among hosiery workers in Pennsylvania in the early 1930s convinced Barbey to move his company. He vowed that Vanity Fair would never run a union shop.[7]

After the towns of Jackson and Monroeville, Alabama, raised the capital to build two factories to Barbey's specifications, Vanity Fair opened its doors to a largely female and almost exclusively white labor force. The company easily accommodated the southern system of occupational segregation by race and gender. For almost thirty years, the production jobs at Vanity Fair were open only to white workers, and the majority of those positions were for white women. In 1940 African Americans held a slight majority over whites in the populations of both Clarke County and Monroe County, the locations of Vanity Fair's first southern plants, but they held few positions in either facility.[8] Although some workers remembered that Cajuns from the nearby town of McIntosh did occasionally earn positions at Vanity Fair, the workers consistently described the labor force in these early years as "all white."[9] A 1955 company photo reveals, however, that six African American men worked at the Jackson factory (figures 10–11). These men appear in the very back of the photo, behind the group of several hundred white women workers and a dozen or so white male

FIGURE 10. A company photo of Vanity Fair employees at the Jackson, Alabama, plant, 1955.

FIGURE 11. A close-up of Vanity Fair employees at the Jackson, Alabama, plant, 1955. Older workers often referred to the plant by its previous name, Clarke Mills, well into the 1990s.

CLARKE MILLS JACKSON, ALA, APRIL 1955

managers. The black men were most likely employed as bundlers or janitors, but their absence in the memories of white Vanity Fair employees
reveals much about the nature of work at the plant. In other apparel factories, especially those found in the North, African American women were
occasionally hired to work as pressers, ironing the garments before they
were packed for shipping.

With respect to gender, the comments of one worker from the earliest
generation of Vanity Fair employees are revealing. Shortly after opening
day, Elizabeth "Buff" McDonald began working in the personnel office of
Vanity Fair's Jackson plant. She remembered the impact of white wom-
en's employment on the rural county. "Initially, women and the sewing
machine were a perfect match," she recollected. "You saw houses being
painted and women had washing machines when Vanity Fair came here.
And it made all the difference in the world." Similarly, Dot Guy, another
longtime sewing machine operator at the Jackson plant, recalled that the
initial group of workers "were all ladies. In my time there was no men."
In this way, from the very beginning, workers understood the production
positions at Vanity Fair to be the privilege of white women.[10]

The story of Vanity Fair was typical, one that highlights the willingness
of runaway factories to adapt and use Jim Crow segregation to achieve
control over workers while continuing the industry's history of relying on
the labor of women seamstresses. The preference for white women workers in the apparel factories that relocated to the South in the years before
the Second World War was hardly unspoken. Employers and civic recruiters made no secret of their predilections.

Employers frequently used race as a weapon against worker solidarity.
In 1937 a wave of strikes hit three women's clothing manufacturers in the
Memphis area. The ILGWU came in to support the white women workers at all of these plants. Nona-Lee, one of the apparel concerns where
workers struck after learning of wage cuts, responded by hiring African
American women as replacements for the striking white women stitchers.
The strike lasted a month and included a fair number of scuffles between
unionists and strikebreakers. Near the end of the strike, two white women
and the company vice president were arrested after an angry confrontation in which the company officer pulled a gun on the workers. Shortly
thereafter, the company and striking white women workers signed a
contract and production resumed. The African American strikebreakers
were dismissed.[11] At Nona-Lee, company officials used the issue of race to

their advantage, knowing that the union-supported white women workers would be outraged at their black replacements. This was hardly a
new practice in the southern textile industry. Decades earlier, in 1897, the
white women employees of the Fulton Bag and Cotton Mill went out on
strike when the company hired twenty black women. Threatened with losing their jobs to black women, the white strikers agreed to return to work
with *increased* hours. The white women strikers sought to preserve the racial order by returning to work and resigned themselves to their defeat.[12]

In the coal mines of Alabama this technique of union-busting became
known as "divide and rule."[13] And it worked. But "divide and rule" had another important effect. It placed African Americans and labor unions in
a difficult and conflicting position. When African American women accepted positions that had been opened to them only because of strikes,
they aligned themselves against the union and other women workers.
Black and white women thus lost sight of the fact both groups were drawn
to the apparel plants by higher wages and a chance to avoid domestic and
agricultural work. Labor unions, in turn, were forced to oppose the black
women workers, reinforcing a racial divide among southern industrial
workers.

Although the vast majority of southern apparel factories hired white
women as sewing machine operators, there were exceptions. In New
Orleans, a city with its own distinctive racial dynamic, African American women frequently found positions in garment plants outside of the
pressing department. Gussie Woodest worked for the Rutter Rex Manufacturing company for well over a dozen years in the 1940s and 1950s. As
a sewing machine operator, Woodest sewed seams in the pants of the
seersucker suits that Rutter Rex was famous for. Day after day, frequently
in sweltering heat, she and hundreds of other African American women
labored in a line of sewing machines that produced thousands of suits every day. Despite the difficult work, she remembered feeling fortunate, as
a black woman, to have gotten a job at Rutter Rex. "I started working, I
think, around '45 . . . in the factory," she recalled. "Of course, it was a popular thing down in New Orleans for black women to get a chance to make
money because in the 'thirties we was getting like a dollar a day doing
housework, all day. So when we got a chance to get in the factories, well,
that was wonderful."[14]

Although she enjoyed the wages at Rutter Rex, Woodest was eventually driven out of the company by a prolonged strike that began in 1954,

after the Amalgamated Clothing Workers of America won a National Labor Relations Board election at Rutter Rex. The strike lasted almost a year, but Woodest strove to avoid the dispute, preferring instead to keep working. But when the company hired strikebreakers the situation changed for Woodest. It was these new workers who compelled Woodest to leave behind the good wages of Rutter Rex and rejoin the ranks of domestic workers of New Orleans. "We were with this strike business for two years," she said. "And that's when [the owner] got these rough women to come in and that broke up everything. . . . They was just low down. They were rough, like [they] came from the projects. We were church women and they would fight and that frightened me. That's why I left."[15] At Rutter Rex, as in other apparel factories, workers were divided along a variety of lines. Employers segregated workers by race and gender. Differences in education, religion, and social status also manifested themselves in workers' attitudes toward each other. The nonchurchgoing, rough project women clearly violated the group norms established by Woodest and her coworkers and friends. Just as race and gender were simultaneously contested identities, class also provided lines of demarcation among garment workers. But even before the strike and the introduction of rough women strikebreakers, workers were segregated at Rutter Rex.

Race, of course, provided an easily identifiable line of separation. Woodest and her black coworkers toiled under the watchful eye of white female supervisors. Unlike other southern garment manufacturing centers, New Orleans had a long history of employing black women.[16] And yet the racial line of segregation was still clear—there were no black women supervisors and, in Woodest's words, "none of us ever thought we'd be promoted."[17] Male workers were also segregated along racial lines. White men were the highly skilled and highly paid cutters, while a handful of black men held pressing, bundling, and janitorial jobs. In the 1940s a combination of race and gender hierarchies determined the occupation of employees at Rutter Rex. But, at least for African Americans in New Orleans, the multifaceted systems of segregation inverted the usual occupational hierarchy of male over female. African American women had access to a better-paying, higher-status position in New Orleans apparel factories than did black men. African American men in the apparel factories found only the lowest-paying and least desirable positions open to them. In 1915 South Carolina enacted a state law that stated, "It shall be unlawful for any person, firm or corporation engaged in the business of cotton textile manufacturing in this State to allow or permit operatives . . . of different race to labor and work together within the same room." The law was not rescinded until 1960, effectively relegating African Americans to the lowest positions in every industry. It was simply impractical to have white and colored sewing rooms. In South Carolina, the law essentially dictated that sewing machine operators would be white.[18]

Eula McGill, a longtime organizer for the Amalgamated Clothing and Textile Workers' Union, pointed out that in the early years of the southern clothing industry companies often "wouldn't hire blacks," and if they did, they tended to "hire all white[s] or all blacks."[19] Established near the turn of the century, New Orleans factories were primarily engaged in the lightweight suit sector of the men's clothing industry. These factories were nominally integrated along lines of race and gender.[20] Rutter Rex employed African Americans and whites, men and women. However, the pattern of occupational segregation, in which men and women, whites and blacks, dominated specific occupations within each factory, meant that the New Orleans clothing industry still conformed to southern practices and racial mores.[21]

The traditional fears of white working-class southerners played a significant role in the rigid enforcement of occupational segregation by race during the New South years. While apparel employers could have undermined occupational segregation by insisting on hiring workers without regard to race, feelings of racial identification with their workers precluded any such actions. Certainly, government-mandated efforts did little to undermine such segregation. For instance, the Fair Employment Practices Commission (FEPC), which was formed during World War II expressly to limit race-based occupational segregation, appears to have had no significant effect in lessening discrimination.

The mobilization and labor shortage that accompanied World War II in the South and the establishment of the FEPC seemed to provide an opportunity for African Americans to enter the apparel industry in much greater numbers. Moreover, the continued expansion of the southern branch of the apparel industry also seemed to indicate that apparel factories would be more likely to employ African American workers.

These realities, however, failed to trigger much occupational desegregation at all. President Roosevelt's 1941 Executive Order 8802, which established the FEPC to ensure that companies with government contracts did not discriminate in employment, had little impact on the hiring patterns of southern apparel companies. In isolated cases the FEPC did have the effect of opening the doors of racially segregated factories to African American southerners. For example, during the FEPC era the New York–based Reliance Manufacturing Company opened a plant in Montgomery, Alabama, with the express desire of hiring black women.[22] But this was an exceptional case. Like other segregated industries of the era, the apparel industry saw an increase in the number and percentage of African American employees during the war. However, the numbers were nothing like those found in other industries, and after the war and demobilization whites in the South and North resumed their dominance of the apparel industry.[23] In fact, the percentage of apparel workers who were African American declined in virtually every southern state, except Louisiana, from 1940 to 1960. In Alabama the percentage of African American workers in apparel factories declined from 10.5 to 3.3 percent. This decline in the percentage of black workers coincided with a dramatic expansion of Alabama's apparel industry. The overall number of employees engaged in clothing manufacture in the state increased over 600 percent during the same period.[24] Clearly there was a great expansion of opportunity for white workers in Alabama's clothing industry, but a similar expansion did not occur for African American workers.

The decline of opportunity for African Americans in the apparel industry from 1940 to 1960 in Alabama and other southern states coincided with the further entrenchment of Jim Crow segregation and increased white resistance to public desegregation in the aftermath of the Supreme Court's *Brown v. Board of Education* decision. The percentage of African Americans in the apparel industry also declined in Mississippi, North Carolina, South Carolina, and Tennessee.[25] The racial exclusivity of the southern apparel industry actually increased in the decades before and after World War II, indicating that the FEPC and other wartime measures to decrease racial discrimination had no lasting impact on the industry.

In most of the post–World War II South, the composition of garment plants was mostly white and female. Companies seeking to establish factories in southern communities frequently cited a desire for white women workers. Employers used racialized and gendered criteria because it facilitated control of workers.[26] In 1946, according to one South Carolina labor activist, the Manhattan Shirt Company "informed the [Charlotte] employment office that they wanted 500 white women as soon as possible."[27] Three years later, the Louisiana Department of Commerce sought a location for a men's clothing manufacturer by emphasizing the company's desire for "250 white women employees." Further, the company "did not want to locate in any community where they will have to compete with similar manufacturers for white female labor."[28] Clearly the manufacturing companies themselves had designated the production positions in their factories by race and gender.

Perhaps because of these divisions, solidarity among southern workers has never been easily achieved. The lines that separated workers often seemed stronger than the ties that bound them together. A 1947 Department of Labor report suggested that unions would have a difficult time gaining a foothold within the South's new industries for a variety of reasons. The report argued that workers in the South were relative newcomers to the modes of industrial labor and thus lacked a tradition of collective action. The region's increased competition for industrial jobs lowered wage levels and diminished prospects for worker solidarity. More important, the division of industrial employment into black and white job categories impeded efforts at unionization. The report concluded that racism among and between workers would have to be overcome in order to achieve a collective identity among southern industrial workers.[29]

A decade before the Department of Labor published this report, the Committee for Industrial Organization (later the Congress of Industrial Organizations) was already hard at work addressing those issues in the South.[30] In 1935 the CIO made headlines across the country with its call for industrial unionism. In addition to the abandonment of traditional, craft-based unionism, the young CIO gained attention for its emphasis on non-discrimination, especially with respect to race. In its very first organizing campaign, the CIO made appeals to African American steelworkers and their wives. John L. Lewis, the leader of the United Mine Workers as well as the first leader of the CIO, brought the ideal of interracial unionism to the CIO's first organizing drive in the steel industry. His forceful masculinity, revealed with great dramatic effect at the 1935 American Federation of Labor (AFL) convention when he physically attacked the president of the carpenters' union, gave a sense of militancy that the new CIO might otherwise have lacked. The Steel Workers' Organizing Committee was successful in the South among both black and white steelworkers. Philip Murray, chosen by Lewis to direct the daily operations of the committee, endeavored to attract the support of the wives of African American steelworkers. The tactic worked, and the CIO had its first, crucial victory. African Ameri-

cans were critical to the success of the Steel Workers' Organizing Committee and other initial efforts of the CIO. This was not the situation in the apparel or textile industries. In the 1930s African Americans accounted for a
small portion of workers in those industries and thus could not serve as
the key to successful organizing in the southern needle trades.[31]

Of the original eight international unions that founded the CIO, two
were apparel unions. The principal U.S. apparel unions, the International
Ladies' Garment Workers' Union and the Amalgamated Clothing Workers of America, had already established themselves as significant forces in
the labor movement, and they lent their considerable prestige to the CIO.
They also provided important financial support to the fledgling CIO.[32] Neither the ILGWU nor the ACWA officially endorsed racial discrimination or
segregation in their organizations, and in that way, too, the apparel unions
seemed to fit the model established by the CIO.[33] Given the reality of discrimination in the apparel industry, the official position of the unions
may seem to have had no real meaning in the 1940s. But even if the policy
was mainly symbolic, the symbolism was important at a time when many
unions in the AFL had little dedication to nondiscrimination. It was that
commitment to nondiscrimination, particularly with respect to race and
ethnicity, that helps to explain the supportive role the clothing workers'
unions would eventually play in the civil rights movement.

Still, it was a surprising choice to pick Sidney Hillman, founder and
president of the ACWA, to head the CIO's Textile Workers Organizing Committee in 1937. That same year, the clothing industry's daily newspaper reported that there were less than "300 [apparel] manufacturing plants in
the South and Southwest, and . . . 75,000 workers in these widely scattered
plants." The *Daily News Record* argued that the overwhelming majority of
southern apparel manufacturers awarded "good wages" to their employees.[34] Because of the "widely scattered" opportunities for apparel organizing, Hillman was chosen to lead the drive to organize apparel's related industry, textiles. In addition to the inherent difficulties of being called on to
direct a campaign in a different, albeit related, industry, Hillman faced the
challenge of not being particularly familiar with the South. In fact, nearly
all of his organizing activities and successes had occurred in the North,
particularly in New York and Chicago. During a 1933 House hearing on the
National Industrial Recovery Act, Hillman made a rare comment on the
nascent southern branch of the apparel industry. In the South, Hillman
argued, the working conditions in garment factories were generally bet-

ter than those found in the North.[35] This statement perhaps arose from organized labor's lingering focus and emphasis on working conditions, as opposed to wages, in the needle trades. The infamous Triangle Shirtwaist Fire of 1911 left the American public with the indelible and appalling images of young women jumping to their deaths from fire-lapped factory windows. In the aftermath of the fire, apparel unions had come to focus as much on factory conditions as wages. In the 1930s the limited number of southern factories were generally newer than their northern counterparts. The relative modernity of the factories may have made the conditions seem better, especially compared with the true sweatshop conditions of the needle trades in New York and Chicago. Despite Hillman's lack of experience in textiles, he was a dynamic, well-respected leader of a high-profile industry. Moreover, he had served in several different labor posts under President Roosevelt. He had friends in high places, and his familiarity with politics coincided with another goal of the CIO: to boost its political influence. Finally, his unwavering opposition to racial and ethnic discrimination within his union made Hillman a good choice for the CIO's southern drive into textiles.

Because there were few apparel factories in the South, the apparel industry did not become a primary focus of the CIO's efforts in the region. In 1937 a little more than 3 percent of the nation's apparel factories were located in the South. By 1947 that figure had grown substantially, and yet the South still held less than 6 percent of the nation's apparel plants.[36] A decade after CIO directors took a labor leader from the apparel industry and redirected him into another field, the CIO once again focused its organizing efforts on the southern textile industry. And once again, the ACWA was a key contributor. In 1946 the creation of a permanent Southern Organizing Committee marked the beginning of a renewed union focus on the South, officially designated "Operation Dixie." With money in its coffers from the ACWA and with ACWA president Jacob Potofsky on the committee, the needle trade's influence on Operation Dixie was undeniable. The ACWA contributed $200,000 to the Southern Organizing Committee, a figure that surpassed the Textile Workers Union of America's contribution of $125,000.[37] Those contributions, however, failed to produce substantial organization of the southern apparel industry, especially when compared to the CIO's efforts to organize the southern textile industry.

Still, even the Southern Organizing Committee's limited efforts to penetrate the southern apparel industry underscored the CIO's commitment to challenging racial discrimination in an age of segregation, one of the hallmarks of Operation Dixie. In fact, in the fall of 1946 Franz Daniel, the Southern Organizing Committee's South Carolina director, lamented to an ACWA official that "our weakness in Charleston has been that we have organized mostly colored workers."[38] Daniel's remarks reflected the CIO's understanding of the difficulty of its task. Organizing black and white workers into a single organization in a region where jobs were designated as white or black was difficult. In fact, it proved to be an insurmountable problem for Operation Dixie, one that was at the center of the drive's failure. Even the CIO's most ardent local activists in the South had a difficult time overcoming the racist tendencies of workers. Daniel recalled that one committee chairman "wanted to put the Ku Klux Klan on a company stooge that was going around. He was a little bit mad when I refused him permission."[39] While the racism of white apparel workers certainly was not the only problem to plague Operation Dixie, it proved to be one of the most intractable. Even in the face of significant opposition from the very people it hoped to organize, the CIO seemed to have stayed true to its principles of nondiscrimination and suffered organizing failures as a consequence. This commitment to nondiscrimination on the basis of race continued to be reflected in the efforts to organize southern apparel workers after World War II.

Without substantial support or direction from the CIO, the apparel unions still focused their attentions southward in the postwar years, following the apparel manufacturers as they relocated to southern towns. As the unions chased the runaway industry in the 1940s and 1950s, they began to adapt their practices to southern ways. Racial segregation characterized much of southern culture in these decades, and the ILGWU and ACWA negotiated a fine line between their dual obligations to nondiscrimination and the attitudes of potential unionists, the vast majority of whom were white. There was a discrepancy between ideological principle at the national level and practical reality at the local level. Apparel union organizers in the South faced a difficult task: to organize white workers, many of whom held beliefs of racial superiority, into a union that had committed itself to nondiscrimination on the basis of race. In the 1940s and 1950s segregation took many forms in southern society, and those divisions threatened to undermine even a fleeting possibility of solidarity among garment workers.

In the early years of the southern apparel industry, race was a dominant concern, especially among southern liberals. Emory Via was an advisor to the Southern Regional Council (SRC) on labor issues. The SRC developed out of the Commission on Interracial Cooperation, an organization of southern liberals founded in Atlanta in 1919 that worked toward ending the lynching of African Americans. In 1944 the commission merged with the SRC, and by 1950 the combined organization began a more direct attack on racial segregation. The membership rosters of the SRC listed several well-known figures, including Howard Odum, Will Alexander, and Lillian Smith. The SRC was principally interested in addressing the economic consequences of racial discrimination and segregation. In the formative years of the civil rights movement, the SRC helped to give a voice to white and black liberals opposed to segregation.[40] With their support, Via traveled throughout the South gathering data on the prevalence of segregation. A series of questionnaires that he distributed in 1956 and 1957 provide insight into the racial practices and attitudes of southern clothing workers prior to federally mandated racial desegregation. The Via surveys covered a number of industries in the South, including the textile industry, the trucking industry, and the apparel industry. From 1956 to 1957, Via studied ILGWU locals in North Carolina, South Carolina, and Georgia and ILGWU organizers in Tennessee and Mississippi.[41]

Via's surveys of ILGWU locals in Georgia and South Carolina, in particular, were quite detailed. Each survey listed over fifty questions, many of which explored issues related to the ILGWU's official opposition to racial segregation. The surveys also requested that respondents describe the racial composition of garment union locals and the concerns of white and black unionists. Taken together, the questionnaires and responses offer a glimpse of the ways in which racial segregation was implemented in southern apparel factories and union locals. The surveys reveal that black and white workers were concerned about race relations and segregation. The surveys further describe the ways in which southern apparel companies systematically implemented racial segregation in the pre–civil rights era. They relate the concerns of black and white workers about their jobs and perceived threats to their occupation stability. The reports from the ILGWU locals in Walterboro, South Carolina, and Atlanta, Georgia, are especially revealing in these aspects.

After a three-month-long strike for union recognition at the Walterboro Dress Corporation in 1956, the ILGWU finally prevailed and established the Walterboro local. The ILGWU local in Walterboro was biracial, and that fact presented difficulties for union operations, especially with respect to matters of racial segregation. In 1956 Walterboro was a Jim Crow community. As an organizer for the ILGWU in the 1950s, Nick Bonanno spent months in the small town, leading the union to victory. To Bonanno, Walterboro represented the heart of "plantation country." In accordance with the ILGWU's official commitment to racial integration, Bonanno insisted on integrated union activities and facilities. Several decades later he recalled with great pride, "My headquarters [in Walterboro] were always integrated, completely and absolutely.... The kitchen, the proceedings, and the meetings, were completely integrated."[42] Immediately after the strike, the integrated local ran into problems when Bonanno tried to arrange for a victory party at the Walterboro armory. The Walterboro community refused to allow a racially integrated group to rent the armory facility. The brand-new local was forced to have its celebration at the union's strike headquarters.[43] Bonanno and other ILGWU representatives worked against the local custom of segregation, and in the process they risked losing everything.

By the end of the strike and the successful NLRB election, however, it appeared that Bonanno's strategy had worked. Less than a year later, Via conducted his survey of the Walterboro local.[44] Garment workers at the Walterboro Dress Corporation reported that the "race issue" did not have much significance among their union local's two hundred white members and fifty African American members.[45] Considering the racial tensions in the South at this time, just three years after the *Brown* decision, the generally peaceful portrait of race relations that emerges from the Walterboro survey is remarkable. The questionnaire made specific mention of good relations between "white and Negro rank-and-file" unionists. Even in the wake of the *Brown* decision and the resulting resistance of some southerners to desegregation, unionists in the Walterboro ILGWU local felt no pressure to officially or formally segregate the local by race.[46]

Despite the ILGWU's efforts and its modest success in creating a racially integrated local in Walterboro, a closer look reveals that racial segregation survived, especially in informal ways. For instance, the Walterboro local reported that it held racially integrated meetings. Bonanno, as mentioned earlier, was particularly proud of his efforts to maintain integrated union offices and meetings. Nevertheless, as Bonanno himself was aware, some union events were segregated. The survey also acknowledged that racially segregated "activities or local functions" were hosted by the Walterboro local.[47] Even during the strike, before Via's survey, the racial divisions were evident. Bonanno argued that African American women played an important role during the strike, but they participated in informally "self-segregated" strike lines. Perhaps in an effort to uphold the ILGWU's commitment to integration, Bonanno argued that the unionists themselves brought about the separation of unionists by race. He said, "Whatever segregation took place was theirs.... There were certain picket groups that were ... segregated, but not by me, not officially. They did it themselves, because they were friends, and they went to churches [together,] and so on and so forth."[48] So, while the ILGWU succeeded in its larger goal of interracial unionism in Walterboro, South Carolina, the union was unable to subvert local commitment to racial segregation.

The ILGWU local itself reported some degree of racial discrimination in union practices. Although relationships between white and black members were apparently good, the local had no African American officers. However, African American women did serve as shop stewards. The presence of African American women shop stewards contributed in a modest way to the overall good relations between white and African American unionists.[49] But without representation on the executive board and at the officer level in their local, African American garment workers were left without a clear voice of their own in union affairs.

The survey also reveals the depth of the racial divide between white and black unionists in Walterboro. While union officials believed that they had fairly and aggressively represented the concerns of African American employees at the clothing plant, African Americans themselves believed otherwise. The most important issue for African American women at the Walterboro Dress Corporation was "segregation by craft." Black women worked exclusively in the pressing department, preparing clothes for sale after they had been sewn together by white women. According to the survey, the union's officers had done nothing to alter the racial division of labor in the Walterboro clothing factory. During contract negotiations the union committee did push the company to increase the wages of the black women pressers, but they failed to challenge the occupational segregation of black women. Quite clearly, jobs in this clothing factory were either white or black; stitching clothes was a white woman's position and pressing garments was a black woman's position. As a result of this occupational segregation by race, black women were restricted to a race-specific line of occupation progression. That is, black women pressers could advance only within the pressing department, thus limiting the actual number of entry-level positions and promotion opportunities available to African Americans at any given time.[50]

The fact that African American men were not hired by the Walterboro Dress Corporation or, as a result, organized by the ILGWU in this small South Carolina town illustrates another dimension of an interconnected system of segregation by gender and race. White and black workers did not work alongside one another. They did not compete with each other for positions within the factory because they worked "in separate departments." The rigid racial segregation of occupations at the Walterboro Dress Corporation effectively denied African American women equality in employment and wages.[51] Local union officers, all of whom were white, simply did not demand the race-based (or gender-based) desegregation of occupational lines. Through their silence on this point, the local effectively supported segregation.

It is perhaps unfair to judge the shortcomings of the union's actions in matters of race-based occupational segregation. After all, most of the employees at the Walterboro Dress Corporation were white women, and their opinions on race relations probably precluded any substantive action in that direction. Via's survey reveals that "many" white women workers were "opposed to Negroes voting [and] school integration." In addition, "many" white women workers reportedly held "antagonistic feelings toward Negroes" and were "in favor of the White Citizens Councils," a mass-membership organization that mobilized southern whites to resist racial desegregation. Despite the support of white women workers, the local White Citizens Council apparently did not have much influence on the Walterboro local. The failure of the union to aggressively pursue occupational desegregation is best explained by the feelings of white workers about the occupational status of black workers. Via reported that "many" white women workers were "opposed to Negroes having the same economic opportunities on the job as white workers."[52] White women workers feared economic competition with African American workers. Presumably they feared that their already meager wages would decrease if the union succeeded in expanding the labor pool to include African American women, who already earned less than white women.

The attitudes of the mostly white and female employees in the ILGWU's Walterboro local ensured the preservation of race-based occupational segregation. And although most white unionists reportedly believed it was the union's responsibility to protect the "equal rights of the Negroes," they believed that responsibility was limited to actions that did not threaten the social and occupational hierarchy of white over black.[53] Union officers believed that the local had supported African Americans when they "fought for [a] higher pay scale for Pressers" during contract negotiations.[54] And in some way they had. By arguing for increased wages for pressers, the committee acknowledged the rights of black workers to have some of their workplace concerns addressed. But the committee failed to address African American women's most significant concern: occupational segregation.

In addition, it does not appear that the union worked to alter the company's role in implementing race-based segregation. When asked about supervisors' attitudes toward African American women employees, the local reported that supervisors "follow[ed] company instruction only," implying that any discriminatory activity came from the upper echelons of management at the Walterboro Dress Corporation. Whether under pressure from senior management or white women workers, the company maintained segregated bathroom facilities. Once again, there is nothing to indicate that the union attacked this provision on the grounds that it violated the international's commitment to racial integration.[55] The fact that white women outnumbered black women by a ratio of four to one caused an imbalance of power that allowed white women to implement strategies and rules that met their needs. By virtue of their majority position in the company and in the union local, white women ensured the racial exclusivity of the sewing machine operator positions at Walterboro Dress Corporation. Even though white women outnumbered black women unionists in the ILGWU local, it is also clear that African American women may have had a greater commitment to union affairs, as they attended meetings more regularly than white members. Only 38 percent of white members typically attended ILGWU meetings in Walterboro, while approximately 50 percent of the local's black members routinely attended union meetings.[56] Despite the discrepancy between African American concerns and white actions within the union, the achievement of a biracial apparel workers' union in South Carolina was remarkable. The ILGWU maintained a successful local in Walterboro for several decades, and the local ceased to function only when the company closed in the 1970s.

In Atlanta's Local 122, the first ILGWU local to be established in the South and one of the largest in the region, issues regarding segregation and discrimination were more apparent and openly discussed than in Walterboro. As in the local in Walterboro, black and white apparel workers were members of the same local. Unlike the arrangement in Walterboro, however, Local 122 brought together workers from a number of different clothing manufacturers in the metropolitan area. As early as 1947 the ILGWU had negotiated uniform contracts with a consortium of clothing manufacturers in the Atlanta area known as the Atlanta Dress Manufacturers Association. The Atlanta local contained approximately five hundred members from a number of companies that belonged to this consortium. The Lithonia-based apparel manufacturer Levy Brothers was one of the earliest members of the consortium. Carla Gay Dress Company, Lee Dress Company, Pleasure Togs, Rita Dress Company, and Dixie Dress Company were listed as members of the Atlanta Dress Consortium in the mid-1960s.[57] White women accounted for the majority of the union's membership, at 70 percent, while African American women constituted a little less than 20 percent of the local's membership. Ten percent of the workforce was white and male, but the Via survey estimated that only 1 percent of the unionists were African American men.[58]

In some ways race relations in this ILGWU local were similar to those found in the Walterboro local. In both unions, prosegregationists feared economic competition from African Americans, and this left a system of race-based occupational segregation in place. But in the ILGWU's Atlanta local the prosegregationist sentiment came not only from the rank-and-file members but also from the local's officers. When considering a proposal to upgrade African American pressers to the position of sewing machine operator, the "majority of Board [members] voted against" the proposal.[59] Occupational segregation by race was such an important issue in the Atlanta ILGWU that it frequently sparked disputes between black and white women unionists about subjects not directly related to apparel manufacturing. The survey described race relations within the local as troubled, with "many" whites advocating segregated schools. White women unionists apparently felt that privatizing (and segregating) public schools was an appropriate response to government-mandated desegregation, although few white unionists disapproved of African American suffrage. In the final analysis, however, only a few white members felt that the labor movement's support of integration was important enough to undermine their support for their union.[60]

Within the local, "many" African Americans challenged the white segregationists and advocated positions that would improve the situation of African American women in the southern apparel industry. Once again, the most important issue for the black women pressers was job segregation. As in the Walterboro Dress Corporation, the Atlanta local reported that African American women found employment only in the pressing departments of Atlanta-area garment factories. As a result, African American women received lower wages than their white counterparts. They pushed their union and executive board to work to promote African American women to sewing machine operators and other higher-wage positions within the apparel factory. In response the Atlanta local reportedly "fought for higher pay" but refused to challenge the occupational segregation of apparel workers.[61] White women unionists' greater numbers undoubtedly made occupational desegregation an unlikely goal for the Atlanta local.

Occasionally the disputes between locals and the international were substantial enough to warrant action. For example, a small ILGWU local in Charlottesville, Virginia, threatened to pull out of the state labor council over the council's support for integration. The local also was rumored to have passed a resolution opposing desegregation.[62]

In 1950 African Americans accounted for only 7 percent of the national apparel workforce.[63] Despite the industry's tendency to hire whites in most production positions, there were scattered exceptions. For instance, in 1954 ILGWU officials described a contract shop manufacturing skirts in downtown Atlanta as an "all Negro shop."[64] In 1956 an ILGWU representative reported that another "new shop employing 75 Negroes has opened in Atlanta."[65] Even the "white" textile industry was not exclusively white. As far back as the turn of the century, nearly 40 percent of one North Carolina rayon factory's workforce was black.[66] Clear lines of occupational segregation, however, undermined what may have occasionally appeared to be integration at the individual plant level. As late as 1950, a shirt manufacturer in Anderson, South Carolina, listed twelve individuals on its company roster as employed in the position of "coloreds."[67] Race was such an overwhelmingly important identifier that "colored" was a job at the Andrews plant. Most likely, these employees worked as bundlers or janitors. The categorization of those positions under the label of "coloreds" underscores the ways in which definitions of occupations within the southern apparel industry were based on racial categories.

While the race-based line of occupational segregation was readily apparent to the managers at Rutter Rex in New Orleans, Woodest's recollection of the strike and the company-hired strikebreakers suggests that there were other lines of segregation that may not have been as apparent to her employers. From a purely race-based or gender-based perspective, the rough women hired by Rutter Rex to replace Woodest and her fellow strikers fit the bill. They were women, they were black. But Woodest was aware of other differences, differences that mattered to her. She called the "rough women" "low down." She accused them of coming from the projects, of not attending church. They were different.

Similarly, workers at a clothing plant in Jackson, Alabama, recognized other important points of difference among the white women workers at their plant. Arcola McLean remembered that the workers who came in from the nearby town of McIntosh were different from her and other workers in the sewing room. In her words, "They were Cajuns."[68] Vivian Long, the personnel secretary at that same plant, echoed McLean's emphasis on that point. Just as importantly, Long was proud of her level of education and the important role she played at Vanity Fair. This was in contrast to the people she hired for the company's production positions. Some workers could not attend high school, she said, "because they was just poor folks." Illiteracy was another mark of difference among white women workers in the apparel industry. Long remembered that some workers who applied to Vanity Fair could not read and write and, as the personnel secretary for the plant, she filled out their applications for them. She said, "There weren't many, but there were some."[69] Literacy, education, class, ethnicity, and religion divided the seemingly homogeneous group of white women sewing machine operators long before government-mandated racial integration.

A segmented labor force is a hallmark of modern industrial development and the result of political and economic forces that divided workers into segments. When workers are divided, they are less able to achieve solidarity and engage in activities that would improve working conditions and wages. One of the key principles in labor market segmentation theory is that once divided, workers cannot cross over to compete in other segments of the labor market. Scholars have argued that these labor market dynamics were sometimes intentional and sometimes a response to larger economic changes.[70] Occupational segregation provided formal divisions according to race and gender in the apparel industry. Class, social, and cultural differences combined with occupational segregation in the apparel industry to divide workers and thwart the development of solidarity.

Race, gender, and class provided the most obvious lines of demarcation within a complex hierarchy of similarities and differences. While it may be useful to examine these categories separately, it is important to recognize that these systems of categorization rarely functioned, or were experienced, separately and distinct from each other. Apparel workers derived their identity from a variety of sources, all of which were interrelated.

In the 1940s Rutter Rex was, on the surface, an integrated apparel factory. The apparel manufacturing company hired men and women, whites and blacks, and even people of different classes. But beneath the surface, occupational segregation reinforced the separateness these categories implied. When the hiring of "rough women" threatened the class-based exclusivity of the position of sewing machine operator, Woodest sought work elsewhere. Rutter Rex had found an effective weapon against worker solidarity. Perhaps the managers at Rutter Rex knew this all along.

In 1956 organized labor's commitment to civil rights and interracial unionism met with strong resistance in McComb, Mississippi. While attempting to organize the McComb Manufacturing Company, which employed only white workers, ILGWU organizers were forced to combat the race-card technique of the company. Antiunion forces in McComb raised the "race issue" to oppose the ILGWU's organizing efforts. Upon hearing of the ILGWU's $10,000 grant to the Civil Rights Committee of the AFL-CIO in 1956, four members of the McComb Organizing Committee resigned their posts.[71] Although the local White Citizens Council eagerly publicized the grant, local newspapers did their part as well. Al Kehrer, the director of the ILGWU's Southeast Regional Office in 1956, recognized the potential negative effect of that kind of publicity. He wrote, "The story on our financial support to the Civil Rights Committee received very widespread coverage in the Mississippi papers. There is no doubt [that] it has had an adverse effect in some quarters." At the national level, organized labor contributed to the civil rights struggle in the 1950s through donations and words of support for civil rights organizations. In response to the activism and critical words of A. Philip Randolph, the president of the Brotherhood of Sleeping Car Porters, the newly merged AFL-CIO created the Civil Rights Committee. Critics argued that the committee did not have the necessary power to effect change rapidly. In fact, the committee's first chairman,

James B. Carey of the International Union of Electrical Workers, resigned
from his post after less than a year, alleging that the committee was unable to effect change on racial matters. Charles Zimmerman, vice president of the ILGWU, replaced Carey as chairman. David Dubinsky, the president of the ILGWU, also served on the committee, as secretary-treasurer.[72]

During another drive in 1957, organizers in North Carolina reported
similar use of the race issue to combat unionization. In the aftermath of
the momentous 1954 desegregation decision by the Supreme Court, the
management of the Ahoskie Garment Company reportedly threatened
white employees with integration of the factory if the factory was successfully organized. The ILGWU organizer concluded that the race card
"stopped the campaign dead in its tracks." Faced with potential unionists
who strongly resented the notion of an integrated workplace, the organizers equivocated on the issue of racial segregation: "We simply stated
that the Union does not hire, or set hiring policies." But, "in other situations," the organizer continued, "we point out that we have a large Negro
membership. . . . We also consistently point out that we don't organize on
the basis of race—that we organize garment workers on the basis of their
being garment workers."[73] In the case of the Ahoskie Garment Company
organizing drive, the ILGWU organizers purposely tailored their response
to accommodate, at least in part, the segregationists within the workforce
by sidestepping the issue of integration. They knew that the company's
threat of an integrated workplace was especially effective in southern
states after the Supreme Court's 1954 decision, and they opted to placate
segregationists while, at the same time, posing no literal threat to the
union's official position on race. Organizers in both North Carolina and
Mississippi reported that the "race issue" was used "more now than it was
before the desegregation decision." In addition, they believed that the employer technique of opposing unionization by arguing that it would force
the company to hire African Americans was "more effective" than it had
been before the desegregation decision.[74]

As evidence of the success of the race-card technique, occupational
segregation in the southern apparel industry persisted for decades after
the industry's arrival in the South. African Americans were few and far
between in both the southern textile and apparel industries, largely employed in small numbers as janitors, bundlers, or pressers until well into
the 1960s.[75] In this way the industries were similar. However, the situation was quite different with respect to gender. From 1940 to 1950, over

75 percent of the apparel workers in the United States were women, while the average for women in the textile industry was less than 50 percent for the same period.[76] And while the CIO placed race at the center of many of its organizing drives, gender did not rank as one of its primary concerns. Nevertheless, by affiliating with the CIO, the ACWA and ILGWU officially committed themselves to the principle of nondiscrimination on the basis of gender in organizing and hiring practices. The original constitution of the CIO pledged to organize "the working men *and* women of America regardless of race, creed, color or nationality."[77] The discrepancy between ideological commitment and practical reality proved great. When Virginia Durr, the famous southern liberal, recalled her interaction with the CIO organizing drive in the South in her autobiography, she highlighted one of the reasons for its failure:

> I identified with the labor movement, but it took me a long time to realize that the labor movement didn't identify with me. I remember going to one of the CIO conventions. I was considerably younger and prettier then and I was very earnest and lobbying a great deal. All the men wanted to do was take me out and buy me a drink. They wanted to have a great time. I had a terrible shock. I thought all labor men were going to be great. . . . They were going to be just as interested as I was . . . in fighting for the rights of labor. I got the biggest shock of my life to see those fat flunkies sitting around guzzling booze and chasing women. That's what they did. That's human, but it was a great disappointment to me. I lost a lot of illusions.

For Durr, the gender inequality of the union environment effectively undermined the class-oriented goals of the CIO.[78]

The ILGWU itself suffered from the same type of behavior by union officials. Nick Bonanno, director of the Southeast Region from 1969 until the 1980s, claimed that the former director of the region, E. T. "Al" Kehrer, "was a womanizer" and that his long list of sexual indiscretions hurt the movement. (Kehrer was director from 1954 to 1964.) And this kind of activity was not limited to the confines of the union's southern office and personnel. According to Bonanno, another regional director "used to bring in these country girls from small towns for sensitivity sessions. They'd sit around holding hands and, you know." Bonanno's own perspective on these activities is particularly revealing. He said, "I'm not opposed to womanizing to a certain extent, don't get me wrong. I'm not a saint."[79] Remarks like these suggest a patriarchal and sexist environment that may not have been particularly conducive to organizing an industry that was overwhelmingly female.

Representations of women workers in apparel union newspapers reveal the ways in which the unions underestimated the power of women workers and placed them in a separate category from male employees. Over and over, union newspapers depicted women operators and unionists as sexualized objects. In 1950 the ACWA's own journal, the *Advance*, published a cartoon that poked fun at women unionists. Showing a seated crowd of men and women at the World's Fair, the cartoon's caption reads, "Things were sort of crowded at the World's Fair." In the foreground a young woman is seated on a man's lap as she listens to him explain, "It's all right for you to sit on my lap, —after all we're all brothers and sisters."[80] This cartoon depicted women workers as gullible, sexualized objects. This representation helped to reinforce the reality of sexual exploitation of women workers at work rather than attacking it.

In the 1940s a regular feature of the *Advance* entitled The Union Member at Home included articles on makeup, dress patterns, and date etiquette. Although this page was certainly an effort to attract women unionists, it was also an approach that highlighted domesticity and women workers' sexuality, not workers' rights, union policy, or politics. Those more serious and therefore masculine issues were the focus of a separate section entitled Men, Books, and Things. The *Advance* gave implicit sanction to traditional gender roles and segregation of the sexes through these two pages. Interestingly enough, in 1941 the editors of the *Advance* occasionally replaced The Union Member at Home with similar section entitled The Lighter Side of Life: A Page for the Ladies. One typical page included articles with the following headlines: "Longer Days Make Children's Bedtime a Big Problem," "Save Some of Your Charm for Your Family!—It Pays!" and "Why Not a New Complexion to Match a New Spring Bonnet." The Lighter Side also included several essays offering advice on domestic and appearance issues. For instance, one article, "A Tip on Charm," warned its readers against sloppy shoes, saying, "Remember, people see your feet as well as your head. Keep your shoes polished and the heels straight. You will get longer wear from your shoes and look smarter."[81]

The *Advance*'s coverage of one southern strike had a similar emphasis on domesticity. In March 1941 approximately 175 women garment workers in the Atlanta Cluett-Peabody plant began a spontaneous walkout. The *Advance* article that covered the origins of what became a three-plant strike stressed the domesticity, as opposed to the solidarity, of women union members. It described the warm, cozy atmosphere provided by the striking women: "Inside a big new tent set up by the Amalgamated, a stove throws out cheerful heat and coffee and sandwiches are served."[82] The domestic image put forth in this assessment of the strike detracted from the achievement of these women workers as unionists. Although the *Advance* did make appeals to women workers, it did so by sending a clear message about appropriate and segregated goals and interests for men and women.

Of course, gender also determined the nature of southern women's work outside of the apparel unions. After World War II clothing manufacturers looking to relocate to the South frequently cited their desire for female labor. In 1954 the secretary of the Georgia Department of Commerce sent a memo to "ILGWU Organizers" explaining that several companies had expressed interest in locating in Georgia. The memo details the requirements of two blouse manufacturers. Both firms requested information on "available female labor pools," and both operations (or their agents) were currently located in New York City.[83] Similarly, southern counties looking to attract garment factories would boast of a pliant female workforce in addition to the community's disapproval of labor unions. Vivian Long worked in the personnel office of Vanity Fair in Clarke County, Alabama, from 1946 to 1983. She pointed out that in the 1930s, local men sold bonds to fund the effort to attract Vanity Fair. The men worked selling bonds, she said, so the women could get jobs. "Employment for ladies in this part of the country was very limited," she added.[84] Of course, the "ladies" to whom Long referred were white women. African American women found no opportunities at Vanity Fair prior to the late 1960s. Ken Hundley, a plant manager at the same factory, explained that Vanity Fair's proclivity for women sewing machine operators was based on a belief that women were simply "more dexterous."[85] Patriarchal assumptions about women's essential characteristics explain the persistence of the craft's identification as women's work. Not only were women perceived to have more dexterity, but the focus on low-wage labor made the choice of women employees seem natural for the industry. These conclusions reflected a gender-specific contradiction. Women were believed to be naturally more "dexterous" than men, but their great dexterity in handling a commercial sewing machine was not regarded as a skill worth high wages. The apparel industry was (and continues to be) notorious for seeking the lowest wage level possible, and female employment became synonymous with low-wage labor.[86] The roots of this attitude can be traced to the earliest years of the apparel industry in America.[87]

In the decade prior to World War II, southern white women joined the ranks of the nation's apparel workers as garment factories opened all across the South, from North Carolina to Texas. History and precedent dictated that clothing workers would be female, but domesticity afforded little protection to women in factory settings.[88] Eula McGill, a clothing worker who later became the first woman business agent for the ACWA, recalled that women workers were often sexually assaulted on the job. "Right there in the mill . . . the bosses took girls back there," she explained.[89] At the Fulton Bag and Cotton Mill in Atlanta, women workers endured sexual harassment and objectification ranging from obscene language to sexual assault.[90] It was this kind of experience that cried out for remedy at the hands of organized labor.

The apparel industry also had its own patterns of racial segregation and separation. As noted earlier, New Orleans was unusual in that African American women were hired as sewing machine operators in the very first clothing factories to be established, near the beginning of the century. But it is also revealing that Rutter Rex and other New Orleans apparel factories hired *only* African American women as sewing machine operators. Similarly, in the rest of the South prior to the 1960s, the great majority of apparel factories hired *only* white women for positions as sewing machine operators.[91] Long explained, "We had some [blacks] apply. . . . We didn't hire any until that [federal] legislation came [in the 1960s], because most of the blacks were doing domestic work. They were maids and things."[92] White women like Vivian Long resisted the employment of African Americans as sewing machine operators because they envisioned another, more appropriate race- *and* gender-specific role for African American women: "maids and things."[93] Labor surveys in Greenville, Mississippi, reveal that local boosters envisioned only white women workers in garment factories. Eager to attract runaway industry from the North, boosters also sought to preserve the racial and sexual divisions of labor in the South.[94]

The rise of the apparel industry in the South brought about significant changes not only in women's work but also in household economies in the communities surrounding apparel factories. The wages that women workers brought home from Vanity Fair's factories were rarely considered to be supplemental or nonessential to household incomes. In most

cases, women worked because they had to. One sewing machine operator recalled, "In the early years, you did find that most all of the people
that went to work for Vanity Fair, they really needed to work. They had to
work, a lot of them, to feed their families."[95] Elizabeth "Buff" McDonald,
who worked in the personnel office and thus was in a position to learn
personal details of workers' lives, recalled with sensitivity that "some of
these women had unpleasant situations at home and this was their only
means of livelihood."[96] From her perspective, the income these women
earned made their difficult lives a bit more tolerable.

Because the southern apparel industry hired only women for the primary production position of sewing machine operator, pregnancy and
childbirth were common experiences that shaped women workers' employment. For most apparel workers, having a child had a negative impact
on wages and family economies. At Vanity Fair, Dot Guy remembered,
when a worker reached the sixth month of her pregnancy, the company
"just exited you. They put you on pregnant leave [and] of course, you
didn't get any money for it." After delivering her first child, Guy "went back
the day my baby was six weeks old. I really needed the money, I had to
go back [in order] for us to be able to live."[97] The working women of the
southern apparel industry provided much-needed wages for their families and for their communities, but their ability to contribute to their family income was limited by a socially constructed belief that women could
not and should not work while pregnant or shortly after childbirth. The
time off from work might have been welcomed if it was accompanied by
regular wages. Instead, women were compelled by the company to refrain
from work. As a result, families suffered from a loss of critical income.

Despite white women's role as significant contributors to the family
economies of Clarke and Monroe Counties, childcare still accounted for
a significant portion of women's daily labors, although it was commonly
a shared responsibility. Many of the earliest generation of women workers
at Vanity Fair expressed gratitude for the African American women who
took care of their children while they worked at the factory. Dot Guy recalled that she "had good luck getting colored ladies to take care of my
children," but in less fortunate families, "the men stayed at home and kept
the children while their wives worked."[98]

Gussie Woodest, the black apparel worker from the Rutter Rex factory
in New Orleans, was the first person in her family to work in a factory. In
that respect her experience was not much different from that of white

women who found employment in large and small sewing shops throughout the South. Most of the white women who came to work in Vanity Fair in the early years had previously worked picking cotton or tending vegetables alongside their husbands and fathers. It is also revealing that after leaving Rutter Rex, Woodest went back to full-time domestic work.[99]

As runaway apparel manufacturers set up new factories in the South during the first half of the twentieth century, they established a system of gender- and race-based occupational segregation. Positions in southern apparel factories were categorized by race and gender. The apparel unions' long-standing commitment to desegregation made organizing in this racially segregated environment more difficult. White women workers benefited from occupational segregation by race in southern apparel factories. By virtue of their whiteness, they were entitled to better positions in apparel factories than African Americans. The emergence of a powerful, grassroots civil rights movement in the 1960s led to changes in the racial composition of the southern apparel industry. One of the great victories of the civil rights movement was the passage of the Civil Rights Act of 1964, which prohibited racial and gender discrimination in employment. It was not until after the passage of the Civil Rights Act that African Americans made significant strides in defeating occupational segregation by race in the southern apparel industry.

Chapter Four

"WHEN THE GOVERNMENT REQUIRED YOU TO HIRE THEM"

RACE, GENDER, AND DESEGREGATION IN THE SOUTHERN APPAREL INDUSTRY

Beginning in the 1960s, as the civil rights movement gained steam and achieved legal protections against racial discrimination, southern apparel employers began to hire African American workers. While there is much evidence to suggest that employers did indeed segregate workers into positions categorized by race and gender, workers themselves also played a role in creating and challenging segregation in ways that may be less obvious. Arcola "Cola" McLean's recollection of the desegregation of the sewing machine room at Vanity Fair's Jackson plant reveals that at least some white women workers found racial integration intolerable. McLean began working at the plant shortly after it opened its doors in 1939. After African American women gained jobs in the sewing machine room, McLean resigned. "They started hiring black people and that's when I didn't like it then," she explained. "The black people didn't care if they done their work good or not."[1] Despite, or perhaps because of, the departure of white women workers who shared McLean's views, shortly after the hiring of African Americans the ILGWU made solid gains in organizing the previously unorganized Vanity Fair plant. The racial integration of the southern apparel industry was the result of both local pressure and national politics.

In August 1962 the House Committee on Labor and Education summoned the president of the International Ladies' Garment Workers' Union to answer to charges of racial and ethnic discrimination within the union.

The print and television media watched as David Dubinsky indignantly responded to the allegations. At one point Dubinsky stood up and shouted at the committee, "There is no discrimination in membership, initiation fees, dues, wages. There is no class A membership, no class B membership. Our members eat together, meet together, dance together, celebrate together and fight together!"[2] In a thick accent that reflected Dubinsky's combined Russian and New York heritages, the union president both flattered and blasted committee members throughout his two days of testimony. In the end, Dubinsky's portrait of harmonious race relations significantly contradicted the testimony of earlier witnesses.

Six days earlier, Herbert Hill, the labor secretary for the National Association for the Advancement of Colored People, set the stage for Dubinsky's outbursts with allegations of massive, systemic discrimination within the ILGWU's New York City locals. In a preemptive strike, Hill distributed a written version of his report to members of the press before his actual testimony. In the report, Hill argued that African American and Puerto Rican ILGWU members were excluded from representation and leadership positions within the union. He cited evidence of segregated locals and sweetheart deals between the union and employers. Perhaps most convincing and damaging of all the charges was Hill's assertion that the union's own constitution prevented the advancement of minorities to positions of leadership. The ILGWU's constitution listed several prerequisites to running for a position on the executive board of the union. Candidates for these positions were required to have held a paid officer position for at least two years and to have served as a delegate to the national convention.[3] The ILGWU's 1934 convention approved similar prerequisites for the position of president and general secretary of the union.[4] In fact, the prerequisites did constitute a structural impediment to the advancement of members of ethnic and racial minorities, a new segment of the garment industry's labor force and the union's membership, and one that was becoming especially prominent in New York City. African Americans and Hispanics were notably underrepresented in the ILGWU's leadership ranks, while Jewish officers continued to serve, even though their representation in the rank and file of some New York City locals had declined. Despite the fact that the committee itself had hired Hill as a special consultant, the congressmen found Hill's report and accusations to be so unsubstantiated that they refused to admit the entire report. Hill was permitted to read only sections of the report into the official record. Although the full report soon appeared in the socialist journal *New Politics*, the damage to the ILGWU's reputation as a leader in the area of civil rights was already done.[5]

Hill's report was not all that was missing from the official record of the hearing. Shortly after beginning his testimony, ILGWU vice president Charles S. Zimmerman lost his temper, stood up, and pointed his finger at the chairman of the committee, Manhattan representative Herbert Zellenko. Zimmerman accused the chairman of reaching a conclusion before the investigation was completed. In one of several similar outbursts, Zimmerman shouted, "What are you trying to do, make a case against us? You have already said on television that there is discrimination in our union, even before the hearing is through. Is that fair?"[6] After some deliberation and with great reluctance, Zimmerman agreed to have his outburst struck from the record. Portions of testimony from Dubinsky, Hill, and numerous others were also removed from the transcript of the hearing.

From the testimony that remained in the official transcript, it is clear that the union was concerned with civil rights and equal opportunity for African Americans and Latinos for at least a decade before passage of the 1964 Civil Rights Act. Numerous contributions to civil rights organizations and institutions evidenced the union's commitment to minority concerns. During his testimony, Dubinsky listed ILGWU contributions to several civil rights organizations. The National Urban League, United Negro College Fund, Negro Labor Committee, Southern Regional Council, Puerto Rican Scholarship Fund, National Committee against Discrimination and Housing, and Southern Tenants and Farmers Union were all recipients of ILGWU contributions.[7] Dubinsky testified that it was difficult to overcome the occupational segregation framework established by employers. ILGWU contracts, he said, forbade employers from discriminating on the basis of "race, creed, color, or national origin." But, he continued, it was also true that the union had a difficult time tackling employers on this point. "We would like to see that the Puerto Ricans and Negroes go to higher brackets, where the earnings are better, but we are not the masters of it. What can you do with employers, frankly, I don't know."[8]

Because the House committee was specifically charged with investigating the union's record in New York City, the congressmen did not consider evidence and testimony relating to the ILGWU's record on race relations in the South. But by 1962 New York City could no longer claim to be anything more than the historic center of the nation's apparel industry. Since the

Second World War, apparel factories had flocked to western and southern states in record numbers. By 1969 over 40 percent of the nation's apparel factories were located in the South.[9] Dubinsky made only one mention of this important southern frontier during his testimony. He defended the charge that African Americans and Puerto Ricans received lower wages by arguing, "When you talk about lower wages, it is not a question of Puerto Ricans and Negroes, it is a question that in some parts of the country, in Atlanta—in Dallas [workers get paid lower wages] because it is nonunion."[10]

Soon after the hearing, debates surrounding Hill's accusations appeared in political and scholarly journals.[11] The ILGWU appointed Gus Tyler, education director for the national office, as the union spokesman to refute Hill's many charges of discriminatory practices. In a 1962 article, "The Truth about the ILGWU," Tyler responded to an accusation of inferior wages for African American workers in one company by remarking that the New York City local was "about as typical of ILGWU conditions as Mississippi is typical of America."[12] Ironically, the southern connection Tyler mocked here could have supported his defense of the ILGWU. The civil rights records of the southern branches of the ILGWU and the ACWA were strong, although not perfect, and would have provided a much different perspective on the clothing unions and African American apparel workers than Hill offered.[13]

In the 1950s and early 1960s, connections between race and the new challenges facing the ILGWU and the ACWA on the southern apparel frontier were real and substantial. Although the needle trade unions organized within a racially segregated environment in the South, union leaders remained committed to the principles of desegregation. The efforts of both the ILGWU and the ACWA to organize southern clothing workers often focused on an alignment with civil rights organizations and targeted African Americans. If Dubinsky and other ILGWU representatives had thought to include the South in their defense, the distasteful portrait of the ILGWU might not have taken hold.

While New Yorkers watched union detractors drag the ILGWU's good name and reputation through the mud, the nation as a whole had its eyes on the South. For as Dubinsky charmed and attacked his accusers before the largely New York–based media, a much more ominous tale of discrimination captured the attention of the entire nation. On the day the House committee heard its last testimony, the nation watched as Mississippi governor Ross Barnett personally denied twenty-nine-year-old James Meredith admission to the University of Mississippi because he was black. Meredith was escorted off campus as hundreds of white Mississippians shouted, "Nigger! Nigger!" Defying three federal court orders, Barnett successfully delayed the desegregation of Ole Miss for another month.[14] Meanwhile, grassroots and student-led efforts to enfranchise thousands of African Americans in the Deep South continued, despite vigorous and often violent opposition by conservative white southerners. The civil rights movement had long been underway, and by 1962 it seemed to be a permanent fixture in the South.

This was the context in which southern apparel factories opened their doors to African Americans in the mid-1960s. As they did so, the apparel unions took on new challenges to organize new potential unionists. The apparel workforce became ethnically more diverse as African Americans and, in smaller numbers, Latinas came to replace a generation of predominantly white women stitchers. Reflecting that increase in ethnic diversity among the needle trades labor force, union membership also grew increasingly diverse. As the ILGWU and ACWA gained southern African Americans and Latinas as members, they also suffered when antiunionists drew connections between desegregation and unionism. The so-called race-card technique became a mainstay of antiunion practices in the southern apparel industry. The apparel unions' connections to established civil rights organizations were extensive and also served to reinforce the association of unionism with African Americans in the South.

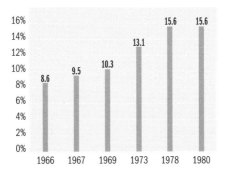

FIGURE 12. African Americans as a percentage of the U.S. apparel industry labor force, 1966–80. U.S. Equal Employment Opportunity Commission, *Equal Employment Opportunity Report: Job Patterns for Minorities and Women in Private Industry*, 1966–80.

Upon the establishment of the Equal Employment Opportunity Commission (EEOC) in 1965 to enforce nondiscrimination in employment, African Americans began to slowly make their way into the southern apparel industry, and the racial exclusivity of the industry declined. For the nation as a whole, the number of black workers in the industry grew from fifty-one thousand workers in 1966 to nearly a hundred thousand workers in 1980, an increase of nearly 100 percent. Other data, obtained through voluntary reports commissioned by the EEOC, showed that the share of African Americans among U.S. apparel workers also increased notably, from 8.6 percent in 1966 to 15.6 percent in 1980 (see figure 12). This increase in African American participation in the apparel industry coincided with a decline in the industry's presence in New York City and surrounding areas.[15] In addition, the number of apparel workers in the nation as a whole suffered a substantial decline during the same time period. Using a separate set of voluntary reports from manufacturers, the Economic Census reported that the number of U.S. apparel workers fell from 1.35 million in 1966 to only 1.18 million in 1982. The increase in African American employment in the needle trades coincided with an overall 13 percent decline in apparel industry employment.

Although the U.S. clothing industry became more ethnically and racially diverse as a whole, at the individual plant level, white, black, and Latina workers in southern apparel factories found the integration to be incomplete. In 1965 Burl C. Robinson, an ILGWU organizer, noted that one South Carolina plant was racially integrated. But at the same time he also recognized a system of occupational segregation. He reported that Capital City, a clothing manufacturer in Columbia, South Carolina, employed "50 to 175 employees. There are approximately 60 to 70 colored operators and 24 to 30 pressers (colored). Supervisor [sic] are all white."[16] The plant was racially integrated, but the categorization of occupations on the floor reinforced racial segregation. Even Nick Bonanno, director of the ILGWU's Southern Regional Office, pointed out that in a typical factory, "black girls were pressers."[17] The pressers, who worked in the hottest rooms of apparel factories, received less pay than the white women who worked at the sewing machines or the male mechanics who fixed the sewing machines. Although desegregation challenged apparel companies to relax their all-white or all-black hiring practices, it did not present a substantial challenge to the pattern of race-based occupational segregation within individual factories.

Black and white workers in the southern apparel industry believed that federal legislation was responsible for opening the factories to large numbers of African American women. Vivian Long, the white personnel secretary at Vanity Fair's Jackson, Alabama, plant, explained that desegregation occurred "when the government required you to hire them." Because the company was unable to ask questions regarding race on applications as it had done previously, Long placed the blame for desegregation of Vanity Fair directly at the feet of the federal government. The laws of the federal government gave African American women a chance at positions within Vanity Fair, and Long resented it.[18] Black women at Vanity Fair also credited the federal government, even specifically the EEOC, with the desegregation of Vanity Fair. Vevlyn "Queenie" Gilchrist, who worked at the Jackson plant for more than fifteen years, recalled that Vanity Fair began hiring black women in the 1960s with the help of the EEOC.[19]

The only published study of African American apparel workers, by Elaine Wrong, similarly points to 1964 as the beginning of the racial desegregation of the industry's workforce. Wrong attributes this change to a combination of factors, including the enfranchisement of increasing numbers of black southerners and a shrinking supply of white labor. Prior to 1960 African Americans in the South were largely disenfranchised. As a result, they were left out of community discussions about the bond issues and tax incentives used to attract apparel manufacturers to the region. But as African Americans gained access to voting booths, they could demand that the numerous apparel factories built or subsidized with local tax dollars employ blacks as well as whites.[20] The traditional explanation for the transition to African American factory employment focused on a shortage of white labor during the 1960s, while newer scholarship emphasizes the role of litigation and federal antidiscrimination legislation in the desegregation of the southern textile labor force.[21] The context created by federal legislation in the 1960s caused the southern apparel industry to integrate its workforce, as evidenced by the many comments about and frequent emphasis on the role of the federal government and its policies.

The precise moment of desegregation in each of the factories is best conveyed by the memories of a whole spectrum of sewing machine operators and factory personnel. While white sewing machine operators frequently complained about the introduction of African American workers, other observers saw a potential alliance of black and white. In a 1981 newspaper article Paula McClendon described the desegregation of the Jackson Vanity Fair factory in the late 1960s as the uniting of African American and disgruntled white workers. In the factory's early years white women were grateful to have jobs, grateful to have an escape from the fields. But as time passed the white women stitchers, many of whom remained with the company for decades, came to resent their low wages and minimal benefits.[22] Other women, especially those among the older generation of employees, felt personally connected and obligated to the company. As one of the original members of the Vanity Fair organizing committee put it, "A lot of the women in there have been there for years and years and years and they were under the impression that if it wasn't for Vanity Fair they'd just dry up and blow away and never be seen again."[23] The white women who began working in the factory in the years surrounding World War II felt a strong loyalty and identification with Vanity Fair, a company that saved them from agricultural work. Moreover, they felt their whiteness entitled them to work at Vanity Fair, an advantage that African American women were not entitled to.

In the 1960s and 1970s African American women were newcomers to Vanity Fair, and they felt much less grateful toward the corporation than the earlier generation of white women stitchers had. One African American sewing machine operator complained that supervisors ordered the women workers to "keep their heads down" and shouted that there should be "no talking" in the sewing room.[24] Another woman recalled, "There were so many people there I would see crying—just crying to no end. . . . I don't like to see people mistreated."[25] It was not simply a case of difficult supervisors and tough management. Sewing was difficult work, as were other positions in the factory. Packing garments into boxes required great skill. And the ever-changing nature of the women's fashion industry resulted in many complaints among sewing machine operators, for as the style being produced changed, the sewing machine operators would be forced to change jobs and machines.[26]

There was also substantial resistance to federally mandated desegregation in the middle of the 1960s. Some white workers resented the demise of their once largely segregated and racially exclusive workplace community. Vivian Long, the personnel secretary of the same Vanity Fair plant for many years, complained that African American women had a poor work ethic. She went on to explain that the quality of production had been better when only white women operated the sewing machines at Vanity Fair.[27] The reluctance of white workers to work alongside African Americans had a long history in the apparel industry.[28] Nearly a decade before integration this feeling was so strong among the workers at a North Carolina plant that an ILGWU campaign virtually evaporated. The organizer reported that "supervisors [told employees] that if [a] union came in, they would have to work with Negroes. This stopped the [ILGWU's] campaign dead in its tracks."[29]

After 1964 interracial workplaces and unions became more common in the southern apparel industry. Eventually the opposition to racially integrated workplaces came to be associated with antiunion sentiment and activities. That connection developed only after the southern apparel industry had begun to integrate and the international offices of the clothing unions sought to improve their organizing efforts by targeting African Americans. Clyde Bush, a Textile Workers Union of America organizer during the Oneita Knitting Mills strike of 1973, commented, "Back in the late 1960s, whenever you went into one plant the first thing that you looked to was how many blacks are working in there. And if there were forty blacks you could count on forty votes." The presence of African Americans in the textile factories resulted in easier union victories, as organizers were able to build on the infrastructure that the civil rights movement developed within African American communities.[30]

In the 1960s the two apparel industry labor unions had to find ways to attract this growing demographic segment of the labor force. Despite the failure of the CIO's southern drive, some believed interracial unionism would arise out of an alliance of African Americans' and white workers' interests. Union leaders had long supported voting rights for African Americans, for they understood that the white southern conservatives who opposed African American civil and voting rights generally voted against labor's interests as well.[31] In 1965 a reporter for the *AFL-CIO Federationist* argued that an alliance between conservative Mississippi businessmen involved in the Balance Agriculture with Industry program and segregationists from the conservative John Birch Society and the White Citizens Council caused organized labor and African Americans to become "natural allies." As Mississippi's industrial labor force grew at a record pace, organized labor came to the Magnolia State to represent the new industrial workers.[32] Mississippi governor Ross Barnett symbolized the combination of the proindustry and segregationist interests perfectly. In 1960 white Mississippians elected Barnett not only for his fierce opposition to desegregation but also for his proindustry stance. Barnett's close association with the White Citizen's Council was no secret. Moreover, Barnett served as governor during a critical period in the history of industrialization of Mississippi. He actively sought industrial development and, while in office, frequently traveled outside the state to attract new companies.[33] The combination of proindustry and prosegregationist voices in the halls of Mississippi's government was undeniable.

In 1960 the AFL-CIO's Industrial Union Department conducted a study on the importance of race in labor organizing. E. T. "Al" Kehrer, then director of the ILGWU's Southeast Region, explained to ILGWU president Louis Stulberg that the study had revealed that "the various southern manufacturers associations, White Citizen's Councils, [and] a wide assortment of Fascist lunatic fringe groups" were linked in the South. He argued that "a public airing of this whole business would greatly help all unions in the South."[34]

The situation was much the same at the local level, as an example from Tuscaloosa, Alabama, shows. In a 1966 memo to Leon Stein, the editor of the ILGWU publication *Justice*, Martin J. Morand, the director of the union's Southern Region, claimed that Robert Shelton, "grand dragon of one Klan or another . . . really dominates and controls the Labor Council." Shelton's "influence [was] so great" that it proved an impressive challenge to organize the garment plants in the area. Morand described the courage of the integrated membership of an ILGWU local in Tuscaloosa that had gone out on strike regardless of the influence of prosegregationists like Shelton on the Labor Council. Despite the use of strikebreakers, the unionists at Andrew Knit remained on strike for months, protesting the "many unfair labor practices committed by the company" shortly after the union won an NLRB election. Morand noted the courage of the black workers in particular, saying that "all the Negro employees have joined the strike and . . . despite intensive efforts by the company there have been no Negro strikebreakers."[35] Given the context of the civil rights movement, the African American workers' courage and solidarity at Andrew Knit was remarkable, and Morand's support underscored the ILGWU's commitment to interracial organizing in the South.

Employers did what they could to turn organized labor's commitment to integrated unions to the advantage of management. In the mid-1960s the race-card strategy of union opposition was hardly new. But the opening of what were once legally segregated positions within southern apparel factories granted the strategy more power. In a recent interview,

Bruce Raynor, the secretary-treasurer of the Union of Needletrades, Industrial and Textile Employees (UNITE!), the successor union to the ILGWU and the Amalgamated Clothing and Textile Workers Union, identified the race-card tactic as one of the most effective weapons utilized by southern employers in their battles against unionization. Looking back, he argued that southern workers faced this potent obstacle routinely, "probably more so in the South than anywhere else." The ability of employers to pit whites and blacks against one another, he maintained, significantly undermined the union's efforts to organize southern apparel workers. "They tell the workers that the union is for black workers and try to separate the white workers. I've never seen a hard-fought campaign in the South that didn't use [the race] issue to divide workers."[36] In the years between the Supreme Court's *Brown* decision and the passage of the Civil Rights Act ten years later, strategies like the race card had more muscle and influence among southern workers, white and black. The civil rights action of this period created an environment in which debates over occupational segregation by race and racial discrimination escalated tensions among southerners.

Many of these issues surfaced after Oneita Knitting Mills closed its factory in New York and reopened in South Carolina. Beginning with the mill's establishment in 1952, nearly every employee of Oneita in Andrews, South Carolina, was white. In the years between the opening of the plant in 1952 and 1965, Oneita hired only two African American men. They worked as janitors in the factory. That pattern of racial exclusion continued until several years after the enactment of the 1964 Civil Rights Act.[37] It was in this nearly all-white environment that the ILGWU organized the Oneita local. Union records indicate that neither the international office nor the union local in Andrews challenged the racial exclusivity of the workforce in the years prior to federally mandated desegregation.[38] Oneita Knitting Mills hired white employees and, as a result, the ILGWU's local in Andrews was made up of white unionists.

In the years before the Civil Rights Act took effect, Oneita managers utilized the race-card technique to challenge the position of the ILGWU as the representative of Oneita's production employees. Frank Urtz, the plant manager of Oneita Knitting Mills, published a bulletin that subtly reinforced occupational segregation by race and gender. The bulletin noted the "RUMOR—That the company intends to fire a number of persons of one race and to replace them persons of another race," adding, "This is false.["][39] Urtz was well known around Andrews for his fierce opposition to the desegregation of Oneita as well as his efforts to prevent a union from taking hold there. Through Urtz's message, Oneita officially denied the charge that the company intended to combat organization of its plant by hiring African American replacement workers. In this way, the company preserved and reinforced the racial exclusivity of the plant. But at the same time, Urtz delivered another message: company managers would protect *white* jobs from union-inspired African American encroachment.[40] Even though the ILGWU had done little to bring African Americans into the Oneita workforce, Urtz used the preconceived association of union membership with racial integration to thwart the efforts of the union to obtain a new contract.[41]

Urtz justified his refusal to hire African Americans until well into the mid-1960s by echoing the sentiment expressed by many white employers in the South in the early twentieth century. He professed that he could not hire African American operators in his factory because he did not want to take away white employees' domestic workers. In an era when there were few mechanical clothes washers in the South, working-class white women frequently hired African American laundresses. In addition, the southern white working class also employed African American women as cooks and, occasionally, even live-in maids.[42] A local civil rights activist and minister argued that white workers in Andrews held the same opinion as Urtz. They believed that African American women belonged in the homes of Oneita's white employees, working as domestics, not in the Oneita factory, working as operatives alongside white workers. Even after the company hired its first black women operatives, whites told them they had "no business" working in the factory.[43]

Once again, the connection between gender, race, and occupational hierarchy is clear. White women were Oneita employees and black women were the employees of those Oneita employees. In 1964 the ILGWU local in Andrews itself reported that of its 142 paid members, only 5 were men.[44] In the early years, working at Oneita was the prerogative of white women. Both race and gender were critical to the definition of employment at Oneita. In fact, the race-card technique was successful because it rested upon the rigidity of race- and gender-based occupational segregation.

Soon after Urtz issued the "race-card" bulletin, the ILGWU local in Andrews ran into some trouble. In 1963, after months of failed contract negotiations with Oneita management, the local struck the plant. For six long months, Oneita's mostly white ILGWU members walked the picket lines and endured life without wages. The ILGWU strike pay helped, but it fell far short of the wages workers earned in the factory. Moreover, there were problems regarding dues payment during the strike. As the weeks and months dragged on, the strike effort dwindled and eventually collapsed. Workers broke ranks, returned to the factory, and sent letters to the ILGWU resigning from the union. Adding to the growing disfavor of the union among the factory's workers, Oneita management offered the president of the Andrews ILGWU local a low-level management position. The president accepted the position and the fate of the ILGWU was sealed. The union local collapsed.[45]

Almost ten years later, after the Civil Rights Act had helped to racially desegregate the Oneita plant in Andrews, the Textile Workers Union of America (TWUA) rekindled the union spirit that the ILGWU had squandered. By 1971, 85 percent of Oneita's workforce was female and three-quarters of Oneita's employees were African American. Two years later the TWUA led a newly integrated Oneita workforce to victory after another nearly six-month-long strike.[46]

Although the ILGWU did little to advertise its support of racial integration in Andrews, the union's reputation was well known. Indeed, Oneita's "race-card" strategy would not have been successful had it not been for the widespread understanding in the South that organized labor supported desegregation. The apparel unions were proud of their opposition to the "race-card" technique of apparel employers. Nick Bonanno, head of the Southeast Regional Office of the ILGWU after federally mandated desegregation, boasted often that the "ILGWU never had segregated locals."[47]

In 1961, faced with an NLRB election, company officials at Bonnie Frances Lingerie Company in Picayune, Mississippi, took the race-card strategy to a new level. Just days before the election, a rumor spread among the mostly white workforce at the factory that if the ILGWU were to win the election, African Americans would be hired as supervisors of the white production employees. To give the rumor credibility, the company had several African Americans pose as job seekers. Although the African Americans were not permitted to complete applications, company officials went out on the production floor after they left and told the employees that the union had sent the black applicants to the plant. As a result, the ILGWU lost the election. Upon hearing of the race-baiting by company officials, however, the NLRB declared the election invalid and ordered another. Although the race-card strategy eventually failed at Bonnie Frances Lingerie, the fact that the company's stunt initially had the intended effect suggests that many white workers in the South were aware of the union's commitment to civil rights for African Americans.

In fact, the ILGWU worked hard to attract African American members throughout the South. In some instances the apparel union targeted African American workers by hiring African American organizers. In a 1956 organizing drive questionnaire, the ILGWU asked organizers to assess the effectiveness of this approach.[48] An emphasis on African American organizing in the ILGWU continued through the civil rights era. In 1965 one unionist emphasized that a sleepwear plant in Greensboro, North Carolina, employed a substantial percentage of African American workers. He further suggested that the presence of African American workers in the plant was a benefit to organizing.[49]

The ILGWU's Southeast Regional Office seemed to be particularly concerned with the racial composition of union locals. From December 1973 through the early months of 1974, the regional office, led by Bonanno, received dozens of reports on the racial composition of ILGWU locals. Reports frequently listed not only the number of African American unionists and their occupations in the sewing plant but also the names of any African American officers in each local. The exhaustive quality of these reports suggests that this accounting must have been fairly important to the union.[50] The effort may also have been part of the ILGWU's attempt to address the weaknesses uncovered by Herbert Hill in the 1962 hearings before the House committee.

Some unionists even contended that African American workers were easier to organize than whites. In a 1963 interview with a business professor from Mississippi State University, Claude Ramsay, head of the Mississippi AFL-CIO, argued that firms with a large number of African Americans were more receptive to unionism than those that were all white.[51] The ILGWU was unable to penetrate Vanity Fair's plant in Jackson, Alabama, until African American women began working there. The longtime personnel secretary at the Jackson plant drew connections between the union and the desegregation of the sewing room.[52] Vivian Long explained the ILGWU's organizing strategy as one that targeted African Americans. From Long's prejudiced perspective, the ILGWU organizers cunningly linked gullible black workers with disgruntled white workers. "You could take a black worker [and] much of them around here don't have too much intelligence. And [the organizers] could motivate them. And if they could find one white person that was dissatisfied, they stuck with that one." To her mind, the combination of black and white workers in a labor organization "festered" like a wound within the Vanity Fair community.[53] From the very beginning of the organizing campaign, the ILGWU's commitment to interracial organizing was clear to unionists and antiunionists alike.

Changes and events at the local level in these rural communities also helped to create an environment that encouraged African American women to apply for positions at the once all-white Vanity Fair plants, thus laying the foundation for a successful organizing campaign. Jackson was just ninety-four miles from Selma, Alabama, the location of the most dramatic episode in the struggle for African American voting rights. While white residents were often ambivalent about events during the civil rights era, saying that Jackson did not experience much formal activity, African Americans remembered the period differently.[54] In sites ranging from churches to restaurants, African Americans in Jackson worked to achieve desegregation. In 1965, the same year in which Alabama police attacked six hundred civil rights marchers on the outskirts of Selma, seven African American men in Jackson formed a group called Men for Dynamic Action. These seven men decided, with very little forethought or formal planning, to challenge the power of Jim Crow by organizing a mixed-race group to enter a local restaurant, Ray's and Tom's, and demand service. Soon after they entered, police cars surrounded the restaurant. Although they were initially put off by the waitstaff while the owner called the mayor for advice, they were eventually served the steak dinners that they had ordered. When the men left the restaurant, they knew that they had achieved "the first official integration in Jackson, Alabama."[55]

Around the same time, Elizabeth "Buff" McDonald heard rumors "that there would be some blacks to attend our church that Sunday." Although no African Americans did arrive that Sunday at McDonald's church, Vivian Long remembered that some African Americans attended white churches without incident.[56]

White residents of Jackson often put a positive spin on the civil rights chapter of their local history. Dot Guy's assessment was typical. She said, "You had a few young [black] people to go into the restaurants. . . . Jackson handled that well. And they showed up at church a few times. Nobody made any moves. In the restaurants they just went ahead and waited on them."[57] Sarah Boykin, one of the first African American sewing machine operators at Vanity Fair, remembered those times quite differently. "Life was hard," she noted.[58] The struggles that occurred in the churches and restaurants of Jackson laid a foundation on which African American women could stand and claim that they had a right to jobs at Vanity Fair.

White workers at Vanity Fair's Jackson plant had mixed reactions to the desegregation of the sewing room. Dot Guy remembered, "The first two blacks that were ever hired sewed on my line. And they were wonderful." While the two African American women "didn't seem to have any prejudice," Guy recalled, "some of the white girls on the line was kinda prejudiced."[59] White workers often resented the demise of their racially exclusive workplace community, and racial prejudices shaped their assessments of the abilities of black workers. In the eyes of the first generation of white women workers, the nature of the work in the sewing plant reinforced the need for racial exclusivity. Sewing at Vanity Fair was a team effort, and individual operators relied on the quick, accurate work of other stitchers on the line to achieve the standard level of production and earn decent wages. A slower worker would mean that garments would not move down the line efficiently and the whole line of sewing machine operators would fall short of the standard. McLean believed that African American women were inferior operators. "If you sewed next to [one of the African American workers], you just had to wait for work. You couldn't make nothing." Racial exclusivity, she believed, led to better cooperation between workers who depended on each other for their wages.[60]

Younger white women remembered the integration of Vanity Fair differently. Sarah Blackwell Philips, a white woman who worked at Vanity Fair's knitting plant in Jackson, remembered that her mother trained some of the newly hired African American women sewing machine operators. "There were a lot of the [black] ladies that learned well. They wanted to work. They wanted to put out a quality product just like [Mother] did."[61] Most of the white women workers did not leave their jobs after integration. Willingly or not, they stayed on at Vanity Fair and worked alongside black women for the first time in their lives.

The process of desegregation was a difficult one for both white and black workers at Vanity Fair. Sarah Boykin remembered, "When I went to work [in 1965] there were about five blacks. [Whites] were as nice as they had to be. A lot of them didn't speak to me."[62] Elizabeth "Buff" McDonald, a white woman who worked in the personnel office at the time, remembered integration as a time of great uncertainty, saying, "We didn't know what was going to happen." In addition to problems on the production lines, white women workers were concerned about the integration of the restrooms at Vanity Fair. According to McDonald, a manager at the plant responded to this concern by mandating that the "first two stalls would be for the blacks. And the rest would be for the whites." McDonald felt that the manager did not really believe that this resolved the problem; he "was simply trying to relieve some apprehensions." Boykin remembered that when she started working at Vanity Fair "prejudiced white person[s] wouldn't go in the stall behind you and stuff like that."[63] Although, like the production lines, the restroom facilities at Vanity Fair were eventually integrated without a substantial incident, African Americans still remembered the sting of discrimination.

By 1965 the Jackson plant was technically integrated, in that African American women worked as sewing machine operators, but at the floor level the categorization of occupations reinforced racial segregation. Vevlyn "Queenie" Gilchrist, a black woman hired shortly after desegregation, felt that she was unable to get certain jobs, especially supervisory positions, because she was black. After being overlooked for a promotion, she told a sympathetic white foreman, "I do think it was prejudice that I didn't get the job."[64] Sarah Boykin also believed that white women had access to training and supervisory positions that black women were kept out of. In this way, the integration of Vanity Fair was incomplete.[65]

The participation of African Americans in southern locals of the ILGWU suggests that however true Hill's criticisms of the union may have been, his assessment applied only to New York City. For it is simply not the case that African American women stitchers in the South were overlooked or forced into segregated locals by ILGWU leaders or the union's rules.[66] Indeed, quite the opposite was true. The union sought the help of African Americans in organizing apparel plants and welcomed them as office-holders in local unions. Organizers listed a number of African Americans on the executive boards of their locals. In 1972 an ILGWU organizer in Spartanburg, South Carolina, reported that while only one of the seven executive board members was African American, nearly half of the local's shop stewards and committee members were black. In 1973 and 1974 locals and business agents sent rosters of African American members of southern ILGWU locals to the union's Southeast Regional Office. Several locals included special mention of the number of "colored" and white union members and officers. For instance, a 1973 report from the ILGWU local in Florence, Alabama, reported that there were "56 colored members. There is one colored member of the Ex. Board." Some locals indicated the race of each employee with a "C" for "colored" and a "W" for "white."[67]

Particularly at the local level, organizers and officers were aware of the need to promote better race relations. In 1969 an ILGWU organizing committee was established by four white women, two black women, and one black man who were employees at Loray Manufacturing in Savannah, Georgia.[68] After Vanity Fair workers requested union assistance, the ILGWU sent two women organizers, a black woman and a white woman.[69] Vanity Fair employees themselves made their commitment to interracial unionism clear. By careful design, the original in-plant organizing and negotiation committee contained equal numbers of black and white women. When they traveled together to Atlanta for an ILGWU conference, the new unionists arranged to share hotel rooms, "one black and one white" per room.[70] President Louis Stulberg praised the southern unionists for their efforts. In a 1973 letter to a member about the conference, Stulberg wrote, "I want you to know that in the wide world of our Union there has never been any discrimination against any group, and we hope that there never will be. Our Union consists of many faces, many groups and many minorities, all of whom are equal."[71] In an effort to combat the "race card" and the

FIGURE 13. Vanity Fair Organizing Committee at the Jackson plant. Courtesy of Sarah Boykin.

FIGURE 14. Richard and Sarah Boykin led the initiative to bring the ILGWU to Vanity Fair's plant in Jackson, Alabama. Michelle Haberland.

"black versus white" perception of antiunionists, organizing committees and the ILGWU itself conveyed a public image of racial harmony under the banner of union activity.

For many African American women workers, union activity and membership were a virtual branch of the civil rights movement.[72] The introduction of African Americans seemed to signal, at least to some white Vanity Fair workers, the arrival of the ILGWU. They believed that African Americans would organize and seek collective action as they had done in earlier civil rights actions. In this way, the white women who opposed desegregation and understood unionism and black empowerment to be one and the same thing were correct. In 1975 Sarah Boykin, the central "ringleader," as antiunionists frequently called her, initiated the first request for union representation by workers at Vanity Fair. Her husband had been an activist in the local civil rights struggle.[73] Boykin described how she came to see unionization as the solution to the way Vanity Fair mistreated workers. One evening her husband asked her, "Why are you crying?" She replied, "If you had seen [what I saw at the factory] you would cry." And then he suggested, "Well, don't cry. What you need to do is get a union."[74] In addition to his civil rights work, Sarah's husband, Richard, was an active member of a United Parcel Service local of the formidable International Brotherhood of Teamsters. Another African American woman on the Vanity Fair organizing committee, Vevlyn "Queenie" Gilchrist, remembered that after she heard about the union's organizing campaign she asked her father what to do. Gilchrist's father was a minister and longtime activist who had experience in collective and political organizing, and his daughter greatly valued his opinion. With his endorsement, Gilchrist joined the Vanity Fair in-plant organizing committee and helped lead the ILGWU to victory at Vanity Fair in 1976.[75] From the beginning of the campaign to organize Vanity Fair, civil rights and labor organizing were mutually reinforcing activities.

A 1968 article in *Newsweek* magazine highlighted the new interracial dimension to union activities in the South. Across the region, black and white workers were joining unions and picketing companies in a racially integrated effort to achieve union recognition and better working conditions and wages. At Wentworth Manufacturing in Lake City, South Carolina, black and white women were part of what *Newsweek* called "a newly integrated attack on antilabor managements all over the South." Black workers in particular brought with them experiences and skills learned "on the streets of Selma and Montgomery, Alabama." After police broke up the strike line and arrested and detained eleven unionists, black women workers demanded their release. They picketed the factory, holding signs that read, "Police are strikebreakers! We demand freedom for our fellow workers NOW!!" The article noted that white workers were eager to follow African American workers in their quest for union representation and contracts. One of the white women workers at Wentworth explained this new attitude, saying, "If we can work with 'em, we can strike with 'em. They stick together better than white people. That's why they've been getting ahead." Interracial organizing posed new threats to business interests in the region.[76]

The ILGWU made no secret of its many affiliations with southern civil rights organizations and causes. In 1965 the director of the ILGWU's Southeast Region, Martin Morand, commented, "The Negro organizations in the South are much closer to the labor movement than in the North."[77] Morand, who would later became the civil rights director for the AFL-CIO, maintained close relations with many civil rights organizations during his tenure as director of the Southeast Region of the ILGWU from 1964 to 1969, a crucial period for the civil rights movement.[78] He routinely and plainly

FIGURE 15. Lake City pickets strike against Wentworth Manufacturing Company for unfair labor practices in 1968. A Wentworth picketer wears a sign that reads "Local 534 ILGWU on strike." International Ladies Garment Workers Union Photographs (1885–1985), Kheel Center for Labor-Management Documentation and Archives, ILR School, Cornell University.

FIGURE 16. African American workers picket with placards announcing their strike against the Wentworth Manufacturing Company and decrying police behavior and arrests of coworkers, 1968. International Ladies Garment Workers Union Photographs (1885–1985), Kheel Center for Labor-Management Documentation and Archives, ILR School, Cornell University.

gave his support for civil rights causes, and he expected the same support for the ILGWU from civil rights organizations. In 1967 the largely African American workforce at Laura Industries in Selma, Alabama, went out on strike. A telegram from the NAACP urged the ILGWU to consider "what is to happen to . . . the Negro workers who may stand to lose their means of livelihood." Morand replied that the strike "has the full support of the leaders in the Negro community" and pointed out that the union meetings had been held in a local African American church.[79] In Selma the ILGWU and NAACP worked together, believing that such an alliance was mutually beneficial.

Other staff in the ILGWU's Atlanta Office also received and accepted invitations to civil rights functions. Jack Handler, regional counsel for the ILGWU's Southeast Region, attended a Southern Christian Leadership Coalition conference in 1966.[80] Early in 1965 a colleague from Pennsylvania wrote Morand to compliment his dedication to the civil rights movement. "I must add a special word of appreciation for your consistent work in the anti-discrimination field," he stated. "Atlanta is doubly fortunate in now having two Martins who share the same ideals in civil rights. Martin Luther King does have a bit of an edge on you with his Nobel Prize recognition but that gives you something to work for." The colleague went on to make special reference to the ways in which Morand's leadership position in the union entitled him to expert status on race relations in the South. "Remember, you will now be an 'expert consultant' on 'civil rights—race relations in the South—etc.'"[81]

The previous director of the Southeast Region, E. T. "Al" Kehrer, was similarly dedicated to civil rights action. Under Kehrer's leadership, relations between the union and civil rights organizations grew stronger. Kehrer was committed to bringing these causes together, seeing both as part of the same quest for social justice. Shortly after he joined the ILGWU's Southeast Regional Office, Kehrer helped to integrate an Atlanta local that had always had separate meetings and officers for black and white workers. Once the local was integrated, Kehrer made certain that African Americans had a seat on the local's executive board. Kehrer was a longtime member of the NAACP and often met with civil rights leaders. In 1961 he closely followed the news of the attempted integration of the University of Georgia. After a court order, Hamilton Holmes and Charlayne Hunter bravely faced racist and violent mobs in attempt to desegregate the university. After their first full day on campus, an angry mob of students and white supremacists threw more than sixty bricks at Hunter's dorm, shattering windows. That evening Dean of Students Joseph Williams informed Holmes and Hunter that they had been withdrawn from the university "in the interest of your personal safety and for the safety and welfare of more than 7,000 other students at the University of Georgia." Kehrer responded by sending University of Georgia president O. C. Aderhold a telegram that read, "I wish to protest the suspension of Negro students under pretext of protecting them. Urge you to suspend hoodlums and morons posing as University of Georgia students." Kehrer participated in the 1963 March on Washington and in 1965 joined Martin Luther King in the pivotal march from Selma to Montgomery, Alabama. In 1964 Kehrer left the ILGWU to lead the AFL-CIO's Civil Rights Department and to teach at the Southern Staff Training Institutes. Reflecting back on those years in a 1995 interview, Kehrer recalled the supportive role the ILGWU played in the civil rights movement, loaning union halls for meetings and frequently providing clerical support to civil rights organizations. But Kehrer insisted that the ILGWU's support was the result of an alliance of interests, that "there wasn't any master plan" to coordinate strategies. "You just grabbed hold."[82]

The ILGWU's commitment to civil rights went far beyond telegrams, committees, and marches. In 1963 an ILGWU business agent from Atlanta wrote Kehrer about his participation in a meeting of the Negro Baptist Ministers Union. Local and regional labor officials were notable attendees. The president of the Atlanta Labor Council attended and other unions, including the ILGWU, sent representatives. At the meeting, a leader of the Atlanta Voters League praised the "Great International Ladies' Garment Workers' Union" for its dedication of "one million dollars for the use of the Atlanta Negro Community in acquiring housing."[83] Clearly, the ILGWU put money behind its many words of support for the civil rights movement.

Relations between civil rights organizations and the ILGWU were hardly trouble-free, though. While the ILGWU never accommodated segregated unions, it was true that the union countenanced informal segregation among union members. Nick Bonanno, the director of the Southeast Regional Office of the ILGWU during the 1970s, noted that white unionists accepted the union's commitment to racial integration. However, Bonanno also pointed out that there was a "certain amount of self-segregation" of black and white unionists in the southern ILGWU locals.[84] There were also concerns in the post-1964 period about the financial irresponsibility of some of the civil rights organizations that the ILGWU had supported.

Bonanno reported that some of the black ministers who received funds from the ILGWU were corrupt. Although most of the tensions between the union and the civil rights movement arose out of financial concerns, the relationship between the ILGWU and a number of civil rights organizations remained strong.[85]

The 1960s and 1970s proved to be a critical era for the southern apparel industry. It was only after the EEOC was established and began keeping records that the clothing factories began to hire African American women as sewing machine operators. But it was also during these years that the ILGWU and the Amalgamated Clothing and Textile Workers Union (ACTWU) won some of their most important victories, including National Labor Relations Board elections at Vanity Fair and Farah Manufacturing in Texas. Those hard-won union triumphs were achieved, in large part, by the participation of Latinas and African American women.

While the unions made it clear, at least officially, that they were committed to ending race-based discrimination, they made few promises about gender. African American women entered clothing factories like Vanity Fair and brought a notion of social justice inspired by the civil rights movement. But gender, the tie that bound them to an earlier generation of white women apparel workers, was not a primary concern of the clothing workers' unions or the industry.

The southern apparel industry, for the most part, had been racially segregated since its very beginnings in the first half of the twentieth century. In this way, the apparel and textile industries are quite similar. With respect to issues of gender-based segregation, however, the apparel industry should not be confused with its related industry, textiles. While the textile industry employed nearly equal numbers of men and women throughout the second half of the twentieth century, women apparel workers generally outnumbered men workers by a ratio of four to one.[86] With the exception of a few positions, such as mechanics, bundlers, and managers, the southern clothing industry was a feminine one. Even today, the position of machine operator in the apparel industry remains one of the most segregated by sex of all the occupations in the United States.

While organized labor supported the racial desegregation of the southern clothing industry, the official record of the clothing unions is less clear on issues of gender. After the failed 1963 Oneita strike in Andrews, South Carolina, the ILGWU offered loans to striking members who were not taken back as employees by the company. The amount of the loan varied according to the gender of the employee. The Southeast Regional Office reported to the ILGWU's headquarters in New York that women could borrow twenty-five dollars while men could borrow thirty dollars. The terms of the loan subtracted any unemployment insurance payments from the maximum loan amounts.[87] While it is certainly true that men, who typically held positions as mechanics and cutters, tended to earn higher wages than women, who typically worked as sewing machine operators, it is also true that the union did nothing to challenge that gender-based occupational segregation of the clothing industry. In this way, the ILGWU itself accommodated an industry that valued men's work over women's.[88]

Domestic obligations limited women's influence in many union locals. As a result of women's dual commitments to work and to family, men simply had more time to devote to union matters. Interestingly, many women unionists in the clothing industry did not have children of their own or reported difficult relations with men. Eula McGill, the first woman business agent in the South for the ACWA, felt mismatched with her husband. While she was on the job, organizing and negotiating, her parents raised her only son. Similarly, Evelyn Dubrow, who became one of the first women lobbyists for the ACWA's political department, suffered "a bad experience with a very brief marriage" when she was young.[89] After a few years' experience organizing and representing her fellow Vanity Fair employees, Emily Woodyard felt that "women are at a disadvantage. They put in their eight hours a day. . . . They go home. They cook supper. They tend to the kids. And they get ready for another day at the plant." Woodyard went on to say that as a result of women's double duty to family and factory, union activism was more of a sacrifice for women than for men.[90] On family and children, Dubrow remarked, "While I love children . . . I never felt that necessity. . . . There's some of us who are domestically inclined and some of us who aren't."[91] The clothing unions attracted women who had some freedom to become activists, often women who did not have husbands or children. Having a family was not an insurmountable barrier to union activism, but it added to the difficulties that female workers faced. The original members of the Vanity Fair organizing committee included both married and divorced people, and most had children. In 1979 interviews the women on Vanity Fair's organizing committee remembered how exhausted they were from their labors for their jobs, the union, and their families.[92] And yet, somehow, these women managed to spread the word and earn the ILGWU a victory at Vanity Fair.

In the political arena, women unionists could be very valuable. The ILGWU persistently sought the active support of its southern women members at the polls. As early as 1957, a bulletin emphasizing the many reasons women should vote in the upcoming election appeared in Alabama. The bulletin asked women, "How well is your house being kept?" and then urged them to "keep politics clean." With a strong emphasis on the metaphor of cleaning house, the Alabama Labor Council's Committee on Political Education synthesized domestic and political images.[93] Another item reminded women that "voting is as much a woman's job as it is a man's. . . . When I hear a woman say . . . 'My husband doesn't want me to vote,' then I begin to think, 'Poor thing, what kind of man is she married to?' I feel sorry for any woman married to a man who thinks his wife should not vote."[94] In this bulletin the Alabama council challenged the depoliticization of women's roles in southern society. An accompanying memo explained how the leaflet would attract women to the polls by discussing political matters "in the everyday terms of housekeeping which every woman will understand." The memo went on to state that the handout "will be particularly effective in those Locals which have a substantial number of women."[95] Clearly, organized labor specifically targeted women unionists for their support of prolabor legislation and politicians.

Given the ambitions of organized labor to have women unionists flock to the polls and vote for a prolabor agenda, the union's reluctance to affiliate with Equal Rights Amendment (ERA) activists seems contradictory. Certainly this was a political crusade, a crusade that sought equity between the sexes in the workplace. Workers from Vanity Fair and organizers for the ILGWU and ACWA reported that the ERA had not stirred up much controversy or support among southern clothing workers.[96] Women who rose to leadership positions in the ILGWU the earliest often opposed the ERA. Rose Schneiderman, one of the most prominent women organizers in the union's early history, denounced the ERA, saying it would undermine protections for women workers that organized labor had worked so hard to put in place. Pauline Newman, the ILGWU's first full-time woman organizer, opposed the ERA for the same reasons. Even Nick Bonanno, director of the Southeast Regional Office during the fight for the ERA, insinuated that the women's movement in general had little effect on his union or the workers the union represented.[97]

Perhaps equal work and equal pay, the primary principles of the ERA, had little meaning for southern women apparel workers, since the clothing industry remained so rigidly segregated by sex and the unions had done so little to change that. Of course, the clothing unions were not the only ones to fail to integrate occupations by gender. In the meat industry, which included a large number of women workers, the United Packinghouse Workers of America failed to challenge industry-wide occupational gender segregation. As women sought access to jobs from which they were excluded, they also challenged union men and their historical dominance of the union. The result of this conflict, whose origins date back to the founding of the union, was a high level of infighting that ultimately undermined solidarity.[98] Just as men dominated the meatpacking industrial unions, so too did men dominate the clothing industrial unions.

Evelyn Dubrow argued that organized labor's reluctance to support the ERA stemmed from the Women's Trade Union League's efforts decades earlier to pass protective legislation for women workers, laws that restricted the number of hours women could work, and that improved the working and safety conditions of women industrial workers. To many, the ERA seemed to threaten hard-earned protections for women in the workplace.[99]

Moreover, advocates of working people sometimes viewed the women's movement as dominated by elite women. Dubrow commented that the ERA supported professional women and worked against organized labor's rank-and-file women unionists. It was a "class piece of legislation."[100] Although Dubrow eventually became active in support of the women's movement (but not the ERA), initially she was unconvinced of the movement's sincerity toward working women. Dubrow felt that the movement "was started by women who were not working in the garment plants. . . . Mostly they were professional women." After initially focusing on what Dubrow saw as "frivolous" cases rather than on important issues like "equal pay for equal work, . . . equal opportunity for jobs and promotions," the movement had to earn Dubrow's support over a long period of time.[101]

Although the clothing unions' support of the ERA was weak and the position of sewing machine operator remains one of the occupations most segregated by sex in the United States, the degree of the segregation eased over time. Vivian Long believed the women's movement resulted in the promotion of a few women to managerial positions and cited this as the only effect that the women's movement had on Vanity Fair.[102]

Gender, race, and ethnicity functioned together in the southern clothing industry. One of the few apparel establishments left in Baltimore,

Maryland, employed a high percentage of women and immigrants. In 1997 an officer from the Union of Needletrades, Industrial and Textile Employees commented of the factory that the workforce was "like a United Nations."[103] As the following chapter will demonstrate, that "United Nations" workforce would figure centrally in the union label and boycott movements throughout the second half of the twentieth century.

Chapter Five

"LOOK FOR THE UNION LABEL"

ORGANIZING WOMEN WORKERS
AND WOMEN CONSUMERS

In 1975 the International Ladies' Garment Workers' Union label became one of the most widely recognized symbols in the history of the American labor movement. Of all the strikes and strategies the U.S. apparel unions have utilized since World War II, none has been as popular or as readily recognized as the ILGWU song and television commercial titled "Look for the Union Label."[1] Created by an innovative advertising team in 1975, the jingle was dubbed "the cry of the American labor movement" and was featured on a host of contemporary television programs. If imitation is the highest form of flattery, then the ILGWU must certainly have been proud when the cast of *Saturday Night Live* parodied the well-known commercial that featured a diverse group of mostly women members of the ILGWU sending a message of solidarity by singing in unison. Although the commercial itself was aired only sixty times between 1978 and 1985, it did much to increase awareness of the union label and to encourage consumers to consider the workers who made their clothing.[2]

A few years before the ILGWU launched its "Look for the Union Label" advertising campaign, the Amalgamated Clothing Workers of America initiated a boycott against Farah Manufacturing, a leader in the production of men's apparel, located in El Paso, Texas. Like the ILGWU, the ACWA relied on a national campaign that encouraged consumers to boycott

Farah products until Willie Farah recognized the right of the largely Latina workforce to be represented by the union. In both the Farah boycott
and the ILGWU label campaign, the moral and political dimensions of
consumption and purchasing power were paramount. In addition, both
apparel unions used the boycott strategy to advance their organizing efforts in the South, where many runaway, nonunion companies had relocated decades earlier. The role of women as the primary consumers of the
household placed them in a critical position to determine the success or
failure of the unions' campaigns. These two important consumer actions
did not, of course, spontaneously develop in the 1970s. Rather, both the
ILGWU and the ACWA drew on a long history of organized consumer actions both within and beyond the clothing industry itself. The history of
this type of consumer protest provides a context for the Farah boycott and
the ILGWU's "Look for the Union Label" campaign.

Although boycotts and label campaigns occupy opposite ends of the
consumption spectrum, they both seek to control consumption in an effort to shape politics and policy. The boycott prohibits consumption of particular goods or services, while the union label strategy encourages consumption. Throughout the course of U.S. history, the boycott has proven to
be one of the most effective and popular consumer actions. Typically, boycotts have taken one of three primary forms. A standard boycott encourages consumers to stop doing business with a single company whose behavior or politics are objectionable. The label is another common but more
complicated strategy related to the boycott. The company affixes a label
to its product to indicate compliance with a specific standard of production. The label strategy depends on the development of a consumer preference for labeled goods and results in a consumer boycott of nonlabeled
goods. Thus the standard boycott prohibits consumption, while the union
label encourages specific consumer behaviors and prohibits others. A third
variation of consumer action is the secondary boycott. This type of boycott
occurs when a group of workers target a second firm, most likely a retailer
or distributor, in an effort to get the second firm to cease doing business
with the primary producer with which activists have a dispute. The apparel
industry, with its complicated structure of contractors, jobbers, distributors, and retailers was—and continues to be—particularly vulnerable to
secondary boycotts.

These avenues of consumer power are deeply rooted in the principles
of laissez-faire capitalism. Indeed, the freedom to give or withhold con-

sumption or labor renders an economy essentially democratic. The right of citizens to engage in consumer actions has been challenged, restricted, and endorsed at different periods in U.S. history, but it has remained a persistent thread in the history of the nation. The potential for groups of consumers to organize and make their voices heard through a consumer action such as a boycott or label campaign functions as a sort of limit on the power of elite corporations and the wealthy.

Boycotts have a long history in the Americas. Far from being the exclusive tool of organized labor, the earliest American boycotts were tools of popular protest. During the Revolution, patriots organized boycotts to express their opposition to the British administration of the colonies. Scholars have noted the political role that ordinary people assumed in the act of refusing to consume British goods. T. H. Breen writes, "Private and personal decisions about the acquisition of manufactured items could be forged into an effective weapon against a despotic authority that appeared deaf to legitimate constitutional grievances." In addition to the legendary tea boycotts of the Revolution, wealthy women patriots refused to wear English-made cloth and created public and political statements by wearing less finely made domestic cloth. Women held public spinning demonstrations to illustrate their support for the patriots' cause. Even as far back as the Revolutionary era, women were understood to be responsible for determining a significant portion of a household's consumption. Linda Kerber argues that the "politicization of the household economy" through the purchase or boycott of certain products depended in large measure on the loyalty of women. Sara Evans points out that women's participation in colonial boycotts reflected an understanding of their role as "political actors."[3] Not only did the success of the patriots' boycott of British goods depend on the solidarity of women, but the boycotts themselves provided women with an avenue toward political expression and identity.

The label strategy also has long roots in American history. Few contemporaries of the Farah boycott or the "Look for the Union Label" campaign recognized that the origins of the union label strategy dated back to the nineteenth century.[4] Fewer still realized that the earliest union labels developed as a way of excluding certain groups of workers from an industrial labor pool. In 1875 a group of San Francisco cigar makers faced increased competition from lower-waged Chinese cigar workers. A group calling themselves the Cigar Makers' Association of the Pacific Coast devised a distinctive white label to be placed on cigar boxes that would help consumers identify the source of manufacture. The label read, "CIGAR MAKERS' AS'N. The cigars contained in this box are made by WHITE MEN. This label is issued by authority of the Cigar Makers' Association of the Pacific Coast and adopted by law."[5] In this early example, rather than being primarily an expression of class solidarity or a guarantee of quality, the cigar makers' label was a tool of racial exclusion, a way of competing with a group of workers that white cigar makers deemed to be inferior (and yet still threatening). Later generations of union label supporters dismissed this obvious aim of the cigar makers' label. In a history of the ILGWU, Gus Tyler argues that this early union label was an expression of class solidarity by the cigar makers and a guarantee of production under sanitary conditions. He makes no reference to its racial aims. A contemporary observer, however, argued that the success of the cigar makers' stamp was due to the fact that "the anti-Chinese feeling was strong and the [cigar makers'] association availed itself fully of this aid."[6] The union label strategy was successful in San Francisco, and other unions soon adapted the strategy to the needs of their own industries and concerns. Male can makers, for example, used the union label—or, in their particular case, a stamp on the bottoms of their cans—to combat the encroaching threat that machinery and less expensive women workers posed to their dominance in the industry. Their label promised "hand-made" quality and sanitary conditions, but it also was a way to combat the deskilling of their craft and the threat posed by lower-waged female machine operators.[7]

These very early versions of the union label depended on consumer support and benefited from the Progressive Era's tendency toward reform and social improvement. They emphasized sanitary and safe working conditions—often by exploiting ethnic stereotypes, as in the case of the Chinese cigar makers. By focusing so intensely on the consumer end of the system of production, the union label strategy directly involved non-wage-earning women in the labor movement. Women, whether or not they earned wages themselves, were typically responsible for directing a great percentage of their family's consumption. By the first part of the twentieth century, women were understood to be the primary consumers of the household, and shopping developed into a particularly feminine culture. Initially department store managers lamented the significant presence of women in their stores, but as the stores adapted new marketing techniques they began to recognize the economic importance of attracting women shoppers. Saleswomen often had an edge over their male counterparts with female customers because women shared a cultural bond that only increased the femininity of consumption.[8]

Despite that reality, one early observer of the union label commented in 1910 that if "the demand for the label goods of a union is to be strong, . . . the purchase of the particular goods should be made by the men *and not the women* of the family." Furthermore, he argued, "it would be difficult to name a single article ordinarily purchased by women in which there is a strong demand for label goods. This is a fact of great importance, since a very large part of the ordinary workingman's income, to say nothing of the income of working women, is expended by the women of the household."[9] Convinced that working-class women made poor unionists and lacked the solidarity necessary for a successful boycott, male union leaders directed the early label campaigns at male consumers, especially those involved in the trade union movement. In addition to labels, unions created cooperatives to help working-class trade unionists combine their resources, cut out middlemen and distributors, and create a union-based network of production and consumption. Recent studies of trade union consumption patterns in the 1910s and 1920s show that it was indeed difficult to gain label loyalty, even among women trade unionists or women relatives of trade unionists. Working women, whether wage-earning or not, were responsible for stretching their family's meager earnings to meet the family's needs.[10] Therefore, when an astute contemporary observer remarked, "It is the experience of the unions that the wives of trade unionists do not insist on having the label on the articles which they purchase," he was exactly right.[11] But it was because working-class women were assigned—as a result of their gender—the specific task of buying most of the goods and services to meet the needs of their families within excruciatingly small budgets that they failed to observe union boycotts and purchased outside cooperatives.

Notwithstanding the experience of unionists in the late nineteenth and early twentieth centuries who perceived working-class women as weak supporters of their label campaigns, other unionists, including those in the clothing industry, would later experiment with the union label strategy to attract the support of women workers and women consumers. At the turn of the century, two of the primary garment workers' unions, the ILGWU and the United Garment Workers (UGW), included a label program in their initial charters. When meeting in 1900 to establish the ILGWU as the national union of the women's clothing industry, delegates authorized a union label. However, the label concept was nothing new to the women's clothing industry in 1900. Tailors' and cloakmakers' associations had adopted labels to identify their garments in the late nineteenth century and brought their experiences to the ILGWU convention.[12]

The union label programs of the decades prior to World War II were spottily enforced and therefore generally unsuccessful. Union leaders in various industries often found it hard to obtain rank-and-file cooperation with the early union label campaigns. From the clothing industry to the entertainment industry, union label officers complained and even cited individual unionists or their family members for patronizing manufacturers or performers that were nonunion.[13] The tension between union loyalty and the grim reality of stretching meager wages in an emerging age of consumption was great. In addition, the label campaign's indirect contribution to improving working conditions, especially when compared to the more immediate and visible power of strikes and organizing, made it difficult to gain label support among rank-and-file unionists. Some argued that the label campaigns were evidence of union leaders' collusion with employers, as in the case of the UGW. Near the turn of the century the UGW granted label privileges to several firms that did not employ union workers and paid substandard wages. This dispute, along with other allegations of corruption, led to the establishment of the Amalgamated Clothing Workers of America by a splinter group of the UGW. Carolyn Daniel McCreesh argues that the UGW's label policy and its "dedication to business union principles" made the union susceptible to accusations of collusion with employers and corruption. The dispute over the administration of the UGW label was at the heart of the breakup of the UGW and the establishment of the ACWA. Furthermore, UGW label officials often complained that it was too difficult to organize women clothing workers and would issue labels employing less-expensive and nonunion female sewers. In 1950 an ACWA-authorized history of the union explained the split from the UGW by emphasizing the latter's refusal to support several strikes. UGW leaders repeatedly adhered to a business unionism philosophy and ordered striking workers back to work.[14] Similarly, from its establishment in 1900 through to World War II, the ILGWU also experimented with a union label, but its use was always voluntary and thus not particularly effective.

Near the turn of the twentieth century, as unions and workers began to implement more and more boycotts, employers responded by seeking the assistance of the federal government to combat potential union gains.

First they established the National Association of Manufacturers (NAM), and shortly thereafter the NAM spawned the American Anti-Boycott Association (AABA). The formation of the NAM was a direct response to the increasing solidarity demonstrated among unionists, especially with respect to consumption and boycotts. Solidarity across craft lines had proven beneficial to unionists, especially with respect to boycotts; employers suspected the same would be true for them as well. Indeed it was. The combination of industrialists from a wide variety of economic sectors resulted in a very powerful organization. These two organizations, the NAM and the AABA, pressured the federal government to legally restrict boycotts and other consumer actions. Not surprisingly, the AABA was created specifically to respond to a boycott in the apparel industry. The famous 1902 Danbury Hatters' Case *Lawlor v. Loewe*, in which Dietrich Loewe refused to recognize the United Hatters union, not only led to the creation of the AABA but also resulted in a Supreme Court decision that restricted boycotts across state lines. The United Hatters vigorously boycotted Loewe's distribution network and promoted its boycott from Connecticut to Virginia and all the way to the West Coast. United Hatters organizers and rank-and-file members attacked any establishment that sold hats made by Loewe's scab workers. Shortly after the American Federation of Labor added Loewe hats to its "Don't Patronize List," Loewe and the AABA filed suit against the United Hatters. The AABA amassed a powerful lobby of attorneys who argued that boycotts across state lines constituted a violation of the Sherman Antitrust Act because, just as certain combinations of employers were illegal, so were certain combinations of workers. The courts agreed and ordered the United Hatters to pay three times the actual damages sustained by Loewe.[15]

Only a few years later the federal courts took the Danbury decision a step further by banning virtually all secondary boycotts. The courts found secondary boycotts to be particularly onerous because they violated an important principle of the Gilded Age: the free flow of capital. Some have argued that the judicial ban on secondary boycotts arose from a fear of the mobilization of large numbers of workers across a wide variety of industries and geographic areas.[16] The ban did not last long. With passage of the Norris-LaGuardia Act in 1932, Congress granted permission for unions to compel companies to deal with them by applying pressure to third parties, especially retailers and distributors. The Wagner Act, passed in 1935, similarly reinforced a wide range of freedoms with respect to secondary boycotts.[17] However, in 1947 the passage of Taft-Hartley amendments to the National Labor Relations Act (NLRA) brought that period of freedom to an end. Senator Robert Taft specifically designed the prohibition on secondary boycotts to protect "the business of a third person who is wholly unconcerned in the disagreement between an employer and his employees."[18] Still the courts had some difficulty in determining just what situations constituted secondary boycotts. Finally, in 1959, the Landrum-Griffin amendments provided the courts with an expanded and clearly enunciated definition of what behavior constituted a secondary boycott.[19]

Thus legal restrictions on boycotts and especially the prohibition of secondary boycotts did not originate with the Landrum-Griffin amendments. Rather, the changes to the NLRA made by the Landrum-Griffin amendments simply codified a long-standing judicial precedent dating back to the Danbury Hatters' Case. In fact, the Landrum-Griffin amendments actually provided an exception to the ban on secondary boycotts for a few industries, apparel among them.[20] That exception, however, existed in a hotly contested area of the law, an area so limited as to make boycotts a very dangerous and potentially costly weapon for unions to use against employers.

The federal government itself ushered in a new phase in the label strategy with its innovative government label the Blue Eagle. Begun in 1933 by National Recovery Administration chief Hugh S. Johnson, the Blue Eagle program met with great success and had a high level of public recognition. The concept was simple: manufacturers who voluntarily adhered to a set of standards on working conditions established by the National Industrial Recovery Administration would be granted permission to use the Blue Eagle as a symbol of their compliance.[21] This campaign and its popularity demonstrated to labor leaders that consumers' purchases could be influenced by the presence of a label and the principles that that label signified. The Blue Eagle label was particularly well recognized in American-made clothing, and union leaders in the clothing industry played a role in creating the industry standards that the Blue Eagle signified.[22] This government-led success provided a model for labor unions. ILGWU officials in particular aided the government in the creation of the Blue Eagle campaign.[23] Participation in the Blue Eagle program was not mandatory, however, and the label suffered much the same fate as the early ILGWU label efforts. Consumer recognition did not always translate into consumer loyalty. Nevertheless, the widespread popularity of the Blue Eagle and the labor standards it represented suggested that a union label might prove more effective than it had decades earlier. The ILGWU would build on its experience with the Blue Eagle campaign and make use of the label mandatory for all shops that had a contract with the union.

With a confidence inspired by the booming post–World War II economy and increased union membership levels, both the ACWA and the ILGWU set out to organize southern garment workers, many of whom toiled in runaway shops for much lower wages than their northern counterparts. Although they employed different organizing strategies, both the ACWA and the ILGWU used boycotts and union label campaigns to address the difficulties of organizing in the South. Both strategies grew out of a recognition of the importance of women as arbiters of consumer spending. The post–World War II boycotts and union label campaigns in the clothing industry also reveal an evolution in the attitudes of male union leaders toward women as workers and political actors. In the postwar decades, union leaders began to recognize the untapped potential of their ever-increasing female membership.

The ACWA was the first to use a label campaign to reinforce its postwar hold on the men's apparel industry. At its 1948 annual convention in Atlantic City the ACWA dedicated a half-million dollars to the promotion of its union label with the express idea of gaining consumer support for ACWA-made clothing. Through the use of sophisticated marketing and advertising techniques, union leaders began to extend the range of label propaganda beyond trade unionists to include the general public as consumers of union label products. Union president Jacob Potofsky explained to rank-and-file representatives that the union would direct its appeal to fellow Congress of Industrial Organizations unionists as well as the general public through radio promotions and advertisements in trade and popular journals.[24]

In addition to boosting the demand for union-made goods among consumers and merchants, the ACWA leadership envisioned the union label as a way of organizing reluctant southern garment factories, thereby bringing the South into the ACWA fold. The director of the national union label effort, Charles Weinstein of Philadelphia, argued that the union label would represent "a guarantee against the return of the sweatshop . . . [and] an effective safeguard against the few chiselers who still seek to undermine standards [in the men's clothing industry]."[25] Those chiselers resided in the South. At a 1954 meeting of the CIO Council of Rochester, New York, one union label worker explained how "money from Rochester consumers is going to non-union firms, mostly in the South, where living and working conditions for the employees are very much lower than in Rochester. This undermines the standard of living here."[26] Union activists understood the presence of nonunion firms in the South as a threat to hard-won union standards in the North and elsewhere and looked to the union label campaign as a way to combat that threat.

Indeed, the campaign was somewhat successful. While touring through the South in 1951, Bessie Hillman, then vice president of the ACWA, made the southern connection to the national union label campaign clear: "We are urging people not to buy clothes unless they carry the union label. Most of these [shops that have contractual relationships with the ACWA] are in the North . . . but last year four Southern firms signed up with us. Now we are putting all our energy on getting other Southern firms into the union."[27] The holdout firms to which Hillman referred all had factories located in the South. The largest holdout was the Palm Beach Company, which included operations in Kentucky, Alabama, Tennessee, and South Carolina, followed by the Merit Clothing Company in Mayfield, Kentucky, Haspel Brothers in New Orleans, and A. Sanger and Sons of Baltimore.[28]

Beginning in 1951, cities and towns scattered throughout the South hosted Union Label Weeks. Typically announced by the mayor or town council, these weeks were dedicated to promoting the ACWA and ILGWU labels among southern merchants and consumers. Although big southern cities like Atlanta and New Orleans took the lead in initiating these activities, smaller towns like Gadsden and Bessemer, Alabama, and Laurel, Mississippi, quickly followed suit.[29] In 1954 ACWA activists in Hattiesburg, Mississippi, sponsored a union label essay contest for high school students.[30] In Bogalusa, Louisiana, Labor Day activities in 1958 included a raffle for an ACWA-made suit, and in Charleston five ACWA members appeared on local television demonstrating "how a union-label shirt is made by union members in a union shop."[31] In Atlanta, one southern-born unionist remarked, "There can be no real prosperity where labor is exploited . . . and the South must not try to go forward as the refuge of nonunion industry."[32] In this way the national ACWA union label campaign came to be directed at southerners and endorsed by southern union activists.

Union Label Week was often scheduled to coincide with the Labor Day holiday and eventually signaled a broader support of organized labor beyond the apparel industry. In 1960 Atlanta's mayor, William B. Hartsfield, issued a formal proclamation to designate the week beginning with Labor Day as "Union Label Week." In the proclamation, Hartsfield urged Atlanta consumers to "observe this period as a tribute to organized labor by patronizing stores, shops and service establishments which feature Union Labels, Shop Cards and Service Buttons." The proclamation also stressed that consumer fidelity to the union label would "protect America." Although the threat to America was not identified in the proclamation, the AFL and CIO were specifically named as the sponsors of Atlanta's Union Label Week. Moreover, the 1960 round of the General Agreement on Tariffs and Trade was underway and the reduction of tariffs on imported apparel and textile products was on the agenda. Most analysts expected that the U.S. apparel industry would not be able to hold on to the protectionist tariffs that had been in place since the first General Agreement on Tariffs and Trade was passed in 1947. In this way, the apparel unions' label strategy came to be understood as a way to combat the combined threats of runaway industry and cheaper, imported clothing.[33]

Many of the ACWA's first postwar label advertisements were directed at women. Union leaders were not prepared to give women an equal place in positions of leadership in the ACWA, but they did recognize that women would play an important role in a successful boycott of non-union-made men's and boys' clothing. As the ACWA's first postwar union label campaign matured and expanded in the decade after its inception, the appeals became more sophisticated. The union enlisted the assistance of advertising firms that used modern marketing techniques to win label loyalty from both union activists and average consumers. Advertisement after advertisement highlighted the role of women in purchasing or influencing the purchase of men's apparel. To reach this female audience, the ACWA placed an extended series of advertisements in women's journals, like *McCall's* and *Woman's Home Companion*. Indeed, one advertising industry journal proclaimed that these advertisements would "be aimed directly at women [since] . . . they purchase more than 50% of men's shirts and almost all the boys' shirts." In 1955 *Printers' Ink*, an advertising journal, reported that the David J. Mendelsohn Advertising Agency had developed a series of advertisements for the ACWA that "present[ed] the union in warm human terms . . . [and] featured . . . individual men and women who make the clothing—people who are typical of the skilled craftsmen who are members of the union."[34] A handbook distributed by the national union label office in New York City urged local label workers to include "women as well as men . . . on [their union label committees], since it is well known to retailers that women have a tremendous influence on all the family's shopping."[35] The union recognized that the success of the label campaign rested, at least in part, on the support of women consumers.

But the advertisements themselves reflected a traditional conceptualization of the role women could play in the labor movement. Although the ACWA apparently envisioned women as potential targets of its label campaign, the union also tended to focus on a traditional and domestic role for women. Throughout the postwar era, women made up approximately 80 percent of the workers in the American apparel industry.[36] Yet union leaders developed advertisements for the union label campaign that virtually ignored the participation of its female members. Many advertisements suggested that wearing suits bearing the ACWA label increased a man's sexual desirability among women. One 1953 cartoon featured two men in an office reading the famous Kinsey report on American sexuality. The caption read, "Ninety-nine point ten percent of women prefer men with Amalgamated Union Labels in their suits."[37] The 1955 series of advertisements placed in women's journals mentioned earlier highlighted women's domesticity. "Nobody has an eye for a good buy like the ladies," one read. "That's why they now look for the Amalgamated Union label when they shop for shirts for the men in their family. Leave it to the ladies to know how spot a good buy. They have a feel for fashion and quality, an instinct for getting their money's worth."[38] Another ACWA appeal made a play on the image of a wife taking money from her husband's pocket. It portrayed women, especially in their capacity as wives, as a drain on family resources. The advertisement featured a man buying a suit and talking to the salesman about his wife, who appears in the background checking for the union label in a man's suit jacket. The male customer says to the merchant, "'It's the *only* time my wife goes through my pockets!' When a wife looks in her husband's pockets *before* he buys a suit—to make sure the Amalgamated label is there—she's reversing the old family 'custom.' Instead of taking money out, it's like putting money *into* the pocket!"[39]

All in all, the ACWA's union label advertisements portrayed women in essentially domestic or sexual situations. The result was a devaluation of women's contribution to the family economy as well as a misunderstanding of women workers as transitory and pliable to the needs of management.[40] The union's failure to portray women as active union members, ca-

FIGURE 17. Mayor Robert Wagner, Senator Herbert Lehman, Governor Nelson Rockefeller, ILGWU president David Dubinsky, and others watch as Mrs. Mary Rockefeller sews an ILGWU union label into a garment in New York City. International Ladies Garment Workers Union Photographs (1885–1985), Kheel Center for Labor-Management Documentation and Archives, ILR School, Cornell University.

pable of the same kind of militancy and loyalty exhibited by male unionists represents a true shortcoming of the early ACWA union label campaign. The union effectively undermined its own advertising campaign—much of which was directed at women consumers—by reinforcing a domestic role for women, despite the fact that the majority of the union's membership was female.

The ILGWU's postwar label campaign bore a strong resemblance to the ACWA's efforts. When the ILGWU announced the establishment of its Union Label Department in 1958, it hired an experienced advertising firm to publicize the advantages of the label to fellow unionists and the general public.[41] The union promoted its new initiative by having the wife of New York State's governor, Mrs. Nelson Rockefeller, sew the first union label into a woman's garment. Just a few years later, Eleanor Roosevelt fastened the eleven-billionth label to another union-made garment. And like the ACWA, leaders in the ILGWU hoped that the union label campaign would help them increase the union's membership. Pauline Newman, a union label officer, had recognized the connection between organizing women workers and the union label campaign many years earlier. At the 1910 ILGWU convention she explained how the compulsory use of a union label would work to gain women members for the union: "At union meetings you find men only. For, sad as it is, . . . the great mass of working women are not organized as yet. And cannot be reached at the meeting. . . . [S]ociety women and women's clubs were rather anxious to have me come and speak before them. These women have a strong influence upon the big department stores. . . . Through contact with these women I next got the opportunity to speak in the churches; so reaching a great number of unorganized women."[42]

The ILGWU's union label campaign specifically targeted runaway shops. The union believed that the South's right-to-work laws and local probusiness governments made the region a haven for such businesses.[43] Soon after the label campaign was underway the ILGWU's Union Label Department created a sample speech that stressed the potential threat posed by runaway shops in the garment industry. After organizing over 90 percent of the women's apparel industry, the speech began, it had become clear that "the remaining non-union shops, though few in number, are hard to get at. And they constitute a threat to our standards." A typical scenario involved "a non-union jobber located, say, in New York City." When faced with an organizing drive at his usual contracting shop in New York, the jobber switched to contracting operations located in "Birmingham, Alabama . . . [or] Mississippi."[44] For a variety of reasons, unionists came to see the South as a refuge for antiunion, runaway shops. Both the ILGWU and the ACWA hoped that their union label campaigns would make the products from these nonunion runaway shops less desirable by increasing the demand for union-made garments. And in time, they hoped that these nonunion shops would find that in order to create demand for their products, in order to stay in business, they would need to use the union label. In short, they would find having a contractual relationship with the ACWA or the ILGWU preferable to not having one.

Another similarity between the two unions' label campaigns was their focus on women consumers. Representations of women in the early ILGWU label campaign advertisements also focused on the domestic and

FIGURE 18. Women unionists model "Union Label Dresses" with ILGWU president David Dubinsky. International Ladies Garment Workers Union Photographs (1885–1985), Kheel Center for Labor-Management Documentation and Archives, ILR School, Cornell University.

traditional features of femininity, although later appeals featured a different perspective. In the early years of the ILGWU's union label campaign, the union promised to meet the needs of women consumers "for reliable information on fashion." Another model speech written by the Union Label Department explained how the ILGWU would hire fashion experts to explain the fundamentals of "How To Dress Well, How To Combine Colors, How To Dress Economically, [and] How To Tell the Difference Between Fads and Fashions." The union promised to distribute booklets aimed at women consumers and containing information on fashion, and it would further sponsor "fashion films, fashion shows, fashion columns [and] fashion programs on radio and TV and advertising of all sorts."[45] In this case, the union's label campaign was aimed directly at women consumers through an appeal based on fashion.

In the early 1970s a "Wage Record Book" distributed by John Denaro, the director of the Union Label Department, revealed an advertising campaign at odds with the ILGWU's mainly female members. Intended for garment workers to use to keep track of the number of pieces completed and piece rates, the booklet emphasized the substantial buying power of union members in all industries, saying, "It's simple. The trade union member-

ship of this country spends some $100,000,000,000 annually. . . . That's
alot [*sic*] of money and a lot of power." But the unionists to whom this appeal was directed were men, not women. Various slogans and missives
printed throughout the fill-in section of the booklet not only reinforced a
domestic image of women consumers but also depicted women as wives
of unionists, not union members themselves. One page read, "The women
of America hold the pursetrings [*sic*] and are the big buyers of retail goods
in our country. As *wives* of union members they can help most by spending union-earned money for goods and services produced by other union
members."[46] The intended audience for this booklet and the union label
appeal was the ILGWU's own membership, and yet the union directed its
appeal to the wives of union members, not the women unionists themselves. In 1970, 81 percent of garment workers in the United States were
women, and the union's membership reflected that figure.[47] Ironically,
the appeal not only excluded women workers but it also suggested that
"union-earned money" was money earned by men, not women. This appeal could not have attracted many supporters among women garment
workers.

As the boycott strategy matured in the middle of the twentieth century,
other popular reform movements began to realize the benefits of boycotts. The NLRA and all of the amendments to the act restricting the legal-
ity of boycotts did not apply to consumer actions that developed independently from labor unions. Instead the courts ruled that boycott activity
by the general public was protected by the free speech provisions of the
Constitution. The principles established in the very early boycotts of the
Revolutionary era were echoed nearly two hundred years later in the boycotts of the long civil rights movement.[48] During the Harlem Renaissance,
African Americans launched "Don't Shop Where You Can't Work" protests
to combat discrimination in their local economies. Decades later, civil
rights activists resuscitated the boycott strategy to encourage businesses
that sold products to African Americans to hire African Americans. The
boycotts of the civil rights era proved that African Americans accounted
for an important portion of the consuming public, and, as a result, mer-
chandisers and producers began to direct their advertising toward this
newly revealed and lucrative segment of the market. These consumer actions were exempt from the legal restrictions of the NLRA, as they did not
involve workers from a single industry or company. Unlike the situation
of the apparel industry, in these cases the definition of a legal boycott was

broad enough to be effective.[49] It is important to remember that in all of these popular protests, women consumers were central proponents of the boycotts.

However misguided the ILGWU and the ACWA may have appeared in the early stages of their postwar label campaigns, especially with respect to images of women workers and unionists, the later versions of these campaigns incorporated images of women as consumers, workers, and union members. The most famous of these more inclusive and representative appeals was the familiar ILGWU jingle "Look for the Union Label." Created in 1975, after feminism had become a political force, the series of commercials featuring ILGWU members themselves singing the praises of buying union-made women's garments was an instant success. Americans and the labor movement itself embraced the song. In fact, the AFL-CIO, capitalizing on the commercial's success, called the jingle the "cry of the modern American trade union movement."[50] Featuring women garment workers in the commercials made the appeal mechanism clear: women urged other women to buy union-made garments. This portrayal of women as workers and as active union members marked a departure from the inappropriate and unrealistic appeals of previous years. The "Look for the Union Label" song was an appeal by women workers to women consumers, who were often one and the same.

The lyrics of the "Look for the Union Label" jingle were well known to an entire generation of Americans. The song begins with one white woman walking onstage singing a cappella, "Look for the union label." As she continues singing, the camera spans wide and she is joined by a multiethnic chorus of workers.

> Look for the union label
> when you are buying that coat, dress or blouse.
> Remember somewhere our union's sewing,
> our wages going to feed the kids, and run the house.
> We work hard, but who's complaining?
> Thanks to the I.L.G. we're paying our way!
> So always look for the union label,
> it says we're able to make it in the U.S.A.![51]

The message conveyed by both the lyrics and the women themselves is one of pride. Marking a departure from earlier visions of women in the union's advertisements, the workers in this commercial were strong and confident and, as the song explains, they were working for their families, "to feed the kids and run the house." Underscoring the reality that the majority of families in the late 1970s required two incomes "to run the house," the women represented by the "Look for the Union Label" commercial contributed significantly to their household economies. Moreover, they were proud of what they did. "We work hard, but who's complaining?" the women sang. The women represented in the ILGWU's commercial were the breadwinners for their families, with their wages going not to superfluous purchases but to "feed the kids and run the house." The ILGWU's new campaign placed women front and center, as both producers and consumers of women's clothing.

The emphasis on women's role as workers was central to the women's movement of the 1960s and 1970s. The civil rights movement and the collapse of the family wage system both played a significant role in the rise of second-wave feminism and the surge toward collective action to achieve social and economic justice for women. As American families became dependent on dual wage earners in the last quarter of the twentieth century, women demanded greater workplace rights. Nancy MacLean points out that in these years breadwinning lost its gender-specific identification and simply became identified with being an adult. Among the working class, however, women's presence in the waged-labor system was not a new development. Rather, working-class women had struggled to define their work lives both within and without labor unions long before World War II and the subsequent rise of second-wave feminism.

In recent years historians have sought to recast the standard narrative of postwar women's history in which working-class women are viewed as the "other" in a movement that was defined and developed by middle-class and elite, well-educated women. Working-class women in the South did not experience the malaise of elite, well-educated American women that Betty Friedan identified in *The Feminine Mystique* in 1963. Their struggles for economic and social justice took place in union halls and on shop floors, not in coffee klatches and university classrooms. There was a practical dimension to working-class women's efforts to claim greater wages and workplace justice in the 1970s, as echoed in the lines of the "Look for the Union Label" song. But women unionists did find ways to coordinate their struggles with middle-class and elite activists in the women's movement. For example, unionists at J. P. Stevens enlisted the support of the National Organization of Women for their boycott of the southern textile manufacturer in the late 1970s. The members of the National Organization of Women were particularly active in the boycott, staging protests in retail stores and calling on the membership to support the boycott. The feminist organization later attempted to parlay its dedication to the J. P. Stevens boycott into support for the Equal Rights Amendment in the conservative South.[52]

The "Look for the Union Label" advertisement also played a leading role in the ILGWU's larger Buy American campaign, which sought to combat the increasing availability of cheaper imported clothing. In an effort to increase awareness of the new label campaign, the ILGWU bought two full pages of ad space in the leading trade journal, *Women's Wear Daily*. The advertisement appeared in the November 10, 1975, edition, the day before the commercial had its debut. In bold letters that spanned the width of two pages, the ILGWU declared, "9 PM, . . . Tomorrow Night, That's when the International Ladies Garment Workers Union takes the big step. We're going to be telling Americans everywhere . . . just who we are . . . and why they should look for the union label. . . . If you make the clothes, or design them, or buy them, or sell them, you know how important this is for all of us. And it's just the beginning."[53] In the days that followed, the pages of *Women's Wear Daily* featured "Buy American" advertisements by other groups and articles that examined industrial expansion in China.

The version of the commercial most often played on network television opened with a modestly dressed white man discussing the apparel industry in a folksy manner. "There used to be more of us in the International Ladies' Garment Workers' Union, but a lot of our jobs disappeared because a lot of the clothes Americans are buying for women and kids are being made in foreign places," he explained. He closed his introduction with a none-too-subtle message: "When our jobs go, we can't support our families or pay our taxes or buy the things other Americans make. Think of that when your label says import instead of union."[54] The concluding lines of the "Look for the Union Label" song reminded viewers to "always look for the union label, it says we're able to make it in the U.S.A.!" This commercial marked the beginning of what would become a hugely popular movement across the United States to save the nation's industry through the purchasing power of American workers. Throughout the 1980s, few American businesses and industries were immune to the implications of the Buy American crusade. The movement had a particular irony in the South. Just forty years earlier, communities across the region had bene-

FIGURE 19. ILGWU members perform "Look for the Union Label" on the set for the union's
television commercial. International Ladies Garment Workers Union Photographs (1885–
1985), Kheel Center for Labor-Management Documentation and Archives, ILR School,
Cornell University.

fited from runaway shops that fled the North for the low-wage South. Now
southerners were decrying the repeat of that same pattern of industrial
restructuring as communities in Latin America and Asia competed for
what were once southern women's jobs.

The successes of the "Look for the Union Label" song and campaign
overlapped with the ACWA's equally successful boycott of the Farah Manufacturing Company. In March 1972 twenty-six Latina workers protested
their low wages, lack of job security, and oppressive work environment by
walking off their jobs at the Farah Manufacturing plant in El Paso, Texas.
Despite their requests, management refused to meet with them and they
were summarily fired. Within a few weeks, workers at the Farah plant in
San Antonio were also fired for supporting the protest initiated by their
colleagues in the El Paso plant. By the end of May, a group of four thousand workers, most of whom were Mexican American women, had walked
off their jobs at Farah. In so doing, they began one of the most remarkable
chapters in the history of labor solidarity in the South. Very quickly after
the initial dismissals, the ACWA dispatched organizers to El Paso and other

Farah plant locations to organize workers and help them seek redress for their grievances. Within a month after the strike had officially begun, the ACWA launched an impressive national boycott of the Farah Manufacturing Company's products. This boycott was one of the most successful in the history of the American labor movement, as evidenced by its widespread popularity and the attention of the national media. Many observers point to the boycott as the critical factor in the union and workers' victory over Farah. However, it is important to note that although the ACWA had made some inroads into various departments of the five Farah plants in Texas and New Mexico prior to the work action in 1972, the strike was initially the product of the workers' own initiative. It was only after the strike had begun that the ACWA came in to help run it.[55]

There are two dominant images of women in southern labor history: the self-sacrificing, often maternal heroine and the victimized, vulnerable girl striker. Historians have pointed out that union leaders were quick to highlight the vulnerability of young women workers in the South.[56] Both the ILGWU's label campaign and the ACWA's Farah boycott advertisements marked a departure from that trend. The images in the national media of the Farah strike and boycott featured strong women, often in militant stances. The cover of the *Farah Strike Bulletin* and the Spanish-language *Viva la huelga*, both published by the ACWA, showed the silhouette of a young Mexican American woman with her clenched fist raised in defiance of her oppressors. Newspapers and television programs across the nation showed pictures of Mexican American women courageously picketing on the strike lines at the Farah plants.[57] The general secretary-treasurer of the ACWA called the boycott of Farah Manufacturing "without [a] doubt, the most successful such campaign in American labor history."[58] Thus the two primary apparel industry unions had come to realize the intrinsic value of their women members. Through their largely female membership, the clothing unions had direct access to a significant portion of the consuming public.

The public images of the women in both the ILGWU's "Look for the Union Label" commercial and the Farah strike and boycott resulted in great sympathy and support for the garment unions. In media reports on the ILGWU's label campaign, for example, women garment workers were described in sympathetic terms. In an article on the popularity of the union's "theme song," accompanied by a six-inch photo of jubilant garment workers, the *New York Times* presented the situation of one unionist,

VIVA LA HUELGA

Don't Buy Farah Pants!

Support the strike. Help give a taste of justice to thousands of Mexican-American workers at the giant Farah pants company in Texas and New Mexico. These people have lived too long with the bitter taste of injustice and oppression. The American dream should be theirs to share, too.

Their employer, the Farah Company, makes the dream seem more like a nightmare. The U.S. Government has found Farah guilty of firing workers because they want to join a union. But the company continues to break the law. And the mammoth manufacturer has instigated the arrests of over 700 strikers. Many were taken from their homes in the middle of the night. All had to post exorbitant bail. Most of them are charged with standing too close together on the picket line in the first days of the strike.

The strike has been peaceful. In fact, the only threat of violence has come from the unmuzzled police dogs the armed Farah Company guards now use to patrol the plant (and to intimidate the strikers).

Show the Farah workers America's heart is still in the right place. Show the world American consumers won't buy injustice.

Don't buy Farah pants

AMALGAMATED CLOTHING WORKERS OF AMERICA, AFL-CIO

This leaflet is not directed to the employees of any store, and is directed solely to the consumer public

FIGURE 20. "*Viva la Huelga*, Don't Buy Farah Pants!" Flyer urging shoppers to boycott Farah pants, New York, ca. 1972. Amalgamated Clothing and Textile Workers Union Records, Kheel Center for Labor-Management Documentation and Archives, ILR School, Cornell University.

Voncile Kinard from the ILGWU's local in Walterboro, South Carolina. After singing the lead in "Look for the Union Label" at the union's 1980 convention in New York City, Kinard learned that the company she worked for had shut down while she was away. The *Times* article focused on Kinard's optimism in the face of hard times. "But I'll roll the union on regardless of whether I have a job," she said. "I feel strongly about the union and I'll back it anywhere I go." In a series of articles about the strike in 1973, *Time* magazine depicted the women on the Farah strike lines as seeking only "*dignidad*." In "A Bishop v. Farah," the editors of *Time* cited the low wages of the Farah sewing machine operators, pointing out that Farah employees took home "an average of $69 per week, while unionized workers at the Levi-Strauss and Tex-Togs plants in El Paso net $102."[59] In another article, *Time* said that the workers at Farah had a "genuine labor grievance." The article described the work situation for the Mexican American women at Farah, pointing out that the production quotas required workers to sew "six belts per minute onto finished slacks when most [women] say that [it] is possible to do only five."[60] In 1974 the *New York Times* published an op-ed column that described Willie Farah as blatantly defying NLRB decisions and flouting federal law. "The day of 'frontier justice' based on brute strength is past," the *Times* editors argued. "It is time for a conclusive assertion of the primacy of Federal labor law."[61]

Although there is controversy over the lasting effects of the strike and boycott, one thing is certain: the boycott dealt a serious blow to the financial health of Farah Manufacturing Company and figured prominently in the company's decision to sign a union contract in 1974. Exact figures vary, but according to the company's own financial report Farah suffered significant losses. George Meany announced in a letter to AFL-CIO unions that, in contrast to a profit of $6 million for the 1971 fiscal year, Farah reported an $8.3 million loss for the 1972 fiscal year. Others argued that the 1974 contract is best understood as the union's resignation to company demands and fears of plant relocations abroad. Furthermore, many of the Farah strikers felt that they had been left out of the negotiations that led to the 1974 contract and that the decision to end the strike came from the union, not the workers themselves.[62] As unique and initially successful as the Farah strike and boycott may first appear, the reality of the situation was a bit different. For although the strike did result in a union contract and numerous NLRB decisions in the workers' and union's favor, the end result was that most of the Farah plants closed by the mid-1980s, and the Mexican American women who had worked so hard to achieve union recognition and better working conditions lost their jobs. Nevertheless, women garment workers were at the heart of the successes that the ILGWU and ACWA earned in the 1970s because union leadership recognized them as both loyal unionists and successful boycott supporters.

The support for the Farah boycott and the ILGWU's label campaign did not, of course, come from women unionists alone. Indeed, it was the ability to reach beyond the unions themselves that made these labor actions so effective. The Catholic Church was a critical ally. Nearly all of the employees and strikers at Farah were Catholic Mexican Americans, and the church provided important institutional support for the boycott.[63] Father Jesse Muñoz, a local Catholic priest, took great pains to publicize and promote the Farah boycott. He also made his church and office facilities available to union supporters for meetings. Muñoz even went so far as to appear on the ACWA's picket lines himself.[64] Much more important support came from Bishop Sidney Metzger. He wrote position papers emphasizing the veracity of the workers' claims of abuse and union-busting activities at Farah and distributed these papers and letters to a wide network of Catholic bishops. His support lent credibility to the workers' complaints. Metzger stressed that "the persons who made those statements are deeply religious. They are devout Catholic people and it would be against their culture and their faith to deceive the bishop with misinformation." When attacked by a Presbyterian minister for supporting the boycott on religious grounds, the Catholic community replied, "The fact that the present boycott is strengthened by churchmen and church bodies is not a mistake. It is the will of God."[65] Prominent Catholics such as Senator Edward Kennedy and Congressman Thomas O'Neill joined the clergy in supporting the national boycott through their public endorsements. Support from public figures was not limited to Catholics. Many other important politicians, unionists, academics, and celebrities joined the Citizens Committee for Justice for Farah Workers. The list of members included Cesar Chavez, Michael Harrington, Irving Howe, Dolores Huerta, Esther Peterson, Bayard Rustin, Arthur Schlesinger Jr., and Joanne Woodward.[66] Still, the religious connection between the Latinas who walked the picket lines in Texas and other American Catholics helped popularize the Farah boycott.

The Farah boycott did encounter some legal obstacles. Despite the NLRA's exception to the ban on secondary boycotts in the apparel industry, the National Labor Relations Board declared some aspects of the Farah boycott to be unfair labor practices. As part of the boycott, ACWA unionists across the country picketed stores that sold Farah slacks. Farah registered a complaint with the NLRB that resulted in an injunction against that type of picketing. ACWA supporters were outraged, perhaps justifiably, that their constitutional right to free speech was limited by the board's injunction. One supporter wrote, "It's the free speech of the picket line, of the strike, . . . of the boycott. Free speech does not come easy for the labor movement . . . [a]nd we must keep it alive."[67] That injunction effectively kept the union from picketing retail establishments, but the boycott continued until 1974, when Farah was forced to recognize the ACWA as the collective bargaining agent of its employees. Despite the ACWA's defeat on the picketing issue, most of the decisions the NLRB issued on the Farah strike and boycott worked in the union's favor. However, the injunction against picketing retail establishments effectively undermined the apparel exception to the NLRA's ban on secondary boycotts. More importantly, it suggested that free speech could be limited by union membership. For if these picketers had not been union members, their activities would have been protected by the First Amendment to the U.S. Constitution.

The Farah boycott and the "Look for the Union Label" campaigns signaled another step toward a more racially and ethnically inclusive representation of women garment workers. For the first time, the publicity surrounding the union label and boycott campaigns featured the ethnicity of women garment workers. Earlier advertisements sought to reach an almost exclusively white female audience by appearing in journals read by white women and highlighting a white version of domesticity. Even during the early civil rights movement, leaders of both the ACWA and the ILGWU overlooked the importance of including black and Latina women among the targets of their boycott and union label campaigns. No series of union label advertisements by either the ACWA or the ILGWU appeared in the black press during the first postwar label campaigns. This was despite the fact that in 1966, the first year for which reliable industry-wide data exist, just over 8.5 percent of garment workers were African American. By 1978 African Americans accounted for over 15 percent of garment workers (see figure 12).[68] The percentage of Latinas in the domestic apparel industry was also significant, just under 10 percent in the same year (see figure 21). Furthermore, the South—an area identified by both the ILGWU and the ACWA as critical to the clothing unions' future and the focus of organizing activity during the union label campaigns—contained the largest concentrations of African American and Latina workers outside of California.[69]

Whether as a result of the growing presence of minority women in the apparel industry or simply as a response to the civil rights movement and a new national discourse on ethnicity, the Farah boycott and ILGWU "Look for the Union Label" commercials went out of their way to celebrate pluralism. The boycott literature featured Latina women on the front lines of the strike at Farah Manufacturing plants, and the "Look for the Union Label" campaign emphasized the multicultural aspects of the ILGWU membership by featuring women of color in the commercials. The ethnicity of these workers appeared to be a strength or, at the very least, not a detriment to the larger goal of increased labor organization in the clothing industry. The ACWA also advertised in Spanish-language newspapers and printed strike bulletins and pamphlets in Spanish.[70]

Although the successes were short-lived, these new representations of women in the union label and boycott campaigns signified the potential for a new role for women in the American labor movement. It was no accident, of course, that this new perspective on women in the labor movement and workplace coincided with a growing women's movement and national debates over "equal work for equal pay" and reproductive rights. The clothing unions' recognition of the strategic position of women garment workers as strong unionists and primary consumers in the boycott and label movements of the 1970s paved the way for further changes.

From the earliest efforts of the ACWA to encourage consumer identification with its union label to contemporary "Made in America" campaigns, unions struggled with the role women would play in these strategies and, indeed, what role they would play in the larger labor movement. The ACWA and ILGWU came to understand that women garment workers wielded a great deal of power in their dual roles of scrupulous consumer and loyal unionist. Indeed, the successes of those campaigns were due, in large part, to the solidarity of women garment unionists. In later years the apparel industry would use the lessons learned from the boycott and union label movements to lead the ranks of organized labor and condemn foreign imports with the famous "Made in America" slogan. But women would make little progress in gaining access to the upper echelons of union leadership, despite their three-to-one majority in the garment workforce. Instead of marking a linear progression from advertisements that emphasized the domesticity and sexuality of women clothing workers to a representation of women workers as active unionists, the history of the union label and boycott movements in the southern garment industry suggests that union leaders had yet to truly envision a permanent and active role for women clothing workers.

Despite all the popular successes of the Farah boycott and the ILGWU's "Look for the Union Label" advertising campaign, the industry itself was about to topple over a precipice, taking with it the very jobs that those campaigns sought to preserve. In the 1970s and 1980s the apparel industry hemorrhaged jobs as foreign manufacturers gained a greater share of the global marketplace. Between 1969 and 1979 the number of workers employed in the U.S. apparel industry declined by 7.4 percent. In the 1980s the industry lost an additional, staggering 17.5 percent of its jobs.[71] The American apparel industry was on a decline from which it would not recover.

Chapter Six

"SWEATSHOPS IN THE SUN"

A GENDERED VISION OF THE U.S. APPAREL
INDUSTRY'S MOVE TO MEXICO

In the 1930s apparel companies in the Northeast began to consider a move to the U.S. South, where labor costs were less expensive and the obstacles brought about by organized labor could be avoided. Industrial capitalists looked to the U.S. South for an opportunity to make their businesses more efficient and profitable. A few decades later, apparel manufacturers were again looking south, but this time they looked outside the borders of the United States.

America's most recognized clothing producers found that trade agreements fostered their relocation to apparel centers from Mexico to the Pacific Rim.[1] Beginning in the 1960s, when tariffs on imported apparel were lowered, and continuing through the 1990s, American clothing producers shut down domestic operations and relocated their manufacturing facilities outside of the country. A number of trade agreements eased import duties on goods manufactured outside of the United States. Following the passage of the first General Agreement on Tariffs and Trade in 1947, the federal government amended trade policies by reducing or even eliminating financial penalties for importing foreign-produced goods. Enacted in 1963, Item 807 of the U.S. Tariff Code had the greatest impact on the domestic clothing industry. This regulation encouraged U.S. apparel companies to import clothing that was assembled by foreign workers. Under the auspices of Item 807, U.S. apparel manufacturers cut the cloth needed for the garments in the United States using American workers. Then the cloth was exported to a factory abroad where the clothing would be assembled. Finally, U.S. clothing manufacturers would import the finished garment, paying tariffs only on the value added, or the cost of the labor required to assemble the garment. In this way Item 807 encouraged U.S. apparel manufacturers to export assembly production jobs to foreign countries, where labor costs were substantially less.[2] The cost of relocation was much lower for garment plants than for those in more capital-intensive industries like the auto or steel industries, which also benefited from the enactment of similar trade regulations. The apparel industry was labor intensive, not capital intensive, especially when compared to other manufacturing industries.[3] The low-wage structure of the clothing industry, coupled with decreasing trade barriers, made relocation almost effortless.

The implementation of the North American Free Trade Agreement (NAFTA) beginning in January 1994 continued and exacerbated the trend of outsourcing apparel manufacturing. Between 1994 and 2002, the U.S. apparel industry lost roughly 437,000 jobs. The effect of NAFTA was particularly significant in southern states, with the region suffering a 59.7 percent overall decline in the number of apparel jobs. The hit to individual states was striking, with Alabama, Georgia, North Carolina, Tennessee, and Texas each suffering the loss of more than thirty thousand jobs in the clothing industry between 1994 and 2002.[4]

As a result of a long series of tariff reductions and policy changes in post–World War II America, the apparel industry has undergone a wholesale restructuring and relocation. In the 1960s companies in the U.S. apparel industry looked south to Mexico. Eventually apparel manufacturers flocked to many countries of the Global South, from Asia to South America. This chapter will focus on the move to Mexico as a prototypical experience, recognizing that many of the themes developed here apply to U.S. apparel companies' later relocations to other nations in the Global South as well.

As a result of changes made to tariffs and regulations following World War II, the domestic clothing industry in the United States has suffered from a seemingly ever-increasing onslaught of foreign-made, less expensive clothes since the early 1980s. What were once primarily U.S. companies employing U.S. workers became multinational corporations employ-

TABLE 2. Decline in Apparel Industry Employment in Southern States, 1994–2002

State	1994	2002	Jobs lost	Percentage change
Alabama	53,300	21,200	32,100	-60.2
Florida	31,800	15,700	16,100	-50.6
Georgia	56,100	17,300	38,800	-69.2
Kentucky	30,000	14,900	15,100	-50.3
Mississippi	33,400	11,100	22,300	-66.8
North Carolina	70,100	28,700	41,400	-59.1
South Carolina	34,800	13,300	21,500	-61.8
Tennessee	57,400	17,800	39,600	-69.0
Texas	65,200	34,100	31,100	-47.7
Total	432,100	174,100	258,000	-59.7

Source: U.S. Department of Labor, Bureau of Labor Statistics, *State and Area Employment, Hours, and Earnings,* http://data.bls.gov (data were extracted on November 11, 2013, with the series SAS0100004230021, SAS1200004230021, SAS1300004230021, SAS2100004230021, SAS2200004230021, SAS2800004230021, SAS3700004230021, SAS4500004230021, SAS4700004230021, SAS4800004230021).

ing foreign workers abroad and importing finished garments into U.S. markets with minimal or no financial penalties. In the 1960s imported clothing accounted for only 2.5 percent of the clothing sold in the United States. That figure grew at an impressive rate, so that by 1976 nearly a third of the clothing available for purchase by consumers in the United States was foreign made. By the 1980s imports accounted for over 57 percent of U.S. domestic sales of apparel.[5] Looking at imports from a different perspective, the story remains much the same. In 1962 the United States imported $364 million worth of clothing manufactured by women stitchers abroad. By 1972 that figure had more than quadrupled, and the value of imported clothing was $1.7 billion.[6]

Like so many U.S. apparel plants in the 1970s and 1980s, the Vanity Fair factories in southern Alabama fell on hard times. Faced with an unprecedented increase in the amount of cheaper imported clothing allowed into the United States, the company began to close sewing plants and lay off workers. In an effort to remain competitive, apparel companies like Vanity Fair sought to move some of their production operations to countries with lower labor costs. In 1984 Vanity Fair announced that it would temporarily close its two Jackson, Alabama, plants as a result of "a business slowdown." At the same time, however, the company had already begun to shift those plants' operations to Latin American facilities. Announcing an "experimental" program in which workers in Panama would assemble garments, the company admitted that it had been making "agreements with companies abroad for about 20 years."[7] Between 1996 and 1997, six hundred workers lost their jobs at Vanity Fair's sewing plant in Monroeville.[8] After announcements in March 2000, Vanity Fair finally closed the Jackson sewing plant on August 25, leaving the 543 mostly women workers at the plant unemployed.[9] By November 2001 Vanity Fair had closed its last domestic sewing plant, in Atmore, Alabama, at a loss of 510 jobs.

It was certainly no coincidence that shortly after the ILGWU was decertified as the collective bargaining agent of Vanity Fair workers in the Jackson plant, the company promoted Paul Parden, the leader of the antiunion decertification faction, to oversee operations at its new plant in Mexico. Parden's antiunion activities were well known to local observers, and this propelled him to the status of lead plaintiff against the ILGWU in the decertification proceedings. His legal representation was secured by the Center on National Policy, an organization that described itself as "a non-partisan charitable legal foundation that works through the courts to restore individual rights lost through abuse of union power."[10] Vanity Fair rewarded the loyalty of this ardent company supporter with a job, while thousands of others in Alabama lost theirs.

The outsourcing of apparel manufacturing had a dramatic impact on families and communities across the South. The lived experience of the southern women workers who lost their jobs and livelihoods is important because that was where globalization was realized. In Alabama, the southern state with the highest percentage of apparel workers, local media documented women garment workers' reactions to the plant closures. The *Clarke County Democrat* reported, "The announcement last Friday that Vanity Fair Intimates will close its Jackson sewing plant so upset employees that the facility closed before mid-day." The women featured in these articles often discussed the loss of their jobs in terms of the impact on their families. Twenty-five-year-old LaQuina Griffin had worked at the Vanity Fair factory in Jackson for four and a half years when she learned that plant was closing. A single mother to three young children, Griffin was pictured holding her young son in her arms in a front-page article in the *Mobile Register*. "I'll probably have to move somewhere," she explained. Compounding her financial difficulties, she was losing her health insurance, too. Griffin told the *Register* that two of her children required asthma medications that cost $200 a month and she was unsure how she was going to pay for them. Bettie Black, a supervisor at Vanity Fair, said she "cried all day" and expressed the same concerns about the loss of health insurance. Vanity Fair sewing machine operator Kay Beck worried that she would be unable to pay for college tuition for her son in Tuskegee. One local official worried about the impact on families in her community, saying, "I passed by [the factory] and saw no cars there and I just said, 'Oh my goodness, what are the people going to do?' Some of them are head of households."[11]

The closing of southern apparel factories had a ripple effect, hurting local businesses and economies as well. When the Andover Togs plant in Pisgah, Alabama, closed in 1996, more than one hundred sewing machine operators in the small community lost their livelihoods. A local gas station owner and former mayor of the small community expected the layoffs to "slow down the economy big time." He added, "People can't spend money they don't have." A year later, approximately two thousand workers lost their jobs at Fruit of the Loom plants in Jamestown and Campbellsville, Kentucky, and small businesses in the area suffered a decline in sales. After Stone Apparel Co. announced it was closing its Orangeburg, South Carolina, plant in 1998, the *Charleston Post & Courier* predicted that "the closing could threaten every business in town, from grocery stores to beauty shops." The closing of sewing rooms brought economic woes to southern communities and local economies that extended beyond the industry's women workers and their families.[12]

Women who lost their jobs in the southern apparel industry frequently blamed the low wages paid to workers in Mexico. Martha Smith cried as she finished her last day at the Andover Togs plant in Pisgah and lamented that the industry's jobs "are all going to Mexico and overseas." Another resident of Pisgah complained that local workers could not compete with workers in Mexico because "they pay those people down there a dollar and a nickel an hour." After retiring from Vanity Fair, Vivian Long refused to buy Vanity Fair products because the company had shifted operations to Mexico.[13]

As the southern apparel industry closed factories, one by one, union label campaigns and boycotts gave way to a focus on goods "Made in America."[14] Union leaders recognized that their successes with the "Look for the Union Label" campaign and the Farah boycott rested in large part on the efforts and appeals of women garment workers. With the threat of imports looming large, they sought to translate that support into the "Made in America" campaign. Unions learned their lessons well from the successes of the earlier boycott and label campaigns and made women garment workers and unionists central to the new "Made in America" strategy. Ironically, however, the targeting of women workers as consumers ran into some problems precisely because of which women it targeted. Critics have called the rhetoric of the "Made in America" campaign "sterile and unrealistic" and have decried the "offensive jingoism" in its nativist overtones. The American and especially the southern apparel industry employed increasing numbers of immigrant women, often from the very countries vilified by the "Made in America" rhetoric, who would necessarily find such a campaign to have little appeal.[15] And although there is certainly no doubt that from the mid-1960s through to the present garment union leaders have been responding to a real pattern of plant relocations to foreign countries, the ways in which they sought to encourage the participation of rank-and-file workers in the campaign reveals that, once again, they misunderstood the composition of their own membership.

On the other side of the trade equation, the expansion of garment manufacturing industries into Mexico resulted in profound changes in the ways in which certain Mexican communities ordered themselves. The introduction of maquiladora industries in towns from the Yucatan to the U.S-Mexico border regions brought with it changes in the ways that Mexican men and women thought of themselves.[16] Their understandings of the roles prescribed for them changed as maquiladoras brought increased occupational opportunities for women. The increasing feminization of the wage-labor force brought with it a change in the roles for women in Mexican society. With the opening up of the maquiladora factories, women were no longer "marginal" workers in capitalist production. Instead, women who assembled garments assumed jobs that were central to production and, in so doing, they assumed (at least in part) the traditional roles of men.

This experience of women workers challenged a traditional understanding of *marianismo*, or women's role in Mexican culture.[17] Women experienced increased power as a result of the wages they earned, and some engaged in collective action. However, these experiences were not common to all women workers in maquiladoras. Instead, women workers in the garment industries tended to be the most resistant to worker organizations, especially when compared to women in the electronics maquiladoras. Employers hired women workers because they could be paid less than men and because women workers were presumed to be more docile than men. Women workers in the garment factories tended to be the lowest paid of maquiladora workers and the least collectively organized. In addition, they were typically older and more likely to be married than their counterparts in the electronics industry.

As Mexico became increasingly industrialized, the feminization of the industrial workforce became more important, both domestically and abroad. Labor leaders in the United States, as well as governmental committees, have noticed and criticized the development of maquiladoras in Mexico because of the factories' reliance on antiunion activities and cheap labor. Underneath this discourse, however, lies a gendered understanding of Mexico's history and a gendered evaluation of its workers.

U.S. government and trade union publications highlight the American reaction to the development of maquiladoras in Mexico. Initially, U.S. labor leaders embraced the garment industry's expansion into Mexico, viewing it as an opportunity to expand union membership. That optimistic sentiment changed with the passage of time, however, and labor leaders came to oppose this expansion for a variety of reasons. Prior to the implementation of NAFTA, labor leaders used a patriarchal discourse that directly related opposition to the maquiladora industries to the feminization of the Mexican maquiladora workforce.

Refusing to see maquiladora growth as an opportunity for Latin American women, the AFL-CIO reinforced the sexual division of labor in Latin America and the patriarchal system that dominates women's wage employment. In discussions of the nature of the employment of Latin American women, U.S. labor organizers rarely challenged the traditional distribution of household work. In fact, they conceived of women's toil in factories as an extra burden, over and beyond work that women do in the home. Latin American women were doubly victimized by this outlook. First they were required to perform household labor and then they were exploited in the labor force. The American Institute for Free Labor Development (AIFLD), a subsidiary of the AFL-CIO, was established in 1962 to promote labor organization among Latin American workers. Despite its establishment of a training course for women trade unionists in August 1971, the AIFLD made few attempts to address the concerns of women industrial workers in Latin America. In fact, the course seemed to focus on efforts to expand membership by including women workers, not by pushing for pay equity, childcare, or advancement opportunities in the workplace. Indeed, the reality was quite the opposite. Speakers at the first course graduation ceremony urged women to "expand your role in the trade union movement." A year later Wallace J. Legge, inter-American representative of the Postal, Telegraph, and Telephone International, offered the same message. He encouraged women to participate in their union and to seek positions of leadership within their organizations but made no effort to address women workers' particular concerns. He charged women workers with correcting the underrepresentation of women in leadership positions in Latin American unions when he said, "This imbalance ... is unrealistic and suggests a limitation to success that you women have the responsibility to correct." He failed to elaborate on just exactly how women workers were to achieve this, given organized labor's resistance to challenging the patriarchy of factories, society, or even labor unions.[18]

The anti-import movement in the United States is particularly revealing, for it shows how American labor leaders have come to see the expansion of the garment and textile industries to Mexico and the Global South in gendered terms. Labor organizers in the United States repeatedly complained about low wages in multinational export assembly plants, especially those paid to women workers, but they failed to consider the relative purchasing power of these wages in Latin America compared to the United States, and to consider how these wages compared to alternative forms of employment in Latin American countries.[19] They presupposed disempowerment, and as a result, they condemned the low wages of maquiladora women without understanding the context in which these women worked. Furthermore, the anti-import campaign relied on an image of the exploited, often female worker to make its protectionist agenda more compelling.[20] Like the early scholarship on maquiladora women, U.S. labor organizations repeatedly denied women workers in Latin America any agency or initiative. Their reports reflected victimization and exploitation. By denying women workers in Latin America the capacity for self-definition and assertion, labor leaders suggested that women workers were disempowered and helpless in the face of patriarchal and capitalist forces.

A comparison of images of women industrial workers in the United States and Latin America reveals a gendered duality. Although labor organizations in the United States came to recognize and endorse women's double role as producer and consumer, they rejected a similar role for

Latin American women. Women industrial workers in the United States appeared to be responsible for both earning wages and directing family consumption. Labor leaders used this image to their advantage and featured American women workers as the rank and file of the anti-import movement, thus highlighting a gender-specific power that women workers possess. The combination of women's roles as both industrial and household workers reflected an acknowledgment of the critical role women played in the U.S. labor movement. Furthermore, the household was a source of power for women industrial workers in the United States. For Latin American women, by contrast, household work was yet another source of exploitation. The anti-import movement further exploited Latin American women workers by focusing on the ways in which maquiladora workers were victimized by their employers, by their own governments, and by U.S. companies.

This theme of exploitation occurs in article after article in labor union journals. For instance, in 1978 the *AFL-CIO Federationist* ran an article entitled "America's Sweatshops in the Sun" that stressed the victimization of foreign assembly workers. An examination of one Mexican sewing factory revealed that workers were subjected to a wide variety of harassment and abuse:

> Workers who do not meet production quotas must put in unpaid overtime until they do meet them.

> Workers must raise they [*sic*] hands to ask permission to go to the bathroom, and waits of up to half an hour are common.[21]

The article depicted workers in these American-owned "Sweatshops in the Sun" as exploited by a profit-driven management that subjected them to inadequate working conditions. In this way, the American labor media portrayed Mexican women workers as passive, docile participants in a labor system that exploited them. The article featured women workers who seemed to have no recourse, no agency through which to air their grievances.

Overwork and poor working conditions were not the only ways that workers in Latin America were exploited. "Sweatshops in the Sun" paid considerable attention to the sexual exploitation of women workers: "Many in the largely female work force must strip at the end of the day to let management see whether they are stealing anything."[22]

The sexual imagery in this particular critique speaks to a gendered understanding of labor in Latin America. Because of their bodies, women were especially vulnerable in the workplace. Furthermore, the *Federationist* did not come to the logical conclusion that Latin American women in these maquiladoras could benefit from the same protections brought about by labor unions in the United States. The article included only one personal experience and, not surprisingly, the experience was that of an exploited woman worker, trapped by her job and gender. After mentioning that Altagracia, a "veteran seamstress," had her piecework rate reduced without sufficient explanation, the article explained, "She became ill soon after her pay was lowered. And then she discovered she was pregnant again." Like other women workers, Altagracia was exploited by her body, by her capacity and presumably unexplained tendency to reproduce. Altagracia stayed away from work for only a few days "because she needed to keep earning money." Shortly after returning to work, Altagracia was taken ill again and "was forced by chronic vaginal bleeding to stop [work] altogether."[23] The fact that the AFL-CIO would publish such a graphic depiction of Altagracia's medical problems reveals how central women's biological functions were to the organization's conceptualization of women's work in Latin America. It is not simply that workers got sick and were exploited by employers in Latin America. Instead, the underlying meaning of the AFL-CIO's assessment of "America's Sweatshops in the Sun" is that women were disadvantaged by employers and they were especially vulnerable because of their bodies. And the American labor movement would do little more than expose their suffering.

The propaganda and reports of the U.S. labor movement further exploited Latin American women by emphasizing their association with domesticity. Like Devon Gerardo Peña, a sociologist who argued that maquiladora workers could only be "temporary" members of the labor force because of their tendency to get married and capacity to have children, U.S. labor leaders linked this aspect of women's lives to their exploitation in the workforce.[24] In 1974 Denise Thiry, the inter-American representative of the International Federation of Free Teachers' Unions, wrote about this connection between domesticity and work in an essay in honor of International Women's Year published in the *AIFLD Report*. According to Thiry, "Every women [*sic*] who works for wages, whether her work be manual or intellectual, also holds another permanent job: At home, she is a manger, an economist and a human relations expert."[25] Although Thiry did recognize that women's household work represented skills that were marketable, she also suggested that household labor was another "*permanent*" feature of women's working lives. U.S. labor leaders failed to challenge the "permanence" of this arrangement. Interestingly, the experience of U.S. women workers was quite similar. In 1985 the vice president and one of the few women on the executive board of the Amalgamated Clothing and Textile Workers Union, Joyce Miller, argued that that work inside and outside the home are "one and the same" for women workers in the United States.[26] To challenge such inherent assumptions about women's domesticity would present a direct challenge to the male-dominated structure of both business and labor in the United States and, more generally, throughout the world. U.S. labor leaders may have envisioned the household labor of women industrial workers as a sort of additional form of exploitation, but unlike exploitation on the shop floor, household work was a responsibility that could not be addressed, challenged, or removed.

The U.S. labor movement minimized the activity and agency of women workers in maquiladora industries. The anti-import movement in the United States revealed the ways in which different conceptions of women underlie different strategies of solidarity. For example, one of the main lines of defense against the importation of cheaper foreign goods in the United States centers on women's dual role as worker and consumer. In the 1970s labor leaders urged women unionists to "Look for the Union Label" before purchasing goods. The clothing unions' large number of women members, numbering almost 85 percent of overall membership during the anti-import campaign, compelled the unions to develop and use this strategy to their advantage and seemingly led the rest of the trade union movement in the United States to do the same. In September 1985 Nilda Quintanilla, president of the ACTWU local in McAllen, Texas, and a Levi's plant employee for over eight years, testified before a Senate subcommittee panel about her commitment to the boycott of imported clothing: "I went to get my children clothes and I saw this beautiful jean by Levi, that's the first thing I usually do, check for Levi. Then I looked inside at the label, which I never did until I understood this import thing, and the label said 'Made in Mexico,' so I threw it back. I didn't even fold it, I just threw it back. . . . And to me, I felt bad, like I was a traitor or something, but I wasn't going to buy imported goods anymore."[27] Quintanilla's understanding of her roles as consumer, industrial worker, and trade unionist is evident in her boycott activities. As a woman and a mother who bought clothes for her children and as a worker and unionist at a Levi's plant, Quintanilla

was empowered. She went on to say, "I don't have anything against bringing in things from other countries, but not excessively. . . . We need to be
able to work . . . and the best way to do that is not to get so many things
from other parts of the world . . . so that people can have a sense . . . of
pride in doing their own thing here. . . . That has always been the American way."[28] The connection Quintanilla made between patriotism and imported goods underscored her identification as a worker. She envisioned
herself as part of the "American way" and she took "pride in doing [her]
own thing here." This was particularly notable given her own ethnic heritage as a Latina American.[29] She was both worker and consumer, express-
ing her patriotism by rejecting products made in other countries.

While the American labor movement was preoccupied with developing
the "Buy American" campaign, the U.S. apparel industry suffered a serious
decline. The number of U.S. apparel workers decreased from a height of
almost 1.4 million in 1972 to just 829,334 in 1997, a decrease of 39 percent.[30]
The reduction in overall employment in the U.S. clothing industry coincided with substantial growth in the percentage of apparel workers who
were African American and Latina. African American women accounted
for 8.6 percent of the U.S. apparel labor force in 1966. Even though African
American women's rate of employment in the U.S. apparel industry slowed
in the mid-1970s, by 1980, 15.6 percent of American apparel workers were
African American. The rapid increase in African American women's apparel employment occurred in the decade after the enactment of the 1964
Civil Rights Act.[31] The apparel industry similarly increased its reliance on
Latina workers. In 1966, 5.1 percent of U.S. apparel workers were Latina. By
1980 Latinas accounted for 10 percent of the workers in the American apparel industry. So, while the number of U.S. apparel workers declined, the
percentage of workers from minority groups increased significantly.

During the mid-1980s many ACTWU members in the United States participated in protests at retail stores, once again illustrating the connection
between a consumer and worker identity among women industrial workers. The union repeatedly and uniformly celebrated the initiative of its
members in these protests. In the South, where much of the anti-import
campaign was waged, women garment and textile workers targeted the
K-Mart chain for its refusal to limit the amount of imported goods it sold
per year. In Knoxville, Tennessee, over two hundred "shoppers" filled shopping carts full of imported clothing. They then proceeded to the cashier
and waited in line. After their purchases had been rung up, the protesters/

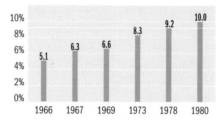

FIGURE 21. Latinas as a percentage of the
U.S. apparel industry labor force, 1966–80.
U.S. Equal Employment Opportunity
Commission, *Equal Employment Opportunity
Report: Job Patterns for Minorities and Women
in Private Industry*, 1966–80.

shoppers "forgot" their credit cards and caused quite a disturbance in the
front of the store. More protesters picketed the store and passed out leaflets.[32] In Americus, Georgia, women from the Manhattan Shirt Company
factory blended their roles as workers, unionists, and consumers when
they demanded that local retailers stop selling imported clothing. Faye
Knight went from store to store in Americus, inspecting the garments on
the racks and shelves of department stores and boutiques. She remembered that most store managers removed the items, perhaps influenced
by the fact that Manhattan Shirt Company was the largest employer in
the area. When she got to Belk, a regional chain of department stores,
the response was different. The store manager refused to remove the imported clothing. In response, Knight and six members of the ACWA local
in Americus immediately established an informational picket. Prohibited
by law from engaging in a secondary boycott of a retail establishment, the
women unionists simply stood in front of Belk and passed out flyers to
shoppers. When the store manager called the police, Knight knew how to
respond. She explained that there was no intent to keep consumers from
shopping at Belk. The picket line was "informational" only, she told the
police officer. Looking back on that day, Knight was proud because "we
did get our point across."[33] Protests like these occurred throughout the
South, with working-class women relying on their simultaneous roles as
consumers, workers, and unionists in an effort to undermine the importation of foreign goods.

The strength and significance of these protests arose out of the fact that the women consumers who participated in these protests were also the women industrial workers who stood to lose their jobs if more and more of the manufacturing jobs available to women in the United States drifted across national borders to foreign countries. In the U.S. South, garment and textile workers were empowered by this dual role of consumer and worker. At Vanity Fair's factory in Jackson, Alabama, workers were keenly aware of their power as mothers who directed the family's consumption and as workers who produced clothing. Rebecca Blackmon, a sewing machine operator, understood that "the women are what made Vanity Fair the company it is. Not only the women doing the work—the actual work—but the women buying the products."[34] In the United States, women stitchers were empowered by their domestic responsibilities, not demoralized.

The portrayal of Latin American women workers in the U.S. labor press revealed a different conceptualization. California Joint Board manager Richard Rothstein made the disempowering of Latin American workers clear in a statement justifying limits on apparel imports. He said, "If workers in El Salvador and other poor countries made enough money to buy the things they produced, their companies could sell products to them instead of flooding the US market with their exports."[35] *Labor Unity* recorded the comments of Arthur Gundersheim, assistant to ACTWU president Murray H. Finley, as he testified before the House of Representatives. He argued that "'the overwhelming majority of workers employed in the *maquila* plants are young women 16 to 25 years of age.' Almost none are male or over 30, 'where the true unemployment problems of Mexico exist.'"[36] What Rothstein hinted at, Gundersheim made clear: labor leaders in the United States did not grant Latin American women the same power that they accorded to women in the United States. Scholars and analysts of the maquiladora industries misunderstand the real value of Latin American women's wages when they mistakenly convert pesos to dollars without considering the relative purchasing power of those arguably small, but not insignificant, wages.[37] Furthermore, the assumption that unemployment was a problem that affected primarily men is misguided. Women maquiladora workers needed their jobs not to supplement their husband's or family's earnings but rather because their wages were typically the primary source of steady income in families where husbands were either absent, unemployed, or underemployed. This misconception of the problem of unemployment reflected an acceptance of a traditional patriarchal understanding of women's work, a belief that it is inferior to men's work and that women's primary responsibility is to ensure the reproduction of the labor force.[38]

All in all, the organized labor press disempowered, exploited, and devalued the role of maquiladora women. The assessment of women industrial workers in Mexico that appeared in the pages of U.S. labor union journals revealed nothing about the potential power these women could wield. The U.S. labor movement has failed to envision maquiladora workers as anything other than passive victims of industrialization. Moreover, as scholars uncovered a developing worker consciousness among women maquiladora workers in Mexico from the 1970s through the 1990s, the perspective of labor leaders remained virtually unchanged. U.S. labor leaders saw women workers in maquiladoras as temporary and secondary components of the Latin American labor force. Labor leaders refused to challenge the patriarchy of the maquiladora system. Efforts to incorporate Latin American women workers in the trade union movement did not coincide with similar efforts to address the needs of women workers in the United States. Instead of improving the lives of women maquiladora workers, American unions helped to reinforce their exploitation.

Epilogue

In the 1980s the southern communities in the United States that had once welcomed apparel factories and their promises of jobs and economic salvation began to notice a change. Apparel factories all across the U.S. South closed their doors forever, leaving more and more women stitchers unemployed. Meanwhile, communities in Mexico and other Global South countries welcomed the apparel industry and looked forward to the fulfillment of the same promises of jobs and economic salvation that had once brightened the future of the U.S. South. In the Global South, the apparel industry has continued its long-standing reliance on female labor, just as it did when it moved from the North to the South in the United States beginning in the 1930s. Although American apparel unions are currently reluctant to organize workers in foreign apparel factories, adhering instead to an older argument that envisions foreign workers as "stealing jobs" from American workers, that attitude may have to change.[1] As the industry continues its decline in the United States, leaders of organized labor may be compelled to envision women workers in the Global South as potential unionists, not antiunionists. Just as the apparel unions followed the industry to the U.S. South in the 1930s, the Union of Needletrades, Industrial and Textile Employees may well be compelled to follow the industry even farther south. It remains to be seen just how much of the industry's history will repeat itself.

The story of the southern apparel industry is one that has considerable meaning for the larger history of industrialization in the twentieth-century U.S. South. Over the course of more than half a century, the industry profoundly transformed the lives of black and white women across the region. No longer relegated to agricultural and domestic work, the women stitchers of the southern apparel industry contributed significantly to household incomes as well as to the economic development of the region. In addition, their individual experiences as industrial workers, and for some, as unionists, helped to both challenge and define new roles for women in the rural South. The history of the southern apparel industry helps to provide an understanding of the impact of industrialization, desegregation, and globalization at a local level. Although these processes are most often discussed at the macro level, they have had the most profound impact at the community level, where the meanings of race, gender, and work were truly transformed.

Nick Bonanno, a longtime director of the Southeast Regional Office of the ILGWU, once pointed out that, historically speaking, "the apparel industry has always sought the lowest level."[2] From the 1930s through to the 1970s, the lowest level was the U.S. South. Beginning in the 1970s, with the removal of trade barriers, American apparel firms headed south once again, still seeking the lowest level. This time they found it in places like Matamoros, Guatemala City, Ashulia, and Karachi. The low-waged, labor-intensive structure of the clothing industry, coupled with decreasing trade barriers, made relocation almost effortless. In some very important ways, the final history in the trilogy of the apparel industry is still being written. It is the story of an industry that goes further afield than ever before in search of the ultimate lowest labor costs and the greatest possible profits.

Industrial relocation and capital flight are often facilitated and influenced by policy decisions. Just as passage of the Taft-Hartley Act and right-to-work laws drew apparel companies to the U.S. South in the 1940s and 1950s, trade policies helped to restructure the apparel industry in the 1970s and 1980s. American apparel unions worked with Congress to pass protectionist measures that would keep the flood of cheaper imported clothing from American retailers. In 1974 the Multi-Fiber Agreement established quotas that slowed the influx of imported clothing, particularly from Asian countries. Meanwhile, corporate mergers and expansions created transnational firms with broad global networks of contractors and suppliers. Companies like Liz Claiborne and Gap routinely produce goods in more than a dozen countries simultaneously. The protectionist measures eroded over time, as an alliance of transnational apparel companies and massive direct retailers like Wal-Mart, Target, and Carrefour helped shape new policies that erased barriers to free trade. In 1995 the international Agreement on Textiles and Clothing replaced the Multi-Fiber Agreement and allowed for the elimination of quotas over a ten-year period. The result is that apparel companies are now able to search the globe for the lowest manufacturing and labor costs. As Ellen Israel Rosen describes the situation in *Making Sweatshops: The Globalization of the U.S. Apparel Industry*, "The pressure to open new markets in lower and lower wage regions of the world has led to a Darwinian struggle, which is producing a race to the bottom."[3]

The apparel industry's continuing dependence on the labor of women has had an impact on the globalization of the industry. Sociologist Jane L. Collins argues that gendered discourse about the nature of women's work facilitated the globalization of the apparel industry, particularly with respect to the quest for lower labor costs. Employers and corporate leaders in the apparel industry made assumptions about women's natural skills that devalued women's skilled labor, often referring to it as unskilled. As Alice Kessler-Harris pointed out in her groundbreaking 1982 book *Out to Work: A History of Wage-Earning Women in the United States*, employers frequently drew connections between women's domestic and industrial work in an effort to justify the deskilling of women's labor.[4]

In part because of its association with women's domestic labor, the position of sewing machine operator pays a low wage across the Global South. In 2002 sewing machine operators in Bangladesh's apparel factories made an average of thirty-nine cents per hour, while workers in China earned eighty-eight cents per hour sewing moderate-to-better apparel.[5] In contrast, sewing machine operators in the United States earned more than ten dollars per hour.[6] Neoliberals argue that even the comparatively low wages earned by women in the Global South have the effect of improving the standard of living of workers and their communities. Rosen successfully challenges that perspective, noting that women production workers in the developing world rarely escape poverty through apparel work. In addition, Rosen faults the race to the bottom and trade policies for the reemergence of sweatshops within the United States in recent years.[7]

The rise of "lean retailing," which provides rich inventory management capabilities through a highly sophisticated information network, shifted much of the cost of production to manufacturers, while sparing retailers. The systemic shift began in the 1970s, but today it continues to place extraordinary burdens on apparel manufacturers in the Global South. In lean retailing, manufacturers and suppliers are given nearly instant data on sales and inventory from the retail side. Bar codes, distribution centers, and almost instant communication allow retailers to avoid the costs of holding large amounts of inventory. Transnational apparel companies expect a nimble and responsive manufacturing network to be able to fulfill retailers' orders quickly. This diminishes dependence on large and costly inventories and reduces risk by decreasing the need to predict future fashions.[8]

The postprotectionist apparel industry depends on the cheap labor of the Global South. The American Apparel and Footwear Association reported that in 2011, 97 percent of clothing purchased by Americans was manufactured internationally. China dominated the American market, exporting more than $32.1 billion worth of clothing. Thirty-two percent of the clothing purchased by American consumers in 2012 was made in China. Labor costs have risen in China in recent years, providing an opportunity for other nations to increase their share of the American clothing market. Vietnam, Indonesia, Bangladesh, and Mexico have all increased their clothing exports to the United States. The apparel industry's reliance on women's labor changed little as countries in the Global South replaced workers in the U.S. South and elsewhere. While some scholars

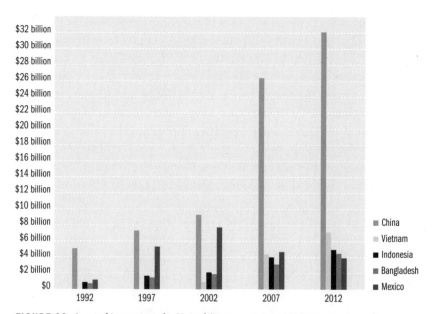

FIGURE 22. Apparel imports to the United States, 1992–2012. U.S. Department of Commerce, International Trade Administration, http://tse.export.gov/TSE/TSEhome.aspx (data extracted using NAICS 315, Apparel).

point to the low wages of women workers in the developing world as a sign of their exploitation, others point to the increased economic citizenship and political awareness that industrial work has provided women workers in the Global South. For instance, one study showed a correlation between an increase in the number of women working in Bangladesh's apparel factories and an increase in the number of girls in school. This highlights the ways in which globalization is experienced at the local level.[9]

Among the countries involved in the global apparel industry, Pakistan and Bangladesh have perhaps received more attention in recent years as their share of the global market has increased. More than 80 percent of the clothing exports from both Pakistan and Bangladesh end up in American or European Union markets. From 1997 to 2001, the value of apparel exports from Bangladesh increased from $3.9 billion to more than $5.5 billion. In 2002, the apparel factories in Bangladesh accounted for 86 percent of the developing nation's total exports. As a result, Bangladesh's national economy has become increasingly dependent on the growing apparel industry. Between 1997 and 2001, Pakistan experienced growth of 18 percent in the value of apparel exports. Most of the garment industry is concentrated in the urban areas of Lahore and Karachi, with some work taking place in workers' homes. Although the textile industry is larger than the apparel industry in Pakistan, the rate of growth in the apparel sector suggests that this might change in the future.[10]

Western consumers are likely less familiar with the specific dimensions of the growth of the apparel industry in Pakistan and Bangladesh than they are with the numerous industrial accidents that have resulted in the deaths of thousands of workers in the region. In September 2012 a fire at a Karachi garment factory took the lives of nearly three hundred workers and reminded the world of the perils and consequences of the free-trade capitalist search for profits at all costs. The *Karachi Dawn*, an English-language newspaper, provided startling coverage of the tragedy as it unfolded. The parallels to the Triangle Shirtwaist Factory fire that claimed the lives of 146 workers in New York City a century earlier were obvious and undeniable. Television screens showed "footage [of] the blaze with people jumping from the factory building in their desperate attempt to escape the leaping flames. Survivors narrating their nightmarish experience to the media claimed that the exits were locked [or] else the casualty toll would not have been so enormous."[11] One worker who jumped to safety lamented to reporters about having to leave behind a pregnant woman.

Another, recounting the horrors of that day, recalled that "the electricity went off with a sound of a blast, followed by four to five more explosions that filled the entire floor with poisonous gas. There was total chaos as people ran for safety but found no way to escape, because the main entrance and the gate on the second floor were closed."[12] Surviving workers and relatives of the dead contend that the accident was preventable and resulted from Pakistan's persistent failure to enforce existing regulations regarding worker safety.[13]

Just a few weeks later, on November 27, 2012, the world awoke to news of another disaster that also bore an eerie resemblance to the Triangle Shirtwaist Factory fire. The front page of Bangladesh's *Daily Star* newspaper featured a simple headline, "Grief-Struck." Reporters described the horrors of a fire that claimed the lives of more than a hundred workers at the Tazreen Fashions factory in Ashulia, a city northwest of Dhaka. As was the case with the Triangle Shirtwaist Factory, the fire began on a lower floor. As the smoke made its way to the upper floors, workers found themselves trapped by locked gates and supervisors who ordered them back to their sewing machines. With no access to the stairwells, some workers decided to jump from the upper floors to escape the flames and suffocating smoke. Many of those who jumped perished, but some workers scrambled through windows and down bamboo scaffolding left by construction workers to safety. Karum Nahar, a sewing machine operator, described how supervisors told her to return to work when the alarm rang out. She waited a few minutes before heading down a staircase. As she made her way to the first floor, she could feel the heat and nearly succumbed to the smoke. Another worker on the fifth floor called her husband on her cell phone and cried, "Please pray for me! I am going to die!" Her husband turned over nearly twenty charred bodies searching for his wife but found no sign of her. More than fifty bodies charred beyond recognition were kept in a local hospital for DNA identification.[14]

Days later, the grim toll of the Tazreen Fashions factory fire was calculated. Government officials reported that 112 workers lost their lives, but labor activists and workers' families put the death toll at more than 200.[15] In the days that followed the fire, grieving families gathered around the factory to demand accountability for the deaths of their loved ones. Subsequent investigations confirmed inadequate safety precautions in both the design of the factory and its procedures. All three of the factory's staircases led to a single exit on the ground floor, and firefighters encountered several locked gates as they rushed to rescue the workers in the five-story factory.

Two weeks after the Tazreen fire, the *New York Times* ran an opinion column that drew connections between the Triangle Shirtwaist Factory fire and the still-unfolding tragedy in Bangladesh. The editors wondered if the garment industry in Bangladesh and elsewhere would finally heed the lessons learned in the Triangle Shirtwaist Factory fire. They called for "comprehensive changes in developing countries that have become the biggest suppliers of clothes to the Western world." Meanwhile, reports emerged that Tazreen Fashions was a leading supplier to Wal-Mart, Carrefour, and IKEA and that the company had earned a "suspicious" rating from international industry safety inspectors. Workers in the Bangladesh garment industry, who routinely earned less than forty dollars a month, deserved better safety precautions. The *New York Times* reported that in its search for the lowest-cost producers, Wal-Mart turned a blind eye toward shortcuts in safety systems. The newspaper made its position plain: "Wal-Mart and other retailers have been unwilling to pay the higher prices for clothes that would be needed to make factories safer. Labor groups say a roughly 3 percent annual increase in prices paid to the factories would be sufficient to make the needed improvements. That is a small expense to safeguard the lives of millions."[16] A small expense, indeed.

For all of the advances in technology, communications, and transportation that have effectively made our world a smaller place, the willingness to ignore the plight of workers abroad is notable. International monitoring agencies and organized labor have been unable or unwilling to respond effectively to multinational companies' desire to maximize profits. Historical echoes of the Triangle Shirtwaist Factory fire abound, but there is no convincing evidence that the global apparel industry will see the kinds of improvements and protections brought about by the garment unions in the United States years after that tragedy. The globalization of the apparel industry has transformed government regulation into collaboration, with transnational trade policies that facilitate profits for apparel companies while minimizing protections for workers.

The human cost of the globalization of the apparel industry became all too clear on April 24, 2013. On that day an eight-story building that held several apparel factories in Rana Plaza in Savar, Bangladesh, just outside of Dhaka, collapsed, killing more than eight hundred workers. In the week after the collapse, as the death toll became apparent and rescue efforts morphed into recovery strategies, workers and consumers around the world were outraged. When cracks had appeared in the building's walls and beams, an inspection had been ordered. Despite the building inspector's conclusion that workers should be kept away from the building, factory owners had compelled the workers to return to their sewing machines. Taslima Akhter, a Bangladeshi photographer and activist, captured an achingly beautiful and sad image of two workers, a man and woman, in a last embrace among the building's rubble. In the photograph, the two figures are entombed by debris, fabric, concrete, and rebar. The man's face is clear, with red blood coming from his eyes like tears. The woman's arm, bearing a modest gold bangle, stretches out only to fall just short of the man's neck. Akhter said the photo "haunts me. It's as if they are saying to me, 'We are not a number—not only cheap labor and cheap lives. We are human beings like you. Our life is precious like yours, and our dreams are precious too.'"[17]

Appendix

Many of the statistical data presented in this volume are based on one consistent group of statistical records: the *Economic Census of Manufactures*. This publication began in 1809 as a way to measure the manufacturing sector of the U.S. economy. Over the course of many years the census underwent substantial revisions, making comparability from one year to another a sometimes complicated issue. Nevertheless, the regularity of the publication, every two years in the beginning and later every five years, provides a relatively consistent perspective on the nation's manufacturing sector.

Working backward, between 1997 and 1954 the data were published every four or five years. The federal government published the census unevenly between 1937 and 1954. The Census Bureau suspended the publication of the census during World War II, resuming it in 1947. There was another fairly long interval of seven years between the first two postwar censuses. The census was scheduled to resume in 1953 but did not actually appear until 1954. So between 1937 and 1947 and between 1947 and 1954, there were no Census of Manufactures reports. And in 1954, when the census resumed publication, the format underwent several important revisions.

From a comparability perspective, there are several problems with the data for 1937. Standard Industrial Classification (SIC) codes were developed after the 1937 census. The SIC is a system for dividing the manufacturing sector into large industry groups. Within each large industry are smaller branches of the same industry. So, for instance, the SIC code for the apparel industry is 23, while the SIC code for the textile industry is 22. The last Standard Industrial Classification system lists apparel under "Major Group 23: Apparel and Other Finished Products Made from Fabrics and Similar Materials." Within the apparel industry group are dozens of subdivisions for different types of men's apparel, women's apparel, and accessories. Projecting the large industry classification backward in time is difficult and may have resulted in some incomparability issues. In order to provide some general level of comparison, though, for this study the data from each smaller branch of industry (from brassieres and corsets to men's, youth's, and boys' clothing) were combined to create an apparel industry total for each state. Each of the branches of the apparel industry that follow was listed separately in the 1937 census.

Branches of the apparel industry included in the reconstruction of the apparel classification for 1937:

Corsets and Allied Garments
Gloves and Mittens
Hats and Caps
Knitted Underwear
Knitted Outerwear
Knitted Outerwear—Contract Factories
Gloves and Mittens, Knitted
Men's and Boys' Cotton, Leather, and Allied Garments—
    Clothing, Leather and Sheep Lined
Men's and Boys' Cotton, Leather, and Allied Garments—
    Clothing, Work, and Sport Garments
Men's and Boys' Cotton, Leather, and Allied Garments—
    Trousers, Wash Suits, and Washable Service App
Men's and Boys' Cotton, Leather, and Allied Garments—
    Shirts, Collars, and Nightwear, Reg. Factories
Men's and Boys' Cotton, Leather, and Allied Garments—
    Shirts, Collars, and Nightwear, Contract Factories
Men's and Boys' Cotton, Leather, and Allied Garments—
    Underwear, Men's—Regular Factories
Men's and Youth's Clothing, Not Elsewhere
    Classified (NEC)—Regular Factories
Men's and Youth's Clothing, NEC—Contract Factories
Millinery—Regular Factories
Miscellaneous Apparel—Furnishing Goods,
    Men's, NEC—Regular Factories
Miscellaneous Apparel—Furnishing Goods,
    Men's, NEC—Contract Factories

Miscellaneous Apparel—Handkerchiefs—Regular Factories
Miscellaneous Apparel—Handkerchiefs—Contract Factories
Miscellaneous Apparel—Suspenders, Garters, etc.
Women's, Misses', and Children's Apparel,
    NEC—Blouses—Regular Factories
Women's, Misses', and Children's Apparel, NEC—
    Blouses—Contract Factories
Women's, Misses', and Children's Apparel, NEC—
    Clothing, NEC—Regular Factories
Women's, Misses', and Children's Apparel, NEC—
    Clothing, NEC—Contract Factories
Women's, Misses', and Children's Apparel, NEC—Coats,
    Suits, and Separate Skirts—Regular Factories
Women's, Misses', and Children's Apparel, NEC—Coats,
    Suits, and Separate Skirts—Contract Factories
Women's, Misses', and Children's Apparel, NEC—Dresses,
    Except House Dresses—Regular Factories
Women's, Misses', and Children's Apparel, NEC—Dresses,
    Except House Dresses—Contract Factories
Women's, Misses', and Children's Apparel, NEC—Dresses:
    House Dresses, Uniforms—Regular Factories
Women's, Misses', and Children's Apparel, NEC—Dresses:
    House Dresses, Uniforms—Contract Factories
Women's, Misses', and Children's Apparel, NEC—Outerwear,
    Children's and Infants'—Regular Factories
Women's, Misses', and Children's Apparel, NEC—Outerwear,
    Children's and Infants'—Contract Factories
Women's, Misses', and Children's Apparel, NEC—Knitted Underwear
Women's, Misses', and Children's Apparel, NEC—Cotton
    Woven Knitted Underwear and Nightwear

There were a few other difficulties working with the pre–World War II data. The census for 1937 did not specify the number of employees in states where there were a small number of apparel factories. Figures for southern states, as well as those for states in the Midwest, were particularly undercut by this omission. Nevertheless, the number of establishments in these states was quite small, especially when compared to apparel industry centers like New York.

In 1967 the Census of Manufactures began to round the figures for each state to the nearest hundred. Therefore, the data for 1967 and later end in zeroes and reflect an approximation. The census statisticians applied this rounding procedure uniformly to all of the industry, state, and national figures. Once again, these differences had a negligible effect on the overall portrait of the apparel industry painted by these figures. Nevertheless, the rounding in the post-1967 census years contrasts with the procedures followed in earlier census years.

In 1997 the Census Bureau began to use the North American Industry Classification System (NAICS), a system developed jointly by Canada, the United States, and Mexico, in place of the SIC system. Created by the three signatories to the 1994 North American Free Trade Agreement, the NAICS provides a consistent standard for measurement and analysis of industrial and economic activity across the continent.[1] Using this system, the 1997 Economic Census identified apparel production as follows:

> Industries in the Apparel Manufacturing subsector group establishments with two distinct manufacturing processes: (1) cut and sew (i.e., purchasing fabric and cutting and sewing to make a garment) and (2) the manufacture of garments in establishments that first knit fabric and then cut and sew the fabric into a garment. The Apparel Manufacturing subsector includes a diverse range of establishments manufacturing full lines of ready-to-wear apparel and custom apparel: apparel contractors, performing cutting or sewing operations on materials owned by others; jobbers performing entrepreneurial functions involved in apparel manufacture; and tailors, manufacturing custom garments for individual clients are all included. Knitting, when done alone, is classified in the Textile Mills subsector, but when knitting is combined with the production of complete garments, the activity is classified in Apparel Manufacturing.[2]

From census to census, figures for previous years were recalculated and corrected. These minor adjustments made little statistical difference to the overall portrait of the apparel industry for each census year.

With the considerations discussed above, the statistical presentations in this volume offer a useful perspective of the apparel industry from a national, state, and regional perspective. The data span over five decades and thus provide an opportunity for time-based analyses.

TABLE A.1. Apparel establishments in southern states, 1937–97

	1937	1947		1954		1958		1963		1967		1972		1977		1982		1987		1992		1997	
	No.	No.	(% change)	No.	(% change)	No.	(% change)	No.	(% change)	No.	(% change)	No.	(% change)	No.	(% change)	No.	(% change)	No.	(% change)	No.	(% change)	No.	(% change)
Alabama	11	97	(782)	139	(43)	146	(5)	189	(29)	220	(16)	262	(19)	345	(32)	354	(3)	397	(12)	395	(-1)	330	(-16)
Florida	–	117	(n/a)	269	(130)	330	(23)	404	(22)	509	(26)	873	(72)	1,279	(47)	1,227	(-4)	1,223	(0)	1,251	(2)	1,139	(-9)
Georgia	59	353	(498)	316	(-10)	346	(9)	432	(25)	468	(8)	541	(16)	622	(15)	639	(3)	644	(1)	644	(0)	585	(-9)
Kentucky	26	88	(238)	105	(19)	104	(-1)	126	(21)	136	(8)	147	(8)	156	(6)	161	(3)	163	(1)	215	(32)	191	(-11)
Louisiana	17	70	(312)	76	(9)	76	(0)	68	(-11)	73	(7)	91	(25)	131	(44)	117	(-11)	103	(-12)	119	(16)	148	(24)
Mississippi	15	55	(267)	100	(82)	112	(12)	142	(27)	158	(11)	191	(21)	221	(16)	214	(-3)	219	(2)	252	(15)	187	(-26)
North Carolina	29	144	(397)	207	(44)	243	(17)	371	(53)	473	(27)	559	(18)	702	(26)	732	(4)	780	(7)	790	(1)	735	(-7)
South Carolina	4	99	(2,375)	137	(38)	163	(19)	216	(33)	238	(10)	269	(13)	319	(19)	345	(8)	380	(10)	387	(2)	351	(-9)
Tennessee	66	138	(109)	175	(27)	209	(19)	256	(22)	298	(16)	358	(20)	443	(24)	458	(3)	485	(6)	545	(12)	473	(-13)
Texas	136	361	(165)	511	(42)	542	(6)	580	(7)	612	(6)	707	(16)	925	(31)	866	(-6)	847	(-2)	1,019	(20)	1,095	(7)
Virginia	51	118	(131)	169	(43)	158	(-7)	184	(16)	200	(9)	238	(19)	287	(21)	292	(2)	332	(14)	336	(1)	329	(-2)
West Virginia	5	27	(440)	37	(37)	34	(-8)	38	(12)	49	(29)	55	(12)	63	(15)	44	(-30)	45	(2)	50	(11)	45	(-10)
Total	**419**	**1,667**	**(298)**	**2,241**	**(34)**	**2,463**	**(10)**	**3,006**	**(22)**	**3,434**	**(14)**	**4,291**	**(25)**	**5,493**	**(28)**	**5,449**	**(-1)**	**5,618**	**(3)**	**6,003**	**(7)**	**5,608**	**(-7)**

Source: U.S. Bureau of the Census, *Economic Census of Manufactures*, 1937, 1947, 1954, 1958, 1963, 1967, 1972, 1977, 1982, 1987, 1992, 1997

Notes

INTRODUCTION. THE PLACE OF APPAREL IN THE
HISTORY OF SOUTHERN INDUSTRIALIZATION

1. Stella M. Hopkins, "Facing Weak Sales, Levi Strauss Plans Factory Shutdowns," *Charlotte (N.C.) Observer*, February 5, 1999; "Small Town, Hard Times: Overseas Competition Shutting Linden's 40-Year-Old Factory," *Birmingham (Ala.) News*, November 4, 1993; "Van Heusen Closing Three Alabama Plants: 1,050 Will Lose Jobs," *Birmingham (Ala.) News*, September 15, 1995; "A Bleak Future: Thousands of Alabamians Have Lost Their Jobs as Apparel Plants Have Closed," *Birmingham (Ala.) News*, September 22, 1996; "Textiles Head South: Imports Unravel Apparel Industry," *Chattanooga Times*, February 29, 1996.

2. King, *"All Labor Has Dignity."*

3. The apparel industry has a distinct classification code as determined by the Office of Management and Budget. In 1987 the Standard Industrial Classification (SIC) system divided the nation's industries into major groups and subgroups. Major Group 23, Apparel and Other Finished Products Made from Fabrics and Similar Materials, was defined to include "the cutting up and needle trades, . . . establishments producing clothing and fabricating products by cutting and sewing purchased woven or knit textile fabrics and related materials, such as leather, rubberized fabrics, plastics, and furs." It is also important to note that this division includes all elements of the complicated apparel industrial structure, from jobbers and contractors to "regular factories." This study will adhere to this definition when considering the history of the apparel industry in the U.S. South. Executive Office of the President, Office of Management and Budget, *Standard Industrial Classification Manual*, 96–106.

4. Sue Davidson makes a similar point in her introduction to an edited volume of essays on the textile and garment industries. Jensen and Davidson, *A Needle, a Bobbin, a Strike*, xii–xiv.

5. According to the U.S. Department of Labor, women accounted for 78.7 percent of apparel workers in January 1960, the first year for which such data exists. In 1970 the figure had risen to 80.7 percent. By January 1990 81.1 percent of apparel

workers in the United States were female. While the textile industry employed around four hundred thousand women between 1960 and 1990, the apparel industry average for those same years hovered around one million women workers. See U.S. Department of Labor, Women's Bureau, *1993 Handbook on Women Workers*, 111, 118–25. See also U.S. Department of Labor, Bureau of Labor Statistics, *Employment, Hours, and Earnings*, 2:1,126, 1,158–59.

6. U.S. Department of Labor, Women's Bureau, *Women's Place in Industry*, 1931), 6–7.

7. Bob Herbert, "In America: Children of the Dark Ages," *New York Times*, July 21, 1995.

8. U.S. Department of Labor, Women's Bureau, *Women's Place in Industry*, 11.

9. American Federation of Labor Legislative Committee, *Subsidized Industrial Migration*, 66–69.

10. In addition, Elaine Wrong's analysis demonstrates that nearly 40 percent of the nation's apparel workers lived in the South in 1969. Wrong, *Negro in the Apparel Industry*, 21.

11. Beginning with the 1947 *Economic Census of Manufactures*, the Department of Commerce instituted a new structure for its analysis of the nation's manufacturing sector. In prior publication years major industries were divided into smaller subsections. As a result, the figures compiled for 1937 represent the combination of thirty-five smaller branches of the apparel industry. Given the absence of an industry-wide total, the figures presented here constitute a best estimate of the actual figures. For more on the comparability of data from one census year to another, please see the appendix.

12. U.S. Bureau of the Census, *Economic Census of Manufactures*, 1992, 1997. The Bureau of the Census publishes the *Economic Census of Manufactures* (later the *Economic Census, Manufacturing and Mining*) every five years.

13. Beginning with Broadus Mitchell's 1921 study *The Rise of Cotton Mills in the South*, historians interested in southern workers often focused their studies on textile workers.

14. W. J. Cash's generative volume on southern history and culture, *The Mind of the South*, argues that textile mills imposed the ugly "defects of progress" on southern workers. Cash's work influenced and inspired a wide variety of scholars in southern history. Hall, Korstad, and Leloudis, "Cotton Mill People"; Hall et al., *Like a Family*. For the quotation, see Cash, *Mind of the South*, 205.

15. In a widely cited 1991 historiographical essay assessing the state of scholarship on the southern textile industry, Robert H. Zieger suggests that two large issues have arisen from the scholarship. First, historians have explored the working-class culture that developed among mill workers. Second, historians have grappled (less conclusively, argues Zieger) with the failure of organized labor to take hold among southern textile workers. In his latest collection of essays in

southern labor history, Zieger tackles the historiography of southern exception-alism. C. Vann Woodward provides an overview of earlier literature on southern textile mills, much of which has a sociological or economic perspective, in his important 1951 study *Origins of the New South, 1877–1913*. Several articles on the weakness of organized labor in the southern textile industry appeared in a special issue of the *Georgia Historical Quarterly*. Articles by Michelle Brattain, Frank J. Byrne, Robert P. Ingalls, and Randall Patton each explore the central issue of organized labor's failure in Georgia's textile industry. Bryant Simon's thoughtful review essay in the same volume explores the question from the broader and more inclusive perspective of the southern workers in general. Robert H. Zieger, "Textile Workers and Historians," in Zieger, *Organized Labor in the Twentieth-Century South*, 35–59; Robert H. Zieger, "Introduction: Is Southern Labor History Exceptional?," in Zieger, *Southern Labor in Transition*, 1–14; Woodward, *Origins of the New South*, 599–601; Brattain, "A Town as Small as That"; Byrne, "Wartime Agitation and Postwar Repression"; Ingalls, "Wagner Act on Trial"; Patton, "A World of Opportunity,"; Simon, "Rethinking Why." See also Marshall, *Labor in the South*; Michael Goldfield, "Failure of Operation Dixie; Griffith, *Crisis of American Labor*.

16. In addition to Broadus Mitchell's *The Rise of Cotton Mills in the South*, good introductions to the development of a mill culture and community among southerners can be found in the classics of modern southern history. W. J. Cash's *Mind of the South*, C. Vann Woodward's *Origins of the New South*, and George Brown Tindall's *Emergence of the New South* trace the basic features of life as a southern textile worker from the last decade of the nineteenth century through the first part of the twentieth century. *Like a Family*, the collaborative work arising from the Southern Oral History Project at the University of North Carolina, remains a standard in the historiography of southern textile workers' community and identity. Like all good history, *Like a Family* inspired dozens of scholars to uncover the boundaries and dynamics of textile workers' communities. Mitchell, *Rise of Cotton Mills in the South*; Cash, *Mind of the South*, 179–86, 202–11; Woodward, *Origins of the New South*, 221–31, 417–20; Tindall, *Emergence of the New South*, 321–52; Hall et al., *Like a Family*; Hall, Korstad, and Leloudis, "Cotton Mill People"; Hall, "Disorderly Women." See also Ayers, *Promise of the New South*; Byerly, *Hard Times Cotton Mill Girls*; Carlton, *Mill and Town in South Carolina*; Clark, *Like Night and Day*; Cobb, *Industrialization and Southern Society*; Cobb, *Selling of the South*; Daniel, *Standing at the Crossroads*, 103–8; Flamming, *Creating the Modern South*; Gaston, *New South Creed*; James A. Hodges, "The Real Norma Rae," in Zieger, *Southern Labor in Transition*, 251–73; David R. Goldfield, *Cotton Fields and Skyscrapers*; Newby, *Plain Folk in the New South*; Tullos, *Habits of Industry*; Robert H. Zieger, "From Primordial Folk to Redundant Workers: Southern Textile Workers and Social Observers," in Zieger, *Southern Labor in Transition*, 273–94.

17. Rick Halpern, "Organized Labor, Black Workers, and the Twentieth Cen-

tury South: The Emerging Revision," in Halpern and Stokes, *Race and Class in the American South*, 43–76. See also Frederickson, "Four Decades of Change"; Minchin, "Color Means Something"; Minchin, *"What Do We Need a Union For?"*; Minchin, *Hiring the Black Worker*. Much of the following scholarship, while not exclusively focused on southern textiles, offers important insights to the larger issues of race relations implied by unionization efforts. See also Bartley, *New South, 1945–1980*, 28–29, 60–62, 72–73; Draper, *Conflict of Interests*; Rick Halpern, "The CIO and the Limits of Labor-Based Civil Rights Activism: The Case of Louisiana's Sugar Workers, 1947–1966," in Zieger, *Southern Labor in Transition*, 86–112; Halpern and Stokes, *Race and Class in the American South*; Michael Honey, "Martin Luther King, Jr., the Crisis of the Black Working Class, and the Memphis Sanitation Strike," in Zieger, *Southern Labor in Transition*, 146–75; Honey, *Southern Labor and Black Civil Rights*; Janiewski, *Sisterhood Denied*; Korstad and Lichtenstein, "Opportunities Found and Lost"; Letwin, *Challenge of Interracial Unionism*; Alex Lichtenstein, "'Scientific Unionism' and the 'Negro Question': Communists and the Transport Workers Union in Miami, 1944–1949," in Zieger, *Southern Labor in Transition*, 58–85. Marshall, *Employment of Blacks in the South*; Marshall, *Labor in the South*; Bruce Nelson, "'CIO Meant One Thing for the Whites and Another Thing for Us': Steelworkers and Civil Rights, 1936–1974," in Zieger, *Southern Labor in Transition*, 113–45; Norrell, "Caste in Steel."

18. While these works occasionally fall outside the scope of the southern textile industry, they draw important conclusions about the role of organized labor and race relations in the South. Michael Goldfield, "Failure of Operation Dixie"; Griffith, *Crisis of American Labor*; Korstad, "Daybreak of Freedom"; Minchin, "Color Means Something," 109–33; Minchin, *"What Do We Need a Union For?"*; Minchin, *Hiring the Black Worker*.

19. To date, there are very few works that substantially explore the development of the southern apparel industry. Although Elaine Gale Wrong's study does not focus on the South exclusively, her work explores the experience of African American apparel workers and thus contains many insights regarding the southern branch of the apparel industry. A few other works have focused more directly on the experience of stitchers in Texas. Wrong, *Negro in the Apparel Industry*; Laurie Coyle, Gail Hershatter, and Emily Honig, "Women at Farah: An Unfinished Story," in Jensen and Davidson, *A Needle, a Bobbin, a Strike*, 227–77; DeMoss, *History of Apparel Manufacturing in Texas*; Honig, "Women at Farah Revisited"; Jensen and Davidson, *A Needle, a Bobbin, a Strike*.

20. Originally the apparel and textile industries each developed their own labor unions. The original apparel worker unions were the International Ladies' Garment Workers' Union (ILGWU), the Amalgamated Clothing Workers of America (ACWA), and the United Garment Workers (UGW). The Textile Workers Union of America (TWUA) was the primary union for textile workers in the twentieth cen-

tury. In 1974 the ACWA merged with the TWUA and became known as the Amalgamated Clothing and Textile Workers Union (ACTWU). Even more recently, in 1994, the ILGWU merged with the ACTWU and became the Union of Needletrades, Industrial and Textile Employees (UNITE!).

21. This point is best illustrated in Timothy Minchin, *Hiring the Black Worker: The Racial Integration of the Southern Textile Industry, 1960–1980*. Minchin examines the process of desegregation in the southern textile industries. In several discussions of Oneita Knitting Mills in Andrews, South Carolina, Minchin makes no reference to the fact that the company expanded its operations from knitted underwear, which technically falls within the Standard Industrial Classification of textile manufacturing, to include children's clothing during the period of his study. However, he does note the predominantly female workforce at Oneita, a typical characteristic of apparel manufacturing. In 1964 the ILGWU listed 142 members of the Oneita local in Andrews, South Carolina. Of the 142 members, only 5 were men. In the caption to a photo of an African American woman operating a sewing machine, Minchin argues, "By the late 1960s, African American women were beginning to break into production jobs in the southern textile industry, particularly in those plants with sewing operations." Burlington Industries, a company well known throughout the South for its textile production, also expanded operations to include apparel production. In companies like Oneita and Burlington, garment manufacturing often occurred in separate sewing plants, a division of processes that underscores the distinctiveness of textile and apparel manufacturing. Minchin, *Hiring the Black Worker*, 176, 180–81, 184, 186–87, 196–204; "Members Paid Through 1963," box 3162, folder 10: "Oneita Knitting Mills, 1963–1965," International Ladies' Garment Workers' Union, Southeast Regional Office Records, Georgia State University Library, Atlanta. For a discussion of Oneita's expansion into apparel manufacturing, see Jim Parker, "125-year-old Oneita's Restructuring Fails; Layoffs Soon," *Charleston Post and Courier*, March 13, 1999, sec. B, p. 1; Jim Parker, "Oneita Nears End after 125-Year Run," *Charleston Post and Courier*, May 16, 1999, sec. G, p. 1; Wrong, *Negro in the Apparel Industry*, 6.

22. James C. Cobb also discusses the labor-intensive nature of the apparel industry in his study of southern industrialization. Wrong, *Negro in the Apparel Industry*, 1–2; Herbert Koshetz, "Human Hands Are Garments' Backbone," *New York Times*, September 27, 1975, p. 37; Cobb, *Selling of the South*, 2, 22, 31.

23. John Holusha, "Squeezing the Textile Workers: Trade and Technology Force a New Wave of Job Cuts," *New York Times*, February 21, 1996.

24. In census data, the textile industry is represented by SIC 22. The apparel industry's SIC is 23. The data presented here on manufacturing in the United States employs various years of the *Economic Census of Manufactures* published by the Bureau of the Census.

25. U.S. Bureau of the Census, *Economic Census of Manufactures*, 1977; Henry P.

Leifermann, "The Unions are Coming: Trouble in the South's First Industry," *New York Times*, August 5, 1973, 21SM.

26. For a discussion of the low wages of southern textile workers and the connections between southern textile and apparel factories, see Tindall, *Emergence of the New South*, 318–20, 480; Woodward, *Origins of the New South*, 134, 225–26, 462–63.

27. Bernstein, *Lean Years*, 40; Cash, *Mind of the South*, 248–49, 364–65; Marshall, *Labor in the South*; Halpern, "Organized Labor, Black Workers and the Twentieth Century South: The Emerging Revision," in Halpern and Stokes, *Race and Class in the American South*; McLaurin, *Paternalism and Protest*; Montgomery, "Struggle for Unions in the South"; Robert J. Norrell, "Labor Trouble: George Wallace and Union Politics in Alabama," in Zieger, *Organized Labor in the Twentieth-Century South*, 250–72; Simon, "Rethinking Why"; Terrill, "No Union for Me"; Minchin, "Color Means Something," 109–33; Minchin, *"What Do We Need A Union For?"*; Minchin, *Hiring the Black Worker*.

28. This is one of the most important conclusions of Hall et al., *Like a Family*.

29. Tera Hunter's groundbreaking study *"To 'joy My Freedom": Southern Black Women's Lives and Labors after the Civil War* explores the important connections between black women and domestic labor from Reconstruction to the dawn of the New South. She explains how ideas of race and class combined to effectively prevent the realization of true freedom for freed bondwomen. Hunter, *"To 'joy My Freedom."*

30. Woodward, *Origins of the New South*, 221–22; Tindall, *Emergence of the New South*, 319, 713–16; Dolores E. Janiewski, "Southern Honor, Southern Dishonor: Managerial Ideology and the Construction of Gender, Race, and Class Relations in Southern Industry," in Baron, *Work Engendered*, 81–82, 90–91.

CHAPTER ONE. "THERE WASN'T ANY JOBS FOR WOMEN"

1. Arcola McLean, interview by author, Jackson, Ala., August 8, 1998.

2. McLean, interview.

3. Vivian Long, interview by author, Jackson, Ala., August 9, 1998.

4. William D. McCain, "The Triumph of Democracy, 1916–1932," in McLemore, *History of Mississippi* 2:93–94. Another study, by Douglas Flamming, utilizes real prices from 1890 as the point of comparison and reveals that from 1915 to 1919 the average price per pound was nearly sixteen cents. Flamming, *Creating the Modern South*, 108–9; Daniel, *Standing at the Crossroads*, 114–15.

5. Long, interview.

6. Dot Guy, interview by author, Jackson, Ala., June 20, 2003.

7. Max McAliley, "Monroeville's Vanity Fair Boasts Many Firsts in 4-Year History," *Mobile (Ala.) Register*, August 11, 1986, sec. B, p. 2.

8. Specific data on the apparel sector in these counties was not published, in an effort to prevent the disclosure of information about individual companies. However, apparel is listed as a primary employer, perhaps the largest manufacturing employer, in Clarke County in 1997. That year Monroe County reported three apparel establishments. Even though the specific employment data was withheld, it is clear that apparel was the second- or third-largest manufacturing employer in the county. U.S. Bureau of the Census, *Economic Census of Manufactures*, 1997. County data available at http://www.census.gov/epcd/www/econ97.html.

9. Ava Baron and Susan E. Klepp, "'If I Didn't Have My Sewing Machine . . .': Women and Sewing-Machine Technology," in Jensen and Davison, *A Needle, A Bobbin, A Strike*, 38–40.

10. Levine, *Women's Garment Workers*, 13–15; Cobb, *Industrialization and Southern Society*, 42–43.

11. George Brown Tindall finds that the post-Depression era witnessed a great proliferation in the number of industries in the region. Tindall, *Emergence of the New South*, 462–63, 471.

12. Cowie, *Capital Moves*; English, *Common Thread*; Massey, *Spatial Divisions of Labor*.

13. Wrong, *Negro in the Apparel Industry*, 19–20.

14. Rodengen, *Legend of VF Corporation*, 23; Vanity Fair Silk Mills (advertisement), *Reading (Penn.) Eagle*, January 18, 1920, 18.

15. Wrong, *Negro in the Apparel Industry*, 19–20.

16. Levine, *Women's Garment Workers*, 342–53.

17. Amberg, "Varieties of Capitalist Development," 236.

18. Braun, *Union-Management Co-operation*, 62.

19. Quoted in Cobb, *Selling of the South*, 11–12.

20. In *The Selling of the South* James C. Cobb details many elements of Mississippi's Balance Agriculture with Industry program and especially notes which features of the program were emulated by other southern communities. In a volume on the history of Mississippi, J. Oliver Emmerich places the BAWI program in the context of Mississippi's recovery from the Great Depression. Another essay by Donald C. Mosely in the same volume discusses organized labor's response to the BAWI program. Cobb, *Selling of the South*, 14–16, 21–33, 61–63; J. Oliver Emmerich, "Collapse and Recovery," in McLemore, *History of Mississippi*, 2:97–119; Donald C. Mosely, "The Labor Union Movement," in McLemore, *History of Mississippi*, 2:250–73.

21. Cobb writes that the Reliance "plant revitalized the area's economy, . . . and, by employing rural women, helped to make farm life a bit more bearable in that part of Depression-era Mississippi." Cobb, *Selling of the South*, 9–10; Jensen and Davidson, *A Needle, a Bobbin, A Strike*, xv; Wrong, *Negro in the Apparel Industry*, 19; Cobb, *Selling of the South*, 110–11.

22. McGill, *South and the Southerner*, 194–95.

23. Wrong, *Negro in the Apparel Industry*, 43.

24. The claim of having an antiunion labor pool was common in the correspondence of residents of southern communities regarding potential industrial concerns. Jules Levy to Robert Cohn, October 17, 1957, box 3043, folder 8: "Advertisements, 1957–1958," International Ladies' Garment Workers' Union, Southeast Regional Office Records, Georgia State University Library, Atlanta (hereafter ILGWU-SERO);D. H. Markstein to R. D. Gilleland, August 12, 1957, ibid.

25. "Committee of 100 Has Accomplished Much in the Augusta Area," *Georgia Magazine*, April–May 1958, 30–31.

26. "Louisiana, the Right-to-Profit State," *Business Week*, June 15, 1968, 70; Gall, *Politics of Right to Work*.

27. These incentive programs and legislative packages were not without their critics. For a good example of the many issues raised in opposition to these programs, see John D. Garwood, "Are Municipal Subsidies for Industrial Location Sound?," *American City*, May 1953, 110–11.

28. Tindall, *Emergence of the New South*, 459–63, 470–71; *Regal Shirt Company and Amalgamated Clothing Workers of America*, 004 NLRB 567–76 (1937).

29. Long, interview.

30. Joseph T. Jordan, "Workers on Strike at Oneita Mills," n.d., ca. 1963, clipping in box 3165, folder 5: "Oneita Knitting Mills, Inc.: News Clippings, 1963," ILGWU-SERO.

31. Jim Parker, "Oneita Nears End After 125-Year Run," *Charleston (S.C.) Post and Courier*, March 13, 1999, sec. G, p. 1.

32. Ibid.

33. Ashbaugh and McCurry, "On the Line at Oneita," 205.

34. F. Ray Marshall argued that this was "the usual strategy" of the ILGWU in dealing with runaway firms in the South after World War II. Murray Seeger, "Runaway Concern Ordered to Bargain," *New York Times*, July 2, 1965, 1, 36; Damon Stetson, "Union Organizing Ordered at Plant," *New York Times*, March 3, 1968, 29. Marshall, *Labor in the South*, 281.

35. As early as 1953 the ILGWU was involved in contract negotiations with representatives from Oneita's Andrews, South Carolina, plant. See various documents in box 3164, folder 10: "Oneita Knitting Mills, Inc.: Negotiations, 1953–1960," ILGWU-SERO.

36. In 1958 the director of the ILGWU's Southeast Regional Office, E. T. "Al" Kehrer, responded to a company invitation to the grand-opening celebration of a new Oneita warehouse by sending the union's business agent in his place. In that same year the president of Oneita Knitting Mills, Robert D. Devereaux, accepted an invitation to an ILGWU banquet. Mr. Wood to E. T. Kehrer, September 3, 1958, box

3162, folder 10: "Oneita Knitting Mills, Inc.: Agreements, 1958–1960," ILGWU-SERO; Robert D. Devereaux to E. T. Kehrer, November 12, 1958, ibid.

37. See letters of withdrawal from Oneita employees, March 10, 1964, through April 17, 1964, box 3162, folder 12: "Oneita Knitting Mills, Inc.: Correspondence, 1963–1964," ILGWU-SERO.

38. Nick Bonanno to Morris P. Glushien, November 15, 1963, box 3162, folder 12: "Oneita Knitting Mills, Inc.: Correspondence, 1963–1964," ILGWU-SERO.

39. *Oneita Knitting Mills, Inc. vs. International Ladies' Garment Workers' Union, Local 371*, testimony of Ronelle Moore, July 31, 1963, box 3162, folder 2: "Oneita Knitting Mills, Inc.: NLRB Case, 1963," ILGWU-SERO.

40. *Oneita Knitting Mills, Inc. vs. International Ladies' Garment Workers' Union, Local 371*, hearing before Honorable James B. Morrison, Georgetown County Court House, transcript, August 30, 1963, box 3162, folder 2: "Oneita Knitting Mills, Inc.: NLRB Case, 1963," ILGWU-SERO.

41. Ibid.

42. In 1971 the TWUA began to organize the Oneita plant in Andrews, South Carolina. In 1973, after two years of failed contract negotiations, Oneita workers once again took to the picket lines. This time the workers were victorious and the company signed a new contract with clearly defined grievance and arbitration procedures. Ashbaugh and McCurry, "On the Line at Oneita," 205–14; Minchin, *Hiring the Black Worker*, 196–204, 255–56.

43. Jules Levy to Robert Cohn, October 17, 1957, box 3043, folder 8: "Advertisements, 1957–1958," ILGWU-SERO.

44. Judy Thomas, Inc. to Robert Cohn, October 4, 1957, box 3043, folder 8: "Advertisements, 1957–1958," ILGWU-SERO.

45. Nicholas Bonanno to Basil Basila, September 20, 1957, box 3043, folder 8: "Advertisements, 1957–1958," ILGWU-SERO.

46. E.T. "Al" Kehrer to Gerson & Gerson, n.d., box 3043, folder 8, "Advertisements, 1957–1958," ILGWU-SERO.

47. Amberg, "Varieties of Capitalist Development," 235–37.

48. Al Kehrer, interview by Marcia Fishman, Atlanta, Ga., February 10, 1995, transcript l1995–12, Voices of Labor Oral History Project.

49. Cobb points out that despite a 185 percent increase in union membership in the South, "unions [in the region] grew only half as fast . . . between 1939 and 1953 as in the rest of the nation." Cobb, *Selling of the South*, 97. Statistics from Marshall, *Labor in the South*, 306.

50. In a discussion of the CIO's Operation Dixie, Michelle Brattain makes a similar point. James C. Cobb argues that developers promised that industrial wages in the South would eventually equal those found in northern factories while pro-

moting the region's abundance of low-wage workers. Brattain, *Politics of Whiteness*, 141–42; Cobb, *Industrialization and Southern Society*, 97.

1. Zieger, *The CIO*, 75–78.

2. The Women's Bureau reported that there were 4,183 total workers in the fifty-three apparel factories studied. Specifically, 91.3 percent (3,818) of workers were women, while 8.7 percent (365) were men. The agents also reported that 2,903 white women (76.0 percent) found work in the clothing factories, while only 898 Mexican women (23.5 percent) and 17 (0.4 percent) were African American. Earnings for a week in 1932 for men's work clothing: white women, $7.15; Mexican, $5.50. U.S. Department of Labor, Women's Bureau, *Women in Texas Industries*, 1–13, 47–8, 53–56.

3. DeMoss, *History of Apparel Manufacturing in Texas*, 146; U.S. Department of Labor, Women's Bureau, *Women in Texas Industries*, 53–56.

4. Bernstein, *Turbulent Years*, 34–35; Babson, *Unfinished Struggle*, 70–71.

5. Salmond, *General Textile Strike of 1934*; Brecher, *Strike!*, 191–92; Rick Spruill, "Seventy-Five Years Later the Chiquola Incident in Honea Path Still Significant," *Anderson (S.C.) Independent Mail*, September 4, 2009; English, *Common Thread*, 129–52; Stoney, Helfand, and Rostock, *Uprising of '34*; "Troops in Georgia Put Strike Pickets in New Prison Camp," *New York Times*, September 18, 1934; Irons, *Testing the New Deal*.

6. McArthur and Smith, *Texas Through Women's Eyes*, 122.

7. Ibid., 122–24.

8. "Garment Workers Making Demands on Manufacturers," *Dallas Morning News*, January 21, 1935; "Portion of Dress Company Workers Go Out on Strike," *Dallas Morning News*, February 8, 1935; "Garment Workers' Pickets and Cops Clash at Factory," *Dallas Morning News*, February 13, 1935; Patricia Hill, "Real Women and True Womanhood"; DeMoss, *History of Apparel Manufacturing in Texas*, 146–49.

9. McArthur and Smith, *Texas Through Women's Eyes*, 122; Patricia Evridge Hill, "Dallas Garment Workers' Strike," *Handbook of Texas Online*, accessed July 22, 2012, http://www.tshaonline.org/handbook/online/articles/oedfb.

10. "Injunctions, Fights Mark Beginning of Dress Plant Strike," *Dallas Morning News*, March 8, 1935.

11. Ibid.

12. DeMoss, *History of Apparel Manufacturing in Texas*, 147; "Dress Strike War Flares Up as Court Meets," *Dallas Morning News*, March 19, 1935.

13. "Injunctions, Fights Mark Beginning of Dress Plant Strike," *Dallas Morning*

News, March 8, 1935; Hill, "Dallas Garment Workers' Strike"; DeMoss, *History of Apparel Manufacturing in Texas*, 150–51.

14. DeMoss, *History of Apparel Manufacturing in Texas*, 144–53.

15. "Women Stripped and 'Spanked' in Strike: Garment Workers Battle Dallas Police," *New York Times*, August 8, 1935.

16. McArthur and Smith, *Texas through Women's Eyes*, 122–24.

17. Ibid.

18. "Women Stripped and 'Spanked' in Strike: Garment Workers Battle Dallas Police," *New York Times*, August 8, 1935.

19. Ibid.

20. "Dress Shop Workers, Pickets Clash in Street," *Memphis Commercial Appeal*, March 9, 1937.

21. Ibid.

22. Gilmore, *Gender and Jim Crow*, 61–118.

23. "Police Patrol Plant after Strike Fights," *Memphis Commercial Appeal*, March 9, 1937; Honey, *Southern Labor and Black Civil Rights*, 80–82.

24. "Memphis C.I.O. Office Will Be Opened Today," *Memphis Commercial Appeal*, March 21, 1937.

25. Honey, *Southern Labor and Black Civil Rights*, 41, 81.

26. "Pickets Win Victory on Contempt Charge," *Memphis Commercial Appeal*, April 6, 1937; Honey, *Southern Labor and Black Civil Rights*, 81; "Clothes Fly," *Memphis Press Scimitar*, March 24, 1937, reprinted in Stein, *Out of the Sweatshop*, 238; Hall, "Disorderly Women."

27. "Memphis C.I.O. Office Will Be Opened Today," *Memphis Commercial Appeal*, March 21, 1937.

28. Bob Marks, "Tupelo Workers Form Unions: Ida Sledge to Contest Move," *Memphis Commercial Appeal*, July 13, 1937; "Strikers at Tupelo Plant Issue Threat," *Memphis Commercial Appeal*, April 14, 1937; Honey, *Southern Labor and Black Civil Rights*, 91.

29. Bob Marks, "Tupelo Workers Form Unions: Ida Sledge to Contest Move," *Memphis Commercial Appeal*, July 13, 1937; Honey, *Southern Labor and Black Civil Rights*, 91.

30. Linda Gordon, *Pitied but Not Entitled*; Elna Green, *Looking for the New Deal*, 96–98; Vassie Lee Hall to Governor Fred P. Cone, March 12, 1937, reprinted in Elna Green, *Looking for the New Deal*, 151.

31. Elna Green, "Relief from Relief."

32. "Merit Clothing Anti-union Acts Exposed at Hearing," *Advance*, March 1940, 19.

33. "Case Work Report of Southern Workers Defense League," March–December 1941, in box 34, "Regional Correspondence," Workers Defense League Papers.

34. Zieger, *The CIO*, 246–48.

35. For excellent discussions of honor and the virtuous victimization of southern women, see Edwards, *People and Their Peace*, 169; and Broussard, "Naked before the Law."

36. "Hi Neighbor" and "Athco Workers Urge Union: Go!," *Athens (Ala.) Limestone Democrat*, February 24, 1953, clipping in box 3046, folder 3: "Clippings, 1953," International Ladies' Garment Workers' Union, Southeast Regional Office Records, Georgia State University Library, Atlanta (hereafter ILGWU-SERO).

37. Gertha Ballard, Jessie Bailiey, et al., letter to the editor, Asheville newspaper, n.d., ca. July 1955, in clipping file—'Strikers Committee Defends Actions," box 3046/4, ILGWU-SERO.

38. "Labor Ills Blamed in Haleyville Blast," *Birmingham Post-Herald*, November 8, 1955, clipping in box 31, folder 8: "Haleyville Textile Co., Inc.: Haleyville, Ala. 1956–58," 5780/058, International Ladies' Garment Workers' Union Records, Cornell University.

39. "Strike Called, Picket Lines Set Up At Plant of Mountain Top Firm" and "Picket Hit By Car in Henderson" (newspaper names not indicated), April 28, 1958, clippings in box 16, folder 5: "Louis Stulberg, General Secretary-Treasurer, Correspondence, 1956–1966 [bulk 1959–1966]," 5780/003, International Ladies' Garment Workers' Union Records, Cornell University; E. T. Kehrer to Louis Stulberg, March 3, 1958, ibid.

40. Ibid.

41. Martha Watford, affidavit, February 25, 1964, Georgetown County, South Carolina, in box 3165, folder 4: "Oneita Knitting Mills, Inc.: NLRB Affidavits, etc.," ILGWU-SERO.

42. Iris Newton, affidavit, August 14, 1963, in box 3163, folder 2: "Oneita Knitting Mills, Inc., NLRB Case, 1963," ILGWU-SERO.

43. "Upholding Mediocrity," *Savannah (Ga.) Morning News*, April 7, 1969, 4a.

44. In 1968 Georgia's union density, the share of nonagricultural workers who were members of labor unions, was far below the national average of 28.2 percent. Only the states of Texas, New Mexico, North Carolina, and South Carolina had lower percentages of unionized nonagricultural workers than Georgia. Hirsch, Macpherson, and Vroman, "Estimates of Union Density by State" (accompanying data online at www.unionstats.com).

45. The Loray Corporation and International Ladies' Garment Workers' Union, AFL-CIO, Decision and Order; *State of Georgia vs. Walter Leste*, Hearing, Recorder's Court of Savannah, Chatham County, Georgia; "Union Man Is Arrested at Plant," *Savannah (Ga.) Morning News*, March 12, 1969, 8D.

46. Ibid.

47. NLRB Rules and Regulations, Sec. 101.18, published November 1959 and amended 1967, http://www.nlrb.gov/reports-guidance/rules-regulations. Thanks

also to National Labor Relations Board deputy regional attorney Andrea Wilkes for her assistance on this point.

48. Lee Schwartz, "beware of what you sign," bulletin, box 3146, folder 4, ILGWU-SERO; The Loray Corporation and International Ladies' Garment Workers' Union, AFL-CIO, cases 10–CA-7759 and 10–CA-7866, National Labor Relations Board, July 20, 1970, Decision and Order.

49. Ibid.

50. Ibid.

51. Ibid.

CHAPTER THREE. "ROUGH WOMEN"

1. The late C. Vann Woodward, the revered scholar of southern history and race relations, defined segregation as the "physical separation of people for reasons of race." Woodward, *Strange Career of Jim Crow*, xi.

2. Kluger, *Simple Justice*, 73–83.

3. Nancy Green, *Ready to Wear and Ready-to-Work*; Glenn, *Daughters of the Shetl*; Tyler, *Look for the Union Label*.

4. Roediger and Esch, *Production of Difference*.

5. Some of the best works on gender roles discuss an earlier period of southern history. Nevertheless, many of the insights offered in these volumes are relevant to the post–World War II South as well. Mary Frederickson, "Heroines and Girl Strikers: Gender Issues and Organized Labor in the Twentieth Century South," in Zieger, ed. *Organized Labor in the Twentieth-Century South*, 84–112; Gilmore, *Gender and Jim Crow*; Hunter, *"To 'joy My Freedom"*; Janiewski, *Sisterhood Denied*; Scott, *Southern Lady*; Wyatt-Brown, *Southern Honor*.

6. An early pioneer in the quest to understand the simultaneous forces of race and gender is Evelyn Brooks-Higginbotham. See her groundbreaking 1992 article in *Signs* for an explanation of the need to "expose race as a metalanguage by calling attention to its powerful, all-encompassing effect on the construction and representation of . . . race, gender, class and sexuality." Brooks-Higginbotham, "African American Women's History," esp. 252.

7. For more on Barbey's hostility to unions and his promises to never work with a union, see Rodengen, *Legend of VF Corporation*, 32–34. See also J. E. Barbey's speech of June 21, 1938, reprinted in "Barbey Toured the South, Picked Monroeville," *Monroe (Ala.) Journal*, June 11, 1987, sec. 2, pp. 1–2.

8. The 1940 Census reported 14,417 (52.1 percent) African Americans and 13,204 (47.8 percent) whites out of a total population of 27,636 in Clarke County. It reported a similar situation in Monroe county, with 15,593 African Americans (52.9 percent) and 13,831 (46.9 percent) whites out of a total population of 29,465. For this and additional census information, consult the Historical Census Browser,

University of Virginia Library, Geostat Center, accessed February 1, 2014, http://mapserver.lib.virginia.edu/.

9. Vivian Long, interview by author, Jackson, Ala., August 9, 1998; Arcola "Cola" McLean, interview by author, Jackson, Ala., August 8, 1998.

10. Elizabeth "Buff" McDonald, interview by author, Jackson, Ala., June 21, 2003; Dot Guy, interview by author, Jackson, Ala., June 20, 2003.

11. Michael Honey recounts this episode in his pioneering book on organized labor and civil rights in Memphis, Tennessee. Honey regards the ILGWU as the only successful CIO union and points out that the white women apparel workers at Nona-Lee and other striking shops illustrated the plight of industrial workers for all of the city of Memphis. Honey, *Southern Labor and Black Civil Rights*, 82–91.

12. Hunter, *To 'joy My Freedom*, 114–20.

13. Daniel Letwin's nuanced study of race and coal mining in Alabama at the turn of the century explores many examples of the "divide and rule" strategy. Letwin, *Challenge of Interracial Unionism*, 90–95, 102–7, 142–44.

14. Gussie Woodest, interview by author, tape recording, New Orleans, La., June 22, 1995.

15. Woodest, interview. On the strike at Rutter Rex, see the *Advance*, January 1, 1950, 1.

16. Wrong, *Negro in the Apparel Industry*, 31, 58.

17. Woodest, interview.

18. Lahne, *Cotton Mill Worker*, 82. See also Frederickson, "Four Decades of Change," 29.

19. Eula McGill, interview by author, tape recording, Irondale, Ala., July 10, 1998.

20. Wrong, *Negro in the Apparel Industry*, 31, 43, 58–59.

21. There are many debates surrounding the history of gender-based segregation of occupations. Ruth Milkman's work was one of the first to posit gender-based occupational segregation as critical to the understanding of U.S. labor history. She argues that despite the ascent of women into "male" jobs during World War II, unions and employers worked to reestablish the essential features of male and female industrial positions after the war. Nearly all of women's labor history deals in one way or another with the issues behind the classification of occupations as male or female. Patricia Cooper, "The Faces of Gender: Sex Segregation and Work Relations at Philco, 1928–1938," in Baron, *Work Engendered*, 320–50; Milkman, *Gender at Work*; Milkman, *Women, Work, and Protest*.

22. O'Farrell and Kornbluh, *Rocking the Boat*, 189–90.

23. Wrong argues that the FEPC and other governmental policies regarding racial discrimination had little impact on the apparel industry prior to the Civil Rights Act of 1964. Wrong, *Negro in the Apparel Industry*, 121. See also Karen Anderson, "Last Hired, First Fired," 89, 95.

24. Wrong, *Negro in the Apparel Industry*, 40–41.

25. Ibid. In Georgia, Florida, and Texas the figures for African American apparel employment remained nearly the same. C. Vann Woodward's groundbreaking study of segregation remains a standard and offers an especially good overview of the passing of segregation in the South. Woodward pinpoints the beginning of the decline of southern segregation with the Supreme Court's *Brown v. Board of Education of Topeka* decision in 1954. Woodward, *Strange Career of Jim Crow*, 149–88. Another excellent interpretation of white resistance is Bartley, *Rise of Massive Resistance*.

26. Roediger and Esch, *Production of Difference*.

27. *Operation Dixie*, reel 16, frame 008.

28. Lepawsky, *State Planning and Economic Development*, 122–23.

29. U.S. Department of Labor, Bureau of Labor Statistics, *Labor in the South*, 174–76.

30. After being expelled from the American Federation of Labor in March 1938, the Committee for Industrial Organization changed its name to Congress of Industrial Organizations at its first constitutional convention, in November of that same year.

31. Foner, *Organized Labor and the Black Worker*, 215–68. Foner highlights the efforts to gain support for from African American women for the Steel Workers' Organizing Committee (p. 220).

32. Robert H. Zieger discusses the role of the ACWA and the ILGWU in the initial year of the CIO's existence. He notes that David Dubinsky, president of the ILGWU, resisted the CIO's separation from the AFL and refused to go along. The *New York Post* also reported that the ACWA was "a heavy contributor to [the CIO's] war chest." Zieger, *American Workers, American Unions*, 44; "Textile Industry Next C.I.O. Goal," *New York Post*, March 4, 1937, reprinted in Amalgamated Clothing Workers of America, *Records*, pt. 3.

33. Zieger, *American Workers, American Unions*, 29–30. Elaine Gale Wrong discusses the racial nondiscrimination policies and activities of the early ILGWU and CIO. Wrong, *Negro in the Apparel Industry*, 30.

34. "Southern Mfrs. Prepare for CIO," *Daily News Record*, March 26, 1937, reprinted in Amalgamated Clothing Workers of America, *Records*, pt. 3.

35. "Full Text of Hillman's Address at Capital Hearing," *Daily News Record*, July 28, 1933, reprinted in Amalgamated Clothing Workers of America, *Records*, pt. 3.

36. For individual state listings as well as regional totals, see table A.1.

37. In *The CIO: 1935–1955*, Robert Zieger provides an excellent overview of the concerns of Operation Dixie, especially within the larger context of the CIO as a whole. Barbara S. Griffith's full-length study of Operation Dixie pays particular attention to the role of religion in both supporting and opposing the CIO's efforts in the South. Zieger and Griffith both attribute the failure of Operation Dixie to a number of factors, including the purge of communists and radical leftists, com-

petition from the AFL, factional disputes within Operation Dixie, and a mistaken emphasis on an industry that was difficult to penetrate, southern textiles. Michael Honey also assesses Operation Dixie, placing race at the center of his analysis. Zieger, *The CIO*, 227–41; Griffith, *Crisis of American Labor*; Honey, "Operation Dixie." See also Marshall, *Labor in the South*, 254–69; Michael Goldfield, " Failure of Operation Dixie."

38. Franz Daniel was appointed to direct the Southern Organizing Committee's drive for the state of South Carolina. In 1946 he received a letter from Gladys Dickason, director of research for the ACWA, in which she stated, "At present, we have only two organizers in the state." In a letter to Dickason a few years later Daniel stated, "The interesting thing is that garment factories are going up all over the state at a terrific rate." *Operation Dixie*, reel 16, frames 001, 008, 084.

39. *Operation Dixie*, reel 16, frame 085.

40. Tindall, *Emergence of the New South*, 177–83, 718–21.

41. See various "Local Union Questionnaires" and "Organizing Drive Questionnaires," box 1277, folder 10: "Surveys: ILGWU (1957)," Via Papers.

42. During an oral interview about the Walterboro local in December 2000, Nick Bonanno referred to the dress manufacturing firm as the Portrait Frocks Company. This was most likely a reference to the name of the runaway New York firm. The Walterboro local listed employees of Walterboro Dress Corporation as its members in 1956. As was common practice, the New York firm probably changed its name to the Walterboro Dress Corporation after setting up shop in the small South Carolina town. Nicholas Bonanno, telephone interview by author, Atlanta, December 12, 2000.

43. "Local Union Questionnaire, ILGWU Local 552," pp. 21–23, box 1277, folder 10: "Surveys: ILGWU (1957)," Via Papers.

44. See box 1277, folder 10: "Surveys: ILGWU (1957)," Via Papers. The questionnaire is undated, but Via is known to have finished the surveys of ILGWU southern locals in 1957.

45. Although the surveys of ILGWU locals in the South clearly requested the title and name of the "person consult[ed] in preparing the answers for this local," none of the surveys listed such information. The information requested on the questionnaires is quite specific, ranging from the racial composition of the union local to a description of relations between the local and the national union. Given the specificity of the information requested, it is likely that Via or his staff interviewed officers of the local union. See "Local Union Questionnaire, ILGWU Local 552," "Local Union Questionnaire, ILGWU Local 122," and "Local Union Questionnaire, ILGWU Asheville, NC," box 1277, folder 10: "Surveys: ILGWU (1957)," Via Papers.

46. See "Local Union Questionnaire, ILGWU Local 552," p. 3, box 1277, folder 10: "Surveys: ILGWU (1957)," Via Papers.

47. Ibid.

48. Bonanno, interview by author, December 12, 2000. See also Nicholas Bonanno, interview by Chris Lutz, September 13, 1995, transcript, pp. 21–22, Voices of Labor Oral History Project.

49. "Local Union Questionnaire, ILGWU Local 552," p. 3, box 1277, folder 10: "Surveys: ILGWU (1957)," Via Papers.

50. Ibid.

51. Ibid., 5.

52. Ibid., 2.

53. Ibid.

54. Ibid., 6.

55. Ibid., 5–6.

56. Ibid., 3.

57. The records of the Southeast Regional Office of the ILGWU indicate that the Atlanta local signed a uniform agreement with "the individual manufacturers making up the Atlanta Dress Manufacturers Association." The membership of the consortium varied over time, as companies came and went. See various documents titled "Agreement," box 3063, folder 9: "Locals and Joint Councils, Local 122, Correspondence and Agreements, 1948–1968," International Ladies' Garment Workers' Union, Southeast Regional Office, Records, Georgia State University Library, Atlanta (hereafter ILGWU-SERO).

58. "Local Union Questionnaire, ILGWU Local 552," p. 5, box 1277, folder 10: "Surveys: ILGWU (1957)," Via Papers.

59. "Local Union Questionnaire, ILGWU Local 122," p. 1, box 1277, folder 10: "Surveys: ILGWU (1957)," Via Papers.

60. Ibid., 2.

61. Ibid., 5–6.

62. "Continuation of Report of Via's Trip to South Carolina, North Carolina, Virginia and Washington," pp. 1–2, box 1278, folder 17: "Reports and Trips thru the South, 1958," Via Papers.

63. Wrong, *Negro in the Apparel Industry*, 22–23.

64. Handwritten note, n.d., n.a., on E. T. Kehrer Union letterhead, box 3051, folder 6: "Organizing Activities, 1954," ILGWU-SERO. See also E. T. Kehrer to Lew Rhodes, October 7, 1954, box 3051, folder 6: "Organizing Activities, 1954," ILGWU-SERO.

65. E. T. Kehrer to Charles Kreindler, VP, ILGWU, August 8, 1956, box 3029, folder 4: "Kehrer, 'Al' E. T., Regional Director: Correspondence, July–December 1956," ILGWU-SERO.

66. Gilmore, *Gender and Jim Crow*, 22, 240n.

67. *Operation Dixie*, reel 16, frame 0126.

68. McLean, interview.

69. Long, interview.

70. Gordon, Edwards, and Reich, *Segmented Work, Divided Workers*; Reich, Gordon, and Edwards, "Theory of Labor Market Segmentation."

71. "Organizing Drive Questionnaire, McComb Manufacturing Company," pp. 1–2, box 1277, folder 10: "Surveys, ILGWU (1957)," Via Papers.

72. Marshall, *Negro and Organized Labor*, 55–57; E. T. "Al" Kehrer to Hannah Haskel, May 29, 1956, box 3029, folder 3: "Kehrer, 'Al' E. T., Regional Director: Correspondence, January–June 1956," ILGWU-SERO.

73. "Organizing Drive Questionnaire, Ahoskie Garment Co.," pp. 1–2, box 1277, folder 10: "Surveys, ILGWU (1957)," Via Papers.

74. "Organizing Drive Questionnaire, McComb Manufacturing Company," pp. 1–2, box 1277, folder 10: "Surveys, ILGWU (1957)," Via Papers.

75. In a very early study, Sterling Spero and Abram Harris argue that there were less than "two hundred Negroes" in the apparel unions. Spero and Harris, *Black Worker*, 346. Wrong's study of U.S. Census data reveals that African Americans accounted for 1.7 percent of U.S. apparel workers in 1910. This figure increased to 7.5 percent by 1960. Wrong's data also reveal that the percentage of African Americans in the southern apparel industry actually decreased from 1940 to 1960, from 5.0 percent to 4.7 percent. Wrong, *Negro in the Apparel Industry*, 30, 40–41.

76. Milkman, *Gender at Work*, 50.

77. Quoted in Foner, *Organized Labor and the Black Worker*, 228; emphasis added.

78. The precise year of the CIO convention is unclear from Durr's biography. This excerpt concludes a chapter based on the years 1933–49. Durr, *Outside the Magic Circle*, 133–34.

79. Nicholas Bonanno, interview by author, Atlanta, March 27, 1998.

80. Frank Hanley, "Convention Sidelights by Frank Hanley, Number 9," *Advance*, June 1940, 25.

81. Specific quotes from The Lighter Side: A Page for the Ladies, *Advance*, May 1941, 29.

82. "700 Workers in Atlanta Launch Movement to Protect Standards," *Advance*, March 1941, 11. Local newspapers also reported on the 1935 Dallas Dressmakers' War in much the same way, emphasizing domesticity and undermining the militant activities of women unionists. See Patricia Hill, "Real Women and True Womanhood," 10–12.

83. Nelson M Shipp, "Memo: Industrial Prospects," September 13, 1954, box 3051, folder 6: "Organizing Activities, 1954," ILGWU-SERO.

84. Long, interview.

85. Ken Hundley Jr., interview by author, Jackson, Ala., August 9, 1998.

86. Bruce Raynor, the former secretary-treasurer of the Union of Needletrades,

Industrial and Textile Employees, has commented that apparel companies have always sought the lowest wage level possible. This explains, in part, the motivations behind the apparel industry's move to the U.S. South and, later, to Mexico. Author's notes on Bruce Raynor comments at session on "Victory at Kannapolis and the Significance for Southern Labor History" (Southern Labor Studies Conference, Atlanta, October 2, 1999).

87. Mercedes Steedman explores this point throughout her study of the apparel industry in Canada. African Americans also suffered from industry-wide assumptions about their "natural" characteristics and abilities. In the textile industry, Glenda Gilmore argues, it seemed natural to hire blacks for certain positions. Textile mill operators in North Carolina argued that white workers were inherently quicker and more efficient workers. Black workers, on the other hand, were slower and required more instruction. Steedman, *Angels of the Workplace*; Gilmore, *Gender and Jim Crow*, 23–24.

88. Joan Jensen argues, "In 1981 sewing remained one of the most sex segregated of all United States occupations: 96.7 percent of all stitchers are women, exceeded in percentages only by secretaries and dental assistants. . . . Median wages were also the third lowest, after waiters and retail sales clerks." Joan M. Jensen, "Inside and Outside the Unions, 1920–1980," in Jensen and Davidson, *A Needle, a Bobbin, a Strike*, 189.

89. Stoney, Helfand, and Rostock, *Uprising of '34*.

90. Gary M. Fink, "Efficiency and Control: Labor Espionage in Southern Textiles," in Zieger, *Organized Labor in the Twentieth-Century South*, 25.

91. In Texas, Latina women made advances into the apparel industry prior to the 1960s. An excellent introduction to one of the most famous episodes of Latina unionism is Laurie Coyle, Gail Hershatter, and Emily Honig, "Women at Farah: An Unfinished Story," in Jensen and Davidson, *A Needle, a Bobbin, a Strike*, 227–77. See also Honig, "Women at Farah Revisited."

92. Long, interview.

93. Tera Hunter notes a similar connection in her study of domestic labor in Atlanta. Poor white factory workers frequently employed African American women as domestic servants. In fact, Hunter argues, "Low wages made domestic workers accessible to virtually the entire white population." Even in times of economic crises, white working-class women frequently envisioned black women's labors in their homes as a necessity. Ironically, white industrial workers in the South, among the poorest wage earners in the nation, paid even lower wages to black domestic workers. See Hunter, *To 'joy My Freedom*, 108–11.

94. Friedman, "What Price Industry?," 6–7.

95. Sarah Philips, interview by author, Grove Hill, Ala., June 19, 2003.

96. McDonald, interview.

97. Guy, interview.

98. Ibid. For additional discussion of African American women childcare workers, see Christine Blackwell, interview by author, Jackson, Ala., June 20, 2003.

99. Mary Martha Thomas argues that African American women in Alabama left agricultural work during World War II to assume jobs as domestics and in other service and trade industries. Woodest, interview; McLean, interview; Thomas, *Riveting and Rationing in Dixie*, 115.

CHAPTER FOUR. "WHEN THE GOVERNMENT
REQUIRED YOU TO HIRE THEM"

1. Arcola "Cola" McLean, interview by author, Jackson, Ala., August 8, 1998.

2. Stanley Levey, "Dubinsky Scores House Inquiry: Denies Bias in Garment Union," *New York Times*, August 25, 1962, sec. A, pp. 1, 10.

3. Herbert Hill, "ILGWU Today," 10–11.

4. House Committee on Education and Labor, *Investigation of the Garment Industry*, 234–35.

5. Nelson, *Divided We Stand*, 232–34.

6. Stanley Levy, "I.L.G.W.U. Inquiry Called Frame-Up," *New York Times*, August 19, 1962, sec. A, pp. 1, 41.

7. House Committee on Education and Labor, *Investigation of the Garment Industry*, 209–10.

8. Ibid., 223.

9. Wrong, *Negro in the Apparel Industry*, 20–22.

10. House Committee on Education and Labor, *Investigation of the Garment Industry*, 211.

11. The debates can be traced through several contemporary documents. First, the transcript of the congressional hearing provides an outline, albeit without stricken testimony, of the official response to Hill's accusations. See House Committee on Education and Labor, *Investigation of the Garment Industry*. Hill and Gus Tyler continued the debates and launched new exchanges in *New Politics*. See Herbert Hill, "ILGWU Today," 6–17; Tyler, "Truth about the ILGWU"; Herbert Hill, "Reply to Gus Tyler." Numerous *New York Times* articles by the reporter Stanley Levey also chronicle the course of the hearings and impart a sense of drama that the official hearing transcripts lack. See Levey, "ILGWU Inquiry Called Frame-Up" *New York Times*, August 19, 1962, sec. A, pp. 1, 41; Levey, "Sweetheart Deal Laid to ILGWU," *New York Times*, August 24, 1962, sec. A, pp. 1, 51; Levey, "Dubinsky Scores House Inquiry: Denies Bias in Garment Union," *New York Times*, August 25, 1962, sec. A, pp. 1, 10. In later years, as a professor at the University of Wisconsin–Madison, Hill expanded his investigation of the ILGWU into an assessment of the rela-

tionship between organized labor and race. See Herbert Hill, "Racial Practices of Organized Labor"; Herbert Hill, "Race, Ethnicity, and Organized Labor"; Herbert Hill, "Myth-Making as Labor History." For a balanced analysis of the House committee hearings see, Benin, *New Labor Radicalism*, 80–98; and Foner, *Organized Labor and the Black Worker*, 343–45.

12. Tyler, "Truth about the ILGWU," 9; Herbert Hill, "Reply to Gus Tyler," 15–17.

13. For an extensive study of the relationship between the forces of civil rights and organized labor, see Honey, *Southern Labor and Black Civil Rights*. See also Korstad and Lichtenstein, "Opportunities Found and Lost"; Rick Halpern provides an excellent overview of the alliances between civil rights and labor concerns. Halpern, "Organized Labour, Black Workers," esp. 379–83.

14. On the final day of the hearing to investigate discrimination in the ILGWU, the *Atlanta Constitution* carried a front-page photo of Ross Barnett captioned, "Governor Handles It Himself." Al Kuettner, "'Registrar' Barnett Turns Away Negro," *Atlanta Constitution*, September 21, 1962, sec. A, p. 1. See also Richard Aubrey McLemore, "Higher Education in the Twentieth Century," in McLemore, *History of Mississippi*, 2:443–44.

15. Wrong, *Negro in the Apparel Industry*, 35, 46–47, 104.

16. This pattern of occupational segregation by race continued an earlier pattern established by minimally integrated apparel factories. See chapter 3 for a fuller discussion of occupational segregation, especially in the early New Orleans apparel industry. For the racial composition of Capital City, see Burl C. Robinson to Martin J. Morand, January 29, 1965, box 3051, folder 8: "Organizing Activities, 1961–1965," International Ladies' Garment Workers' Union, Southeast Regional Office Records, Georgia State University Library, Atlanta (hereafter ILGWU-SERO).

17. Nicholas Bonanno, telephone interview by author, Atlanta, December 12, 2000.

18. Vivian Long, interview by author, Jackson, Ala., August 9, 1998

19. Gilchrist, interview by author.

20. Wrong also argues that southern governments built manufacturing facilities for more garment companies as an incentive for relocating than for any other industry. Although James Cobb's important study of postwar southern boosterism makes no mention of the apparel industry as the *prime* recipient of such local initiatives, repeated references to apparel concerns throughout his book suggest the industry's prominence in the process of attracting industry. Specifically, in his discussion of Mississippi's pioneering program Balance Agriculture with Industry, Cobb states that "four hosiery plants [and] three shirt factories" were among the original twelve firms attracted to Mississippi. There was such a demand for female labor among firms interested in relocating to Mississippi that several bureaucrats felt they should "search energetically for firms that would employ males." In

the 1950s the apparel industry "created more new jobs than any other industry in [Tennessee]." See Wrong, *Negro in the Apparel Industry*, 43; Cobb, *Selling of the South*, 9–10, 22–24, 31, 54, 61, 69, 97–98, 102–4, 105, 111, 113, 116.

21. Herbert R. Northrup and Richard R. Rowan's 1970 study of African American participation in southern industry emphasizes a shortage of white labor in the 1960s as the impetus behind the entrance of African Americans into manufacturing positions. The University of Pennsylvania's Wharton School funded many such studies of the racial policies of American industry, including Elaine Wrong's 1974 study of African American participation in the apparel industry. James J. Heckman and Brook S. Payner's study of South Carolina concludes that federal legislation may have come about because it was what industrialists wanted; they needed to hire blacks to ease the labor shortage. In short, "discrimination was becoming costly." Timothy J. Minchin's *Hiring the Black Worker: The Racial Integration of the Southern Textile Industry, 1960–1980* challenges the emphasis on a labor shortage through a careful study of federal court records and suggests that federal legislation played a more important role in decreasing the racial exclusivity of southern textile factories. Northrup and Rowan, *Negro Employment in Southern Industry*; Heckman and Payner, "Determining the Impact of Federal Antidiscrimination Policy"; Minchin, *Hiring the Black Worker*; Minchin, "Color Means Something," 109, 116.

22. Paula McLendon, "Union Turns Loners into Leaders," *Anniston (Ala.) Star*, n.d., n.p., reprint in McLendon's personal clipping file in author's possession.

23. Rebecca Blackmon and Emily Woodyard, interview by Paula McLendon, Leroy, Ala., December 16 1979, selected transcription, original in McLendon's personal clipping file in author's possession.

24. Vevlyn "Queenie" Gilchrist, interview by Paula McLendon, Frankville, Ala., November 1979, tape summary, original in McLendon's personal clipping file in author's possession.

25. Quoted in Paula McLendon, "Time and Time Again," 10.

26. Ibid, 11.

27. Long, interview.

28. Drawing on World War II–era Gallup Poll research, Robert H. Zieger notes that, "in general, workers held to positions on a wide range of issues considerably to the right of their leaderships, that of race being the most dramatic example." At Vanity Fair, one white worker said she made more money working alongside other white women than she did with African American women. Zieger, *The CIO*, 162, 422–23n; McLean, interview.

29. "Organizing Drive Questionnaire," box 3105, folder 2: "Ahoskie Manufacturing Company: Organizing, 1956," ILGWU-SERO.

30. In an essay on changes in the textile industry, Mary Frederickson argues, "After black workers entered the [southern textile] mills in . . . larger numbers

in the mid-1960s, their initial response to unionization was so overwhelmingly positive that the unions tended to take that firm commitment for granted." The Oneita Knitting Mills expanded its operations from underwear to children's apparel, T-shirts, and sweatshirts in the years after initial desegregation. In his study of the desegregation of the textile industry, Timothy J. Minchin cites several textile union organizers who agreed that the presence of African Americans in the mills guaranteed the union "yes" votes. Frederickson, "Four Decades of Change," 77; Ashbaugh and McCurry, "On the Line at Oneita," 210; Minchin, *Hiring the Black Worker*, 247–54.

31. Draper, *Conflict of Interests*, 86–106.

32. Bill Barton, "Mississippi: Battlefront for Labor," *AFL-CIO Federationist*, October 1965, 20.

33. James C. Cobb, the author of an important study of southern industrial boosterism, points out that Barnett had to work "hard to convince white citizens that his obstructionism [to federally mandated desegregation] had not hampered his efforts to sell Mississippi to new industries." See Neil McMillen, "Development of Civil Rights, 1956–1970," in McLemore, *History of Mississippi* 2:159. See also McMillen, *Citizens' Council*; Cobb, *Selling of the South*, 134.

34. E. T. Kehrer to Louis Stulberg, July 21, 1960, box 16, folder 3: "Louis Stulberg, General Secretary-Treasurer, Correspondence, 1956–1966 [bulk 1959–1966]," #5780/003, International Ladies' Garment Workers' Union Records, Cornell University.

35. Martin Morand to Leon Stein, memorandum, July 19, 1966, Southeast Region, Records, 1937–70, box 42, folder 2, #5780/058, International Ladies' Garment Workers' Union Records, Cornell University.

36. Quoted in Shelia Poole, "Q & A: Union Leader Sees Southern Opportunity," *Atlanta Journal-Constitution*, January 25, 1998, F5.

37. Ashbaugh and McCurry, "On the Line at Oneita," 205; Minchin, *Hiring the Black Worker*, 180.

38. See box 3162, folders 8–9, 11, and box 3164, folders 1, 4–5, ILGWU-SERO.

39. Frank Urtz, "Notice to Employees," n.d., box 3162, folder 8: "Oneita Knitting Mills, Inc., 1957–1960," ILGWU-SERO.

40. The recent conceptualization of "whiteness" and its relationship to class and gender figures nicely on this point. David Roediger argues that whiteness should be considered to be a part of a race-centered analysis. His collection of essays on this subject points to the strides made by those who place race and gender at the center of their studies, such as Nancy Hewitt, Vicki Ruiz, Dana Frank, and Dolores Janiewski. Roediger, *Towards the Abolition of Whiteness*.

41. Timothy J. Minchin points out that in the southern textile industry, pro-union white workers and union organizers often believed that African American support for the union would lead to union victories in NLRB elections. However,

he also points out that the initial union victories in plants with recently desegre-gated workforces soon gave way to union losses. In fact, he argues that, in some important ways, desegregation eventually made it more difficult to organize in the South. In the textile industry, white workers came to see the union as a vehicle for improving the position of African Americans, not textile workers as a group. Minchin, *Hiring the Black Worker*, 254–60.

42. In an important study of African American women's labor, Tera Hunter stresses that wealthy white southerners were not the only ones to employ black women as domestic workers. Hunter, *To 'joy My Freedom*, 108–11.

43. Quoted in Minchin, *Hiring the Black Worker*, 180–81.

44. See Minchin, *Hiring the Black Worker*, 196–97; "Members Paid through 1963," box 3162, folder 10: "Oneita Knitting Mills, Inc., 1963–1965," ILGWU-SERO.

45. For worker defections from the ILGWU, see various letters in box 3162, folder 12: "Oneita Knitting Mills, Inc.: Correspondence, 1963–1964," ILGWU-SERO.

46. For an account of the 1973 strike led by the TWUA, see Ashbaugh and Mc-Curry, "On the Line at Oneita," 205–14.

47. Nicholas Bonanno, interview by author, tape recording, Atlanta, March 27, 1998. See also Nicholas Bonanno, interview by Chris Lutz, September 13, 1995, transcript, Voices of Labor Oral History Project.

48. "Organizing Drive Questionnaire," box 3105, folder 2: "Ahoskie Manufactur-ing Company: Organizing, 1956," ILGWU-SERO.

49. As early as the 1930s, the ACWA also reported successes in organizing Afri-can American workers. In Baltimore, Maryland, one unionist asserted that "col-ored workers in Baltimore are eager to organize." Quoted in Argersinger, *Making the Amalgamated*, 165; Morton Shapiro to Martin Morand, Atlanta, January 10, 1965, box 3051, folder 8: "Organizing Activities, 1961–1965," ILGWU-SERO.

50. See box 3049, folder 6, "Membership: African-Americans in Locals, 1973–1974," ILGWU-SERO.

51. Donald C. Mosley, "The Labor Union Movement," in McLemore, *History of Mississippi*, 2:270–271.

52. Long, interview; McLean, interview.

53. Long, interview.

54. For recollections of local civil rights activity by white residents, see Long, interview; McLean, interview.

55. Richard Boykin was one of the seven members of Men for Dynamic Ac-tion in Jackson. Nearly forty years later, his recollection of this incident triggered strong feelings of pride. Choking back tears, he said, "It's hard for me to talk about this." Richard Boykin, interview by author, Jackson, Ala., June 20, 2003.

56. Elizabeth "Buff" McDonald, interview by author, Jackson, Ala., June 21, 2003; Long, interview.

57. Dot Guy, interview by author, Jackson, Ala., June 20, 2003.

58. Sarah Boykin, interview by author, Jackson, Ala., June 20, 2003.

59. Guy, interview.

60. McLean, interview.

61. Sarah B. Philips, interview by author, Grove Hill, Ala., June 19, 2003.

62. Sarah Boykin, interview.

63. Ibid.; McDonald, interview.

64. Gilchrist, interview by author.

65. Sarah Boykin, interview.

66. Herbert Hill dedicated much of his political and academic careers to uncovering and ending discrimination in labor unions. His 1962 attack on the ILGWU resurfaced during the late 1990s in the last few issues of *New Politics*, in a bitter exchange with Nelson Lichtenstein, author of the acclaimed biography of Walter Reuther, *The Most Dangerous Man in Detroit: Walter Reuther and the State of American Labor*. Hill alleges that Lichtenstein's presentation of Walter Reuther exaggerates and misunderstands organized labor's role in the civil rights movement, especially with regard to support of Title VII of the 1964 Civil Rights Act. Lichtenstein's rejoinder to Hill's critical review of his book competently and sharply refutes most of Hill's assertions. See Herbert Hill, "Lichtenstein's Fictions"; Lichtenstein, "Walter Reuther in Black and White"; Herbert Hill, "Lichtenstein's Fictions Revisited."

67. See various documents in box 3049, folder 6: "Membership: African-Americans in Locals, 1973–1974," ILGWU-SERO.

68. Walter Leste to Ramelle MaCoy January 28, 1969, box 3146, folder 4: "Loray Corporation: NLRB Cases, 1969," ILGWU-SERO.

69. Gilchrist, interview by author.

70. McLendon, "Time and Time Again," 14. See also Wilda Blackmon, interview by Paula McLendon, Jackson, Ala., November 1979, tape summary, original in McLendon's personal clipping file in author's possession.

71. Louis Stulberg to Mary E. Abbott, September 12, 1973, Southeast Region Records, 1937–70, #058, Louis Stulberg, President, Correspondence, 1945–1977 [bulk 1966–1975], box 19, folder 4B, #5780/004, International Ladies Garment Workers Union Records, Cornell University.

72. Michael K. Honey's *Southern Labor and Black Civil Rights: Organizing Memphis Workers* stands out as one of the most important works on the clear connections between the labor and civil rights movements. In Memphis, Honey argues, the crusaders for both causes were often one and the same. Timothy J. Minchin also discusses the ways in which some "black workers . . . saw union activity as an extension of the civil rights movement." Minchin, "Color Means Something," 128–29. See also Minchin, *"What Do We Need a Union For?"*; Minchin, *Hiring the Black Worker*; Draper, *Conflict of Interests*.

73. McLendon, "Time and Time Again," 11.

74. Ibid., 9–10.

75. Gilchrist, interview by author. See also Gilchrist, interview by McLendon.

76. "The Color Line Is Green," *Newsweek*, October 21, 1968, reprinted in Stein, *Out of the Sweatshop*, 313–14.

77. Martin Morand to Eliott M. Shirk, n.d., ca. January 1965, box 3029, folder 6: "Morand, Martin J., Regional Director: Personal Correspondence, 1965," ILGWU-SERO. Timothy J. Minchin similarly concludes that for African American textile workers, union work was an extension of civil rights work. Minchin, "Color Means Something," 128–29.

78. Southern Christian Leadership Coalition to Martin Morand, July 28, 1966, box 3024, folder 7: "Handler, Jack G. Regional Counsel: Personal Correspondence, 1966," ILGWU-SERO.

79. Martin Morand to NAACP, March 14, 1967, box 3029, folder 7: "Morand, Martin J., Regional Director: General Correspondence, 1965–1969," ILGWU-SERO.

80. Ibid.

81. Elliot M. Shirk to Martin Morand, January 8, 1965, box 3029, folder 6: "Morand, Martin J., Regional Director: Personal Correspondence, 1965," ILGWU-SERO.

82. E. T. "Al" Kehrer was assistant to the director of the Southeast Region from 1953 to 1954. He spent the next ten years as the director of the Southeast Region. For a discussion of the AFL-CIO's Southern Staff Institutes, see "Staff Training with a Southern Accent," *AFL-CIO Federationist*, September 1965, 19–22; E. T. "Al" Kehrer to O. C. Aderhold, telegram, January 12, 1961, box 25, folder 4, #5780/003, International Ladies' Garment Workers' Union Records, Cornell University; Al Kehrer, interview by Marcia Fishman, Atlanta, Ga., February 10, 1995, transcript L1995–12, Voices of Labor Oral History Project; Pratt, *We Shall Not Be Moved*, 87–94; "E. T. Kehrer, AFL-CIO Official Active in Labor, Civil Rights Movements," Obituaries, *Atlanta Journal-Constitution*, June 12, 1996.

83. Albert I. Gross to E. T. "Al" Kehrer, June 19, 1963, box 3029, folder 5: "Kehrer, 'Al' E. T., Regional Director: Personal Correspondence, 1963," ILGWU-SERO.

84. Bonanno, interview by author, March 27, 1998; Bonanno, interview by Lutz.

85. Bonanno, interview by author, March 27, 1998.

86. From 1966 to 1980 the percentages of men and women in the U.S. apparel industry remained relatively constant, with men accounting for roughly 19–21 percent and women accounting for 79–81 percent of the industry's workforce. These figures are derived from U. S. Equal Employment Opportunity Commission, *Equal Employment Opportunity Report*, 1966, 1967, 1969, 1973, 1978, 1980, 1990. For a graphical representation of this data, see figure 1.

87. Nick Bonanno to Mitchell Yager, March 2, 1964, box 3162, folder 12: "Oneita Knitting Mills, Inc.: Correspondence, 1963–1964," ILGWU-SERO.

88. Wilda Blackmon, interview by McLendon.

89. Eula McGill, interview by author, Irondale, Ala., July 10 1998; Kleiner, *Oral*

History Interview with Evelyn Dubrow, 30–31; Eileene Browne, interview by author, Oxford, Ala., July 24, 1998.

90. Blackmon and Woodyard, interview by McLendon.

91. Kleiner, *Oral History Interview with Evelyn Dubrow*, 30–31.

92. McLendon, "Time and Time Again," 14.

93. Alabama Labor Council Committee on Political Education, "She Said: Politics Is Such a Dirty Business," n.d., box 3043, folder 11: "Committee on Political Education (COPE), 1957," ILGWU-SERO.

94. Alabama Labor Council Committee on Political Education, "The Story of Jim and Anna," n.d., box 3043, folder 11: "Committee on Political Education (COPE), 1957," ILGWU-SERO.

95. E. J. Barnett, Barney Weeks, and Leroy Lindsey to All Alabama Local Unions, AFL-CIO, December 4, 1957, box 3043, folder 11: "Committee on Public Education (COPE), 1957," ILGWU-SERO.

96. Long, interview; McLean, interview; Browne, interview; McGill, interview.

97. Deslippe, *"Rights, Not Roses"*; Bonanno, interview by author, March 27, 1998.

98. Fehn, "Chickens Come Home to Roost," 341.

99. Kleiner, *Oral History Interview with Evelyn Dubrow*, 7–8.

100. Ibid.

101. Ibid., 45–46.

102. Long, interview.

103. Quoted in Argersinger, *Making the Amalgamated*, 185. The Union of Needletrades, Industrial and Textile Employees (UNITE!) was formed in 1995 when the Amalgamated Clothing and Textile Workers Union merged with the ILGWU.

CHAPTER FIVE. "LOOK FOR THE UNION LABEL"

1. For the complete lyrics, see Paula Green, "Look for the Union Label," UNITE HERE! website, http://unite-archive.library.cornell.edu/resources/song.html, accessed February 1, 2014.

2. Tyler, *Look for the Union Label*.

3. Breen, "Will American Consumers Buy a Second Revolution?"; Breen, *Marketplace of Revolution*; Kerber, *Women of the Republic*, 37–38; Evans, *Born for Liberty*, 48–50.

4. Dana Frank examines the undercurrents of exclusion behind labels and boycotts throughout U.S. history. In *Buy American: The Untold Story of Economic Nationalism*, she uncovers the history of anti-immigrant sentiments behind labels and boycotts.

5. Quoted in Spedden, *Trade Union Label*, 10.

6. See Tyler, *Look for the Union Label*, 291; Spedden, *Trade Union Label*, 11.

7. Spedden, *Trade Union Label*, 16–18.

8. Benson, *Counter Cultures*, 5, 99. Elaine Abelson's *When Ladies Go A-Thieving: Middle-Class Shoplifters in the Victorian Department Store*, focuses on the ways in which retail establishments in the nineteenth century attracted women shoppers and how those women shoppers sometimes fell to the temptation of stealing. Abelson uncovers a feminine class distinction among department store thieves. In the nineteenth century, with the advance of advertising and sophisticated merchandise displays, wealthy women thieves were considered to have fallen victim to a psychological disorder, kleptomania, while poorer women were simply treated as criminals.

9. Quoted in Spedden, *Trade Union Label*, 72; emphasis added.

10. Frank, *Purchasing Power*, 6–7, 117–19.

11. Spedden, *Trade Union Label*, 72.

12. Levine, *Women's Garment Workers*, 103; Tyler, *Look for the Union Label*, 291; McCreesh, *Women in the Campaign*, 47.

13. Dana Frank discovered that union officers sanctioned rank-and-file members of a Seattle musicians' union when their wives attended performances in nonunion theaters. She further argues that patterns of citations and fines in union records prove that "men could not control the consumption patterns of their wives and also suggests the possibility that men used their supposed lack of control over their wives to escape punishment for their own transgressions." Frank, *Purchasing Power*, 119.

14. See McCreesh, *Women in the Campaign*, 48, 82, 118, 120–24, 196–97; Bookbinder, *To Promote the General Welfare*, 24.

15. Forbath, *Law and Shaping of the Labor Movement*, 63–65, 92–93. For more on the Danbury Hatters' Case, see Daniel R. Ernst, "The Danbury Hatters' Case," in Tomlins and King, *Labor Law in America*, 180–200.

16. Forbath, *Law and Shaping of the Labor Movement*, 83–84.

17. I am especially indebted to Joe McMann, the former assistant regional director of the National Labor Relations Board in Atlanta, Georgia, for his gracious assistance and insightful understanding of the evolution of federal regulation of secondary boycotts. Joe McMann, telephone interview by author, September 9, 1998, notes in author's possession. See also Dereshinsky, Berkowitz, and Miscimarra, *The NLRB and Secondary Boycotts*, esp. 2–3.

18. Quoted in Dereshinsky, Berkowitz, and Miscimarra, *The NLRB and Secondary Boycotts*, 3–4.

19. Ibid., 5–6.

20. For the prohibition on secondary boycotts, see National Labor Relations Act, 29 *U.S. Code*, Title 29, Chapter 7, Subchapter II, Sec. 8b4.

21. Roger Biles includes a comprehensive discussion of the Blue Eagle cam-

paign's successes and numerous shortfalls in his study of the New Deal. Erin Mackenzie Page's 1993 dissertation suggests that the usual tendency to blame the ultimate failure of the Blue Eagle campaign and the National Industrial Recovery Act on the significant role employers played in establishing industry-wide standards may not be correct. Biles, *New Deal for the American People*; Page, "Intersectoral Incidence of the National Industrial Recovery Act."

22. Carpenter, *Competition and Collective Bargaining*, 640–41.

23. Tyler, *Look for the Union Label*, 176–85, 292.

24. See the foreword to volume 13 of the ACWA Red Book, reprinted in Amalgamated Clothing Workers of America, *Records*, pt. 3, reel 8, frame 0078. The *Daily News Record*, one of the primary garment industry trade publications, also reported on the opening of the ACWA's union label campaign. See "Parley Approves $500,000 for ACWA Label Promotion," *Daily News Record*, May 14, 1948, reprinted in Amalgamated Clothing Workers of America, *Records*, pt. 3, reel 8, frame 0272.

25. July 13, 1949, *New York Times* article, reprinted in Amalgamated Clothing Workers of America, *Records*, pt. 3, reel 8, frame 0274.

26. "CIO Plans Drive for Union Labels," *Rochester (N.Y.) Times Union*, February 16, 1954, reprinted in ibid., pt. 3, reel 9, frame 0777.

27. Byron Riggan, "Clothing Workers Struggle to Bring Labels to South," *Birmingham (Ala.) Post-Herald*, April 28, 1951, reprinted in ibid., pt. 3, reel 8, frame 1124.

28. "Union Label Drive Helps ACWA Crack 4 Big Open Shop Holdouts," *CIO News*, December 18, 1950, California edition, reprinted in ibid., pt. 3, reel 8, frame 0315.

29. See various clippings from southern newspapers in ibid., pt. 3, reel 8, frames 1136–40, reel 9, frame 0791, reel 10, frame 0071. See also "Palm Beach & CIO Sign Agreement Covering 8 Plants," *Danville (Ky.) Advocate Messenger*, November 29, 1951, reprinted in ibid., pt. 3, reel 8, frame 0354.

30. "Union Label Essay Contest Underway," *Hattiesburg (Miss.) American* November 3, 1954, reprinted in ibid., pt. 3, reel 9, frame 0778.

31. "Labor Day Prizes Announced," *Bogalusa (La.) News*, August 28, 1958, and "Charlestonians See How Shirt Is Made," *Advance*, April 15, 1957, reprinted in ibid., pt. 3, reel 10, frames 0796, 0790.

32. "South Has Much to Offer Industry, Meacham Says," *Atlanta Journal*, August 31, 1951, reprinted in ibid., pt. 3, reel 8, frame 1136.

33. William B. Hartsfield, "Proclamation," August 19, 1960, box 3063, folder 7: "Locals and Joint Councils: Proclamations, City of Atlanta (Union Labor/Label Week), 1960, 1962," International Ladies' Garment Workers' Union, Southeast Regional Office Records, Georgia State University Library, Atlanta (hereafter ILGWU-SERO).

34. For a discussion of the use of modern advertising techniques, see "Union Label Promoted as Quality Trademark," *Printers' Ink*, December 2, 1955, reprinted in Amalgamated Clothing Workers of America, *Records*, pt. 1, reel 25, frame 0036.

35. Amalgamated Clothing Workers, Union Label Campaign Guidebook, 1953, 1, reprinted in Amalgamated Clothing Workers of America, *Records*, pt. 1, reel 24, frame 0967.

36. According to the U.S. Department of Labor, women accounted for 78.7 percent of apparel workers in January 1960, the first year for which such data exists. In 1970 the figure had risen to 80.7 percent. By January 1990, 81.1 percent of apparel workers in the United States were female. See U.S. Department of Labor, Women's Bureau, *1993 Handbook on Women Workers*, 111, 118–25. See also U.S. Department of Labor, Bureau of Labor Statistics, *Employment, Hours, and Earnings*, 2:1126, 1158–59.

37. "Stitches," *Advance*, December 15, 1953, reprinted in Amalgamated Clothing Workers of America, *Records*, pt. 3, reel 9, frame 0776.

38. "Look for the Amalgamated Union Label," ca. 1955, reprinted in ibid., pt. 1, reel 25, frame 0026.

39. "It's the Only Time My Wife Goes Through My Pockets," ca. 1955, reprinted in ibid., pt. 1, reel 25, frame 0108.

40. Sue Davidson discusses the traditional perception of women as an economic liability in the introduction to *A Needle, a Bobbin, a Strike*. She argues that, even though women "took in boarders, sewed, and engaged in other market activities . . . the idea that women were primarily consumers and nurturers grew after [the] mid-[nineteenth]-century." Jensen and Davidson, *A Needle, a Bobbin, a Strike*, xii.

41. Tyler dedicates only a handful of pages to the union's most famous label campaign, but he offers a compelling, insider's perspective on the origins of the label and its transformation from a union label campaign to a "Made in America" campaign. Tyler himself helped with the union label campaign and held various other leadership positions in the ILGWU. Tyler, *Look for the Union Label*, 291–97. During its postwar campaign the ILGWU employed the services of at least two advertising agencies: Duyle, Dayne, Bernbach and the Solow/Wexton agency. Tyler, *Look for the Union Label*, 294. See also "How Labor Uses Advertising," *Advertising Age*, November 21, 1971, box 3061, folder 5: "Union Label Department, 1973–1975," ILGWU-SERO.

42. Quoted in Tyler, *Look for the Union Label*, 292.

43. Gilbert Gall's full-length study of the passage and implementation of right-to-work laws, both before and after the passage of the Taft-Hartley Act in 1947, reveals a concentration of antiunion sentiment throughout the southern states, especially in North Carolina, Georgia, Virginia, Tennessee, and Texas. Gall, *Politics of Right to Work*. James Cobb, in his work on the probusiness activities of

southern towns and cities in the postwar era, argues that city councils throughout the South promoted their towns as desirable location for new industry with
promises of tax breaks and a plentiful and stable supply of labor, and even with
commitments to provide custom-built manufacturing facilities. Cobb, *Selling of
the South.*

44. ILGWU Union Label Department, "Speech," n.d., ca. 1960–65, box 3061,
folder 5: "Union Label Department, 1973–1975," ILGWU-SERO.

45. ILGWU Union Label Department, "All about Our Label," n.d., ca. 1960–65,
box 3061, folder 5: "Union Label Department, 1973–1975," ILGWU-SERO.

46. ILGWU Union Label Department, "Wage Record Book," n.d., box 3061, folder
5: "Union Label Department, 1973–1975," ILGWU-SERO; emphasis added.

47. U.S. Department of Labor, Bureau of Labor Statistics, *Employment, Hours,
and Earnings*, 2:1126, 1158–59.

48. Coined by Jacquelyn Dowd Hall, the term "long civil rights movement" re-
casts and expands the traditional focus of civil rights historians beyond the decades of the 1950s and 1960s. Hall, "Long Civil Rights Movement."

49. A good overview of the links between African Americans' pursuit of civil
rights, gender, and consumer actions can be found in Greenberg, "Don't Buy
Where You Can't Work."

50. Tyler, *Look for the Union Label*, 290–91, 294–95.

51. Paula Green of the advertising firm Green Dolmatch wrote the union label
song at the ILGWU's request. Paula Green, "Look for the Union Label," UNITE HERE!
website, http://unite-archive.library.cornell.edu/resources/song.html, accessed
February 1, 2014.

52. Chafe, *American Woman*; Evans, *Personal Politics*; MacLean, "Postwar
Women's History" Deslippe, *Rights, Not Roses*; Minchin, *"Don't Sleep with Stevens!"*,
96–99. For working-class feminism in the South, see Allured, "Louisiana, the
American South, and the Birth."

53. "9PM," *Women's Wear Daily*, November 10, 1975.

54. Quoted in Frank, *Buy American*, 137.

55. The best study of the Farah strike and boycott comes from a team of mul-
tidisciplinary scholars who interviewed approximately thirty Farah strikers and
employees in 1977. Twenty years later Emily Honig completed a follow-up study in
which she traced the lasting effects of the strike experience for a handful of former
Farah employees. See Laurie Coyle, Gail Hershatter, and Emily Honig, "Women at
Farah: An Unfinished Story," in Jensen and Davidson, *A Needle, a Bobbin, a Strike*,
227–77; Honig, "Women at Farah Revisited."

56. Mary Frederickson, "Heroines and Girl Strikers: Gender Issues and Organized Labor in the Twentieth Century South," in Zieger, *Organized Labor in the
Twentieth-Century South*, 84–112.

57. *Farah Strike Bulletin / Viva la huelga* (Amalgamated Clothing Workers of

America); the bulletin was published irregularly from the summer to the winter of 1973. See also the Spanish-language leaflet intended to attract support for the Farah boycott, "Viva la huelga: No compre pantalones Farah," 1972, box 789, folder 17, Amalgamated Clothing Workers of America, Southern Region Records, Georgia State University Library, Atlanta.

58. Quoted in Lapides, *Battle of the Boycott*, 2.

59. "A Bishop v. Farah," *Time*, March 26, 1973.

60. "Farah Knuckles Under," *Time*, March 11, 1974.

61. "Back to the Thirties," *New York Times*, February 15, 1974, 32.

62. "Meany Presses Farah Boycott until Victory," *Farah Strike [Bulletin]*, [ca. 1973]), 2. For the perspective of Farah strikers, see Laurie Coyle, Gail Hershatter, and Emily Honig, "Women at Farah: An Unfinished Story," in Jensen and Davidson, *A Needle, a Bobbin, a Strike*, 263–64, 275, 277n8.

63. The El Paso Committee for Fairness at Farah stated that 98 percent of the strikers and employees were Catholic and Latina. Committee for Fairness at Farah, "Response of the El Paso Committee for Fairness at Farah to the Pro-Farah Pamphlet Entitled 'For the Defense of Workers,'" n.p., n.d., box 789, folder 19, Amalgamated Clothing Workers of America, Southern Region Records, Georgia State University Library, Atlanta.

64. Laurie Coyle, Gail Hershatter, and Emily Honig, "Women at Farah: An Unfinished Story," in Jensen and Davidson, *A Needle, a Bobbin, a Strike*, 251–52.

65. Quoted in "For Justice at Farah for Employees and Management, or, the Other Side of the Coin," n.p., n.d., ca. 1974, box 789, folder 19, Amalgamated Clothing Workers of America, Southern Region Records, Georgia State University Library, Atlanta.

66. *Farah Strike [Bulletin]*, [ca. 1973], 4. Unionists rallied behind the support of Senator Kennedy. See "We Will Win," July 7, 1972, box 789, folder 19, Amalgamated Clothing Workers of America, Southern Region Records, Georgia State University Library, Atlanta.

67. Lapides, *Battle of the Boycott*, 1–2.

68. In 1966 the Equal Employment Opportunity Commission published its first report on patterns of employment by race and sex. This series of reports continues to be an invaluable source for tracing the occupational history of several different groups in American history. Still, the data presented in these reports is somewhat problematic. From the very beginning of the series, employers were required to submit data to the EEOC only if they had one hundred or more employees. The U.S. garment industry is composed of mostly smaller establishments, and thus many of these firms are not (and were not) required to submit data to the EEOC. The average number of employees in an apparel industry firm is less than fifty. U. S. Equal Employment Opportunity Commission, *Equal Employment Opportunity Report*, 1966, 119–29; U.S. Equal Employment Opportunity Commission, *Equal Em-*

ployment Opportunity Report, 1980, 23–25. Elaine Wrong discusses the shortcomings of EEOC data in *Negro in the Apparel Industry*, 2.

69. Wrong argues that as apparel manufacturers moved southward they initially repeated the textile industry's pattern of employing largely white laborers. By 1950 and 1960, however, black employment increased in apparel factories in southern cities. Wrong, *Negro in the Apparel Industry*, 22–23, 32–45.

70. *Viva la huelga* (Amalgamated Clothing Workers of America). See also the Spanish-language leaflet intended to attract support for the Farah boycott, "Viva la huelga: No compre pantalones Farah," box 789, folder 17, Amalgamated Clothing Workers of America, Southern Region Records Georgia State University Library, Atlanta.

71. Lauren A. Murray, "Unraveling Employment Trends in Textiles and Apparel," *Monthly Labor Review*, August 1995, 62–72.

CHAPTER SIX. "SWEATSHOPS IN THE SUN"

1. Rosen, *Making Sweatshops*; James Green, "Gone South," 51; Cowie, *Capital Moves*; Adler, *Mollie's Job*; Edna Bonacich and David V. Waller, "The Role of U.S. Apparel Manufacturers in the Globalization of the Industry in the Pacific Rim," in Bonacich et al., *Global Production*, 80–103; Bhagwati, *In Defense of Globalization*; van Liemt, *Industry on the Move*; Craypo and Nissen, *Grand Designs*; Joan Anderson, "Causes of Growth"; Tiano, "Export Processing, Women's Work, and the Employment Problem"; Frank, *Buy American*.

2. On this point, Dana Frank argues that "federal trade policy deliberately encouraged the shift of the domestic apparel industry abroad." The federal government loosened restrictions at the height of the Cold War, and Frank argues that this was no coincidence. Rather, the loosening of trade restrictions was an attempt by the federal government influence foreign countries through commercial and economic policies. Frank writes, "U.S. strategists deployed free trade strategically to keep other nations within a U.S.-dominated capitalist sphere." Frank, *Buy American*, 148–50.

3. Wrong, *Negro in the Apparel Industry*, 5–6.

4. For similar data, see Alfred E. Eckes, "The South and Economic Globalization, 1950 to the Future," in Cobb and Stueck, *Globalization and the American South*, 36–65; Tami Friedman, "'A Trail of Ghost Towns across Our Land': The Decline of Manufacturing in Yonkers, New York," in Cowie and Heathcott, *Beyond the Ruins*, 19–43.

5. For statistics, see Dana Frank's pioneering study of the "Buy American" movement in the United States. Frank uncovers the nationalistic and often racist and ethnocentric spirit behind the union-led consumer movement. Frank, *Buy American*, 132–33.

6. Wrong, *Negro in the Apparel Industry*, 126–27.

7. "VF to Shut Down for December," November 15, 1984, clipping from Paula McLendon's Vanity Fair file in author's possession. The clipping does not list an author, journal title, or publisher.

8. Monroeville figure cited in Karen Tolkkinen, "City of Jackson Struggles to Fill the Gap," *Mobile (Ala.) Register*, March 20, 2000, sec. A, p. 4

9. Jim Cox, "County Braces for Vanity Fair Closing," *Clarke County (Ala.) Democrat*, March 16, 2000, sec. A, pp. 1, 5; Karen Tolkkinen, "Plant Closing Hits 543 Workers," *Mobile (Ala.) Register*, March 11, 2000, sec. A, pp. 1, 4.

10. Quoted in McLendon, "Time and Time Again," 15. For Parden's position at Vanity Fair's Mexican plant, see Vivian Long, interview by author, Jackson, Ala., August 9, 1998.

11. Jim Cox, "County Braces for Vanity Fair Closing," *Clarke County (Ala.) Democrat*, March 16, 2000; Karen Tolkkinen, "Plant Closing Hits 543 Workers," *Mobile (Ala.) Register*, March 11, 2000; Karen Tolkkinen, "Uncertain Future after Plant Closes," *Mobile (Ala.) Register*, March 20, 2000.

12. John Holusha, "Squeezing the Textile Workers: Trade and Technology Force a New Wave of Job Cuts," *New York Times*, February 21, 1996.

13. Shelia M. Poole, "Kentucky Town in Despair over Losing Apparel Plants," *Atlanta Journal and Constitution*, November 27, 1997; John Holusha, "Squeezing the Textile Workers: Trade and Technology Force a New Wave of Job Cuts," *New York Times*, February 21, 1996.

14. John Denaro, director of the ILGWU's Union Label Department, led this transition from "Look for the Union Label" to "Buy American." See "Case Study: How One Union Builds Preference for Its Products," *Public Relations News*, n.d., ca. 1973, box 3061, folder 5: "Union Label Department, 1973–1975," International Ladies' Garment Workers' Union, Southeast Regional Office, Records, Georgia State University Library, Atlanta; Jensen and Davidson, *A Needle, a Bobbin, a Strike*, xx.

15. Jensen and Davidson, *A Needle, a Bobbin, a Strike*, xx; Frank, *Buy American*.

16. In this work, "maquiladora" refers to Mexican factories and industries dedicated to the assembly of foreign goods. Maquiladoras can be involved in the assembly of anything from clothing to electronics to automobiles. This chapter concentrates on the garment maquiladoras.

17. A useful introduction to and overview of the principal themes within the concept of *marianismo* can be found in Stevens, "*Marianismo*."

18. "First Women Trade Union Seminar Termed Success," *AIFLD Report* 9:8 (August 1971): 1–2; "Women Unionists Urged to Fight for Justice and Equality," *AIFLD Report* 10:8 (August 1972): 2.

19. Lim, "Women's Work in Export Factories," 114.

20. Linda Lim criticizes the efforts of "the labor, feminist, and church move-

ments" of the United States that "support protectionism." She argues that these movements present a "disparaging... [view] of export industries in developing countries" as part of a larger effort to protect women industrial workers in the United States. In short, the protectionist agenda of these activists makes them unable to understand the employment of women in Latin America as anything other than exploitation. Lim rightly argues that the origins of such a perspective lie in "a simple ethnocentrism that values jobs in the developed countries much more highly than the same jobs in the Third World." ibid., 117, 119.

21. Michael Flannery, "America's Sweatshops in the Sun," *AFL-CIO Federationist*, May 1978, 16.

22. Ibid.

23. Ibid.

24. Peña, "Las Maquiladoras," 195, 229.

25. Denise C. Thiry, "Women Trade Unionists Are in the Vanguard of International Women's Year," *AIFLD Report* 12 (August 1974): 4.

26. *Labor Unity* (Amalgamated Clothing and Textile Workers Union) 71 (December 1985): 5.

27. "Imports = Economic Murder, Members Tell Senate Panel, *Labor Unity* 71 (August–September 1985): 3.

28. Ibid.

29. It should be noted that the ACTWU article makes no explicit mention of Nilda Quintanilla's ethnicity.

30. Data from U.S. Bureau of the Census, *Economic Census of Manufactures*, 1947, 1954, 1958, 1963, 1967, 1972, 1977, 1982, 1987, 1992.

31. Bruce Raynor, a secretary-treasurer for the Union of Needletrade, Industrial and Textile Employees, made a similar point during his presentation at the 1999 Southern Labor Studies Conference. Author's notes on Bruce Raynor, comments at session on "Victory at Kannapolis and the Significance for Southern Labor History" (Southern Labor Studies Conference, Atlanta, October 2, 1999).

32. "Chaos at K-Mart as Union Hits Chain's Opposition to Trade Bill," *Labor Unity* 71 (July 1985): 2.

33. Faye Knight, Louise Warren, and Betty Bendimire, interview by Philip LaPorte, Americus, Ga., March 31, 2010, transcript L2010–03, pp. 38–39, Southern Labor Archives, Special Collections and Archives Department, Georgia State University Library, Atlanta.

34. McLendon, "Time and Time Again," 15.

35. "California Jt. Bd. Rallies to Aid of Strikers in El Salvador," *Labor Unity* 72 (November 1986): 2.

36. "Union Raps Reagan Scheme to Export Jobs to Mexico," *Labor Unity* 73 (January 1987): 3.

37. Lim, "Women's Work in Export Factories," 114.

38. Tiano, "Export Processing, Women's Work, and the Employment Problem"; See also Tiano, *Patriarchy on the Line*, 54–56.

EPILOGUE

1. Author's notes on Bruce Raynor comments at session on "Victory at Kannapolis and the Significance for Southern Labor History" (Southern Labor Studies Conference, Atlanta, October 2, 1999).

2. Nick Bonanno, interview by author, March 27, 1998.

3. Bonacich et al., *Global Production*, 3, 50–58; Russell Mitchell, "Inside the Gap," *Business Week*, March 9, 1992, 58–64; Rosen, *Making Sweatshops*, 250.

4. Collins, "Mapping a Global Labor Market," 924–27; Collins, *Threads*; Kessler-Harris, *Out to Work*.

5. International Trade Commission, *Textiles and Apparel*, 3-1–3-9.

6. U.S. Department of Labor, Bureau of Labor Statistics, Occupational Employment and Wages, 51-6031 Sewing Machine Operators, May 2012, accessed May 8, 2013, http://www.bls.gov/oes/current/oes516031.htm.

7. Rosen, *Making Sweatshops*, 226–27, 239–51.

8. Abernathy, Dunlop, Hammond, and Weil, *A Stitch in Time*.

9. "The End of Cheap China," *Economist*, March 10, 2012; Ascoly and Finney, *Made by Women*; Brooks, *Unraveling the Garment Industry*; American Apparel and Footwear Association, "AAFA Releases ApparelStats 2012 Report," press release, October 19, 2012, accessed November 11, 2013, https://www.wewear.org/aafa-releases-apparelstats-2012-report/.

10. International Trade Commission, *Textiles and Apparel*, F-3–F-14, F-36–F-52.

11. "Nation's Worst Industrial Tragedy Swallows at Least 258," *Karachi Dawn (Pakistan)*, September 13, 2012.

12. Faiza Ilyas, "Survivors Narrate Nightmarish Experience," *Karachi Dawn (Pakistan)*, September 13, 2012.

13. "Karachi Fire: Police Seek Owners as Relatives Bury Dead," *BBC News Asia*, September 13, 2012, accessed May 9, 2013, http://www.bbc.co.uk/news/world-asia-19582647.

14. Shaheen Mollah, "Grief-Struck," *Daily Star (Bangladesh)*, November 27, 2012; Sohel Parvez, "An Agonizing Wait Outside," *Daily Star (Bangladesh)*, November 27, 2012.

15. S. M. Mizanur Rahman, "Official Death Toll in Ashulia Factory Fire 112, Trade Unions Claim More," *Dhaka Daily Sun (Bangladesh)*, November 27, 2012.

16. "Western Brands Accused in Ashulia Garment Fire," *Dhaka Independent (Bangladesh)*, November 26, 2012; "Fire Safety in Garment Factories," *New York Times*, December 9, 2012.

17. Taslima Akhter, "A Final Embrace: The Most Haunting Photograph from Bangladesh," *Time*, May 8, 2013, accessed May 9, 2013, http://lightbox.time.com/2013/05/08/a-final-embrace-the-most-haunting-photograph-from-bangladesh/#end.

APPENDIX

1. U.S. Census Bureau, *History of the 1997 Economic Census*, July 2000, http://www.census.gov/prod/ec97/po100-hec.pdf. See also Paul Miller, "Ready or Not? Here Comes NAICS," *Catalog Age* 14:12 (November 1997): 53.

2. U.S. Census Bureau, "315: Apparel Manufacturing," 1997 Economic Census, http://www.census.gov/epcd/ec97/def/315.TXT.

Bibliography

INTERVIEWS

Mary Alice
Christine Blackwell
Nicholas "Nick" Bonanno
Richard Boykin
Sarah Boykin
Eileene Browne
Vevlyn "Queenie" Gilchrist
Dot Guy

Sarah Hill
Ken Hundley Jr.
Vivian Long
Elizabeth "Buff" McDonald
Eula McGill
Arcola McLean
Sarah Blackwell Philips
Gussie Woodest

MANUSCRIPT AND ARCHIVAL COLLECTIONS

Amalgamated Clothing Workers of America. *Records*. Part 1, *Papers of Sidney and Bessie Hillman, 1911–1970*. Bethesda, Md.: University Publications of America, 1989.

———. *Records*. Part 3, ACWA *Scrapbook & Press Releases, 1910–1961*. Bethesda, Md.: University Publications of America, 1989.

Amalgamated Clothing Workers of America. Southern Region Records, 1939–76. Southern Labor Archives, Special Collections and Archives Department, Georgia State University Library, Atlanta.

International Ladies' Garment Workers' Union. Records, 1884–2006. Kheel Center for Labor-Management Documentation and Archives, Martin P. Catherwood Library, Cornell University, Ithaca, N.Y.

International Ladies' Garment Workers' Union. Southeast Regional Office. Records, 1945–78. Southern Labor Archives, Special Collections and Archives Department, Georgia State University Library, Atlanta.

Kehrer, E. T. Papers, 1940–89. Special Collections and Archives Department, Georgia State University Library, Atlanta.

Knight, Faye, Louise Warren, and Betty Bendimire. Interview by Philip LaPorte.

Americus, Ga. March 31, 2010. Transcript L2010–03. Southern Labor Archives, Special Collections and Archives Department, Georgia State University Library, Atlanta.

Lucia, Carmen. Papers. Southern Labor Archives, Special Collections and Archives Department, Georgia State University Library, Atlanta.

Operation Dixie: The C.I.O. Organizing Committee Papers, 1946–1953. Sanford, N.C.: Microfilming Corporation of America, 1980.

Springer-Kemp, Maida. Papers, 1944–87. Civil Rights, Amistad Collection, Tulane University, New Orleans.

Via, Emory. Papers. Southern Labor Archives, Special Collections and Archives Department, Georgia State University Library, Atlanta.

Voices of Labor Oral History Project. Southern Labor Archives, Special Collections and Archives Department, Georgia State University Library, Atlanta.

Workers Defense League. Papers, 1913–71. Archives of Labor and Urban Affairs, Walter P. Reuther Library, Wayne State University, Detroit.

PERIODICALS

Advance (Amalgamated Clothing Workers of America)

AFL-CIO Federationist

American City

American Institute for Free Labor Development

Anniston (Ala.) Star

Atlanta Journal-Constitution

Birmingham News

Business Week

Charlotte Observer

Charlotte Post and Courier

Clarke County (Ala.) Democrat

Daily Star (Bangladesh)

Dallas Morning News

Dhaka Daily Sun (Bangladesh)

Economist

Farah Strike Bulletin / Viva la huelga (Amalgamated Clothing Workers of America)

Georgia Magazine

Karachi Dawn (Pakistan)

Labor's Heritage

Labor Unity

Memphis Commercial Appeal

Mobile Register

New Orleans Times-Picayune

New Politics

New York Times

Savannah Morning News

South Alabamian

Southern Changes

Women's Wear Daily

GOVERNMENT DOCUMENTS AND REPORTS

Executive Office of the President. Office of Management and Budget. *Standard Industrial Classification Manual.* Washington, D.C.: Government Printing Office, 1987.

House Committee on Education and Labor. *Investigation of the Garment Industry*, 87th Cong., 2nd sess., 1962.

International Trade Commission. *Textiles and Apparel: Assessment of the Competitiveness of Certain Foreign Suppliers to the U.S. Market.* Washington, D.C., 2004.

The Loray Corporation and International Ladies' Garment Workers' Union, AFL-CIO. Decision and Order. July 20, 1970. Cases 10–CA-7759 and 10–CA-7866. National Labor Relations Board.

National Labor Relations Act. 29 *U.S. Code*, Title 29, Chapter 7, Subchapter II, Sec. 8b4.

National Planning Association. Committee of the South. *Selected Studies of Negro Employment in the South, Prepared for the NPA Committee of the South.* Washington, D.C.: National Planning Association, 1953.

U. S. Bureau of the Census. *Economic Census of Manufactures.* Washington, D.C.: Government Printing Office, 1937, 1947, 1954, 1958, 1963, 1967, 1972, 1977, 1982, 1987, 1992, 1997.

U.S. Department of Labor. Bureau of Labor Statistics. *Employment, Hours, and Earnings, United States, 1909–94*, Vol. 2. Washington, D.C.: U.S. Department of Labor, 1994.

———. *Labor in the South.* Bulletin No. 898. Washington, D.C.: Government Printing Office, 1947.

U.S. Department of Labor. Women's Bureau. *1993 Handbook on Women Workers: Trends and Issues.* Washington, D.C.: U.S. Department of Labor, 1994.

———. *Women in Texas Industries: Hours, Wages, Working Conditions, and Home Work*, by Mary Loretta Sullivan and Bertha Blair. Bulletin No. 126. Washington, D.C.: Government Printing Office, 1936.

———. *Women's Place in Industry in 10 Southern States*, by Mary Anderson. Washington, D.C.: Government Printing Office, 1931.

U.S. Equal Employment Opportunity Commission. *Equal Employment Opportunity Report: Job Patterns for Minorities and Women in Private Industry.* Washington, D.C.: Government Printing Office, 1966, 1967, 1969, 1973, 1978, 1980, 1990.

MONOGRAPHS, REPORTS, AND ESSAYS

Abelson, Elaine S. *When Ladies Go A-Thieving: Middle-Class Shoplifters in the Victorian Department Store.* New York: Oxford University Press, 1989.

Abernathy, Fredrick H., John T. Dunlop, Janice W. Hammond, and David Weil, *A Stitch in Time: Lean Retailing and the Transformation of Manufacturing: Lessons from the Apparel and Textile Industries.* New York: Oxford University Press, 1999.

Adler, William. *Mollie's Job: A Story of Life and Work on the Global Assembly Line.* New York: Scribner, 2000.

Allured, Janet. "Louisiana, the American South, and the Birth of Second-Wave Feminism." *Louisiana History* 54:4 (2013): 389–423.

Amberg, Stephen. "Varieties of Capitalist Development: Worker-Manager Relations in the Texas Apparel Industry, 1935–1975." *Social Science History* 30:2 (Summer 2006): 231–62.

American Federation of Labor Legislative Committee. *Subsidized Industrial Migration: The Luring of Plants to New Locations.* Washington, D.C.: American Federation of Labor, 1955.

Anderson, Joan. "Causes of Growth in the Informal Labor Sector in Mexico's Northern Border Region." *Journal of Borderland Studies* (1988): 1–11.

Anderson, Karen Tucker. "Last Hired, First Fired: Black Women Workers during World War II." *Journal of American History* 69 (June 1982): 82–97.

Argersinger, Jo Ann E. *Making the Amalgamated: Gender, Ethnicity, and Class in the Baltimore Clothing Industry, 1899–1939.* Baltimore: Johns Hopkins University Press, 1999.

Ascoly, Nina, and Chantal Finney. *Made by Women: Gender, the Global Garment Industry and the Movement for Women Workers' Rights.* Amsterdam: Clean Clothes Campaign, 2005.

Ashbaugh, Carolyn, and Dan McCurry. "On the Line at Oneita." In *Working Lives: The Southern Exposure History of Labor in the South*, edited by Marc S. Miller, 205–14. 1974. Repr., New York: Random House, 1980.

Ayers, Edward L. *The Promise of the New South: Life after Reconstruction.* New York: Oxford University Press, 1992.

Babson, Steve. *The Unfinished Struggle: Turning Points in American Labor, 1877–Present.* Lanham, Md.: Rowman & Littlefield, 1999.

Balser, Diane. *Sisterhood and Solidarity: Feminism and Labor in Modern Times.* Boston, Mass.: South End Press, 1987.

Baron, Ava, ed. *Work Engendered: Toward a New History of American Labor.* Ithaca, N.Y.: Cornell University Press, 1991.

Bartley, Numan V. *The New South, 1945–1980: The Story of the South's Modernization.* Baton Rouge: Louisiana State University Press, 1995.

———. *The Rise of Massive Resistance: Race and Politics in the South during the 1950s.* Baton Rouge: Louisiana State University Press, 1969.

Belzer, Michael H. *Sweatshops on Wheels: Winners and Losers in Trucking Deregulation.* New York: Oxford University Press, 2000.

Benin, Leigh David. *The New Labor Radicalism and New York City's Garment Industry: Progressive Labor Insurgents in the 1960s.* New York: Garland, 2000.

Benson, Susan Porter. *Counter Cultures: Saleswomen, Managers, and Customers in American Department Stores.* Urbana: University of Illinois Press, 1986.

Bernstein, Irving. *The Lean Years: A History of the American Worker, 1920–1930.* Boston: Houghton Mifflin, 1960.

——. *The Turbulent Years: A History of the American Worker, 1933–1940.* 1969. Repr., Chicago: Haymarket Books, 2010.

Bhagwati, Jagdish. *In Defense of Globalization.* Oxford: Oxford University Press, 2004.

Biles, Roger. *A New Deal for the American People.* DeKalb: Northern Illinois University Press, 1991.

Bonacich, Edna, Lucie Cheng, Norma Chinchilla, Nora Hamilton, and Paul Ong, eds. *Global Production: The Apparel Industry in the Pacific Rim.* Philadelphia: Temple University Press, 1994.

Bookbinder, Hyman H., and Associates. *To Promote the General Welfare: The Story of the Amalgamated.* New York: Amalgamated Clothing Workers of America, 1950.

Brattain, Michelle. "'A Town as Small as That': Tallapoosa, Georgia, and Operation Dixie, 1945–1950." *Georgia Historical Quarterly* 80 (Summer 1997): 395–425.

——. *The Politics of Whiteness: Race, Workers, and Culture in the Modern South.* Princeton, N.J.: Princeton University Press, 2001.

Braun, Kurt. *Union-Management Co-operation: Experience in the Clothing Industry.* Washington, D.C.: Brookings Institution, 1947.

Brecher, Jeremy. *Strike!* Cambridge, Mass.: South End Press, 1997.

Breen, T. H. *The Marketplace of Revolution: How Consumer Politics Shaped American Independence.* New York: Oxford University Press, 2004.

——. "Will American Consumers Buy a Second Revolution?" *Journal of American History* 93:2 (September 2006): 404–8.

Brooks, Ethyl Carolyn. *Unraveling the Garment Industry: Transnational Organizing and Women's Work.* Minneapolis: University of Minnesota Press, 2007.

Brooks-Higginbotham, Evelyn. "African American Women's History and the Metalanguage of Race." *Signs* 17:2 (Winter 1992): 251–74.

Broussard, Joyce L. "Naked before the Law: Married Women and the Servant Ideal in Antebellum Natchez." In *Mississippi Women,* edited by Martha H. Swain, Elizabeth Anne Payne, and Marjorie Spruill, 2:57–76. Athens: University of Georgia Press, 2010.

Byerly, Victoria E. *Hard Times Cotton Mill Girls: Personal Histories of Womanhood and Poverty in the South.* Ithaca: ILR Press, New York State School of Industrial and Labor Relations, Cornell University, 1986.

Byrne, Frank J. "Wartime Agitation and Postwar Repression: Reverend John A. Callan and the Columbus Strikes of 1918–1919." *Georgia Historical Quarterly* 80 (Summer 1997): 345–69.

Carlton, David L. *Mill and Town in South Carolina, 1880–1920.* Baton Rouge: Louisiana State University Press, 1982.

Carpenter, Jesse Thomas. *Competition and Collective Bargaining in the Needle Trades, 1910–1967.* Ithaca: New York State School of Industrial Labor Relations, Cornell University, 1972.

Cash, W. J. *The Mind of the South*. 1941. Repr., New York: Random House, 1969.

Chafe, William. *The American Woman: Her Changing Social, Economic and Political Roles, 1920–1970*. Urbana: University of Illinois Press, 1972.

Clark, Daniel J. *Like Night and Day: Unionization in a Southern Mill Town*. Chapel Hill: University of North Carolina Press, 1997.

Cobb, James C. *Industrialization and Southern Society, 1877–1984*. Lexington: University Press of Kentucky, 1984.

——. *The Selling of the South: The Southern Crusade for Industrial Development, 1936–1990*. 2nd ed. Urbana: University of Illinois Press, 1993.

Cobb, James C., and William Stueck, eds. *Globalization and the American South*. Athens: University of Georgia Press, 2005.

Cobble, Dorothy Sue. *Dishing It Out: Waitresses and Their Unions in the Twentieth Century*. Urbana: University of Illinois Press, 1991.

Collins, Jane L. "Mapping a Global Labor Market: Gender and Skill in the Globalizing Garment Industry." *Gender & Society* 16:5 (December 2002): 924–41.

——. *Threads: Gender, Labor and Power in the Global Apparel Industry*. Chicago: University of Chicago Press, 2003.

Cowie, Jefferson. *Capital Moves: RCA's Seventy-Year Quest for Cheap Labor*. Ithaca, N.Y.: Cornell University Press, 1999.

Cowie, Jefferson, and Joseph Heathcott, eds. *Beyond the Ruins: The Meanings of Deindustrialization*. Ithaca, N.Y.: Cornell University Press, 2003.

Craypo, Charles, and Bruce Nissen, eds. *Grand Designs: The Impact of Corporate Strategies on Workers, Unions, and Communities*. Ithaca, N.Y.: ILR Press, 1993.

Daniel, Pete. *Standing at the Crossroads: Southern Life in the Twentieth Century*. 1986. Repr., Baltimore: Johns Hopkins University Press, 1996.

DeMoss, Dorothy. *The History of Apparel Manufacturing in Texas, 1897–1981*. Garland Studies in Entrepreneurship. New York: Garland, 1989.

Dereshinsky, Ralph M., Alan D. Berkowitz, and Philip A. Miscimarra. *The NLRB and Secondary Boycotts*. Rev. ed., Labor Relations and Public Policy Series, no. 4. Philadelphia: Trustees of the University of Pennsylvania, 1985.

Deslippe, Dennis Arthur. *"Rights, Not Roses": Unions and the Rise of Working-Class Feminism, 1945–1980*. Urbana: University of Illinois Press, 2000.

Draper, Alan. *Conflict of Interests: Organized Labor and the Civil Rights Movement in the South, 1954–1968*. Cornell Studies in Industrial and Labor Relations, no. 29. Ithaca, N. Y.: ILR Press, 1994.

Durr, Virginia Foster. *Outside the Magic Circle: The Autobiography of Virginia Foster Durr*. Edited by Hollinger F. Barnard. 1985. Repr., Tuscaloosa: University of Alabama Press, 1990.

Dye, Nancy Schrom. *As Equals and Sisters: Feminism, the Labor Movement, and the Women's Trade Union League of New York*. Columbia: University of Missouri Press, 1980.

Edwards, Laura F. *The People and Their Peace: Legal Culture and the Transformation of Inequality in the Post-revolutionary South.* Chapel Hill: University of North Carolina Press, 2009.

English, Beth. *A Common Thread: Labor, Politics and Capital Mobility in the Textile Industry.* Athens: University of Georgia Press, 2006.

Evans, Sara. *Born for Liberty: A History of Women in America.* 2nd ed. New York: Simon & Schuster, 1997.

―――. *Personal Politics: The Roots of Women's Liberation in the Civil Rights Movement and the New Left.* New York: Alfred Knopf, 1979.

Faue, Elizabeth. *Community of Suffering and Struggle: Women, Men, and the Labor Movement in Minneapolis, 1915–1945.* Chapel Hill: University of North Carolina Press, 1991.

Fehn, Bruce. "'Chickens Come Home to Roost': Industrial Reorganization, Seniority, and Gender Conflict in the United Packinghouse Workers of America, 1955–1966." *Labor History* 34 (Spring–Summer 1993): 324–41.

Flamming, Douglas. *Creating the Modern South: Millhands and Managers in Dalton, Georgia, 1884–1984.* Chapel Hill: University of North Carolina Press, 1992.

Foner, Philip S. *Organized Labor and the Black Worker, 1619–1981.* 2nd ed. New York: International Publishers, 1982.

Forbath, William E. *Law and the Shaping of the American Labor Movement.* 1989. Repr., Cambridge, Mass.: Harvard University Press, 1991.

Frank, Dana. *Buy American: The Untold Story of Economic Nationalism.* Boston: Beacon Press,1999.

―――. *Purchasing Power: Consumer Organizing, Gender, and the Seattle Labor Movement, 1919–1929.* Cambridge: Cambridge University Press, 1994.

Frederickson, Mary. "Four Decades of Change: Black Workers in Southern Textiles, 1941–1981." In *Workers' Struggles, Past and Present: A 'Radical America' Reader,* edited by James Green, 62–71. Philadelphia: Temple University Press 1983.

―――. "'I Know Which Side I'm On': Southern Women in the Labor Movement in the Twentieth-Century South." In *Women, Work and Protest: A Century of U.S. Women's Labor History,* edited by Ruth Milkman, 156–80. Boston: Routledge & Kegan Paul, 1985.

Friedman, Tami J. "'What Price Industry?': Southern Organizing and the Runaway Shop, 1946–1966." Paper presented at the annual Southern Labor Studies Conference, Williamsburg, Va., September 1997.

Gabin, Nancy. *Feminism in the Labor Movement: Women and the United Auto Workers, 1935–1975.* Ithaca, N.Y.: Cornell University Press, 1990.

Gall, Gilbert J. *The Politics of Right to Work: The Labor Federations as Special Interests, 1943–1979.* New York: Greenwood Press, 1988.

Gaston, Paul M. *The New South Creed: A Study in Southern Mythmaking.* New York: Knopf, 1970.

Gilmore, Glenda Elizabeth. *Gender and Jim Crow: Women and the Politics of White Supremacy in North Carolina, 1896–1920*. Chapel Hill: University of North Carolina Press, 1996.

Goldfield, David R. *Cotton Fields and Skyscrapers: Southern City and Region*. 1982. Repr., Baltimore: Johns Hopkins University Press, 1989.

Goldfield, Michael. "The Failure of Operation Dixie: A Critical Turning Point in American Political Development?" In *Race, Class, and Community in Southern Labor History*, edited by Gary Fink and Merle Reed, 166–89. Tuscaloosa: University of Alabama Press, 1994.

Gordon, David M., Richard Edwards, and Michael Reich. *Segmented Work, Divided Workers: The Historical Transformation of Labor in the United States*. London: Cambridge University Press, 1982.

Gordon, Linda. *Pitied but Not Entitled: Single Mothers and the History of Welfare, 1890–1935*. New York: Free Press, 1994.

Glenn, Susan A. *Daughters of the Shetl: Life and Labor in the Immigrant Generation*. Ithaca, N.Y.: Cornell University Press, 1991.

Glickman, Lawrence B., ed. *Consumer Society in American History: A Reader*. Ithaca, N.Y.: Cornell University Press, 1999.

Green, Elna C. *Looking for the New Deal: Florida Women's Letters during the Great Depression*. Columbia: University of South Carolina Press, 2007.

———. "Relief from Relief: The Tampa Sewing Room Strike of 1937 and the Right to Welfare." *Journal of American History* 95:4 (March 2009): 1012–37.

Green, James. "Gone South." *American Prospect* 11:24 (November 20, 2000): 51–53.

Green, Nancy. *Ready to Wear and Ready-to-Work: A Century of Industry and Immigrants in Paris and New York*. Raleigh, N.C.: Duke University Press, 1997.

Greenberg, Cheryl. "Don't Buy Where You Can't Work." In *Consumer Society in American History: A Reader*, edited by Lawrence B. Glickman, 241–73. Ithaca, N.Y.: Cornell University Press, 1999.

Griffith, Barbara. *The Crisis of American Labor: Operation Dixie and the Defeat of the CIO*. Philadelphia: Temple University Press, 1988.

Hall, Jacquelyn Dowd. "Disorderly Women: Gender and Labor Militancy in the Appalachian South." *Journal of American History* 73 (September 1986): 354–82.

———. "The Long Civil Rights Movement and the Political Uses of the Past." *Journal of American History* 91:4 (March 2005): 1233–63.

Hall, Jacquelyn Dowd, Robert Korstad, and James Leloudis. "Cotton Mill People: Work, Community, and Protest in the Textile South, 1880–1940." *American Historical Review* 91(April 1986): 245–86.

Hall, Jacquelyn Dowd, James L. Leloudis, Robert Rodgers Korstad, Mary Murphy, Lu Ann Jones, and Christopher B. Daly. *Like a Family: The Making of a Southern Cotton Mill World*. Chapel Hill: University of North Carolina Press, 1987.

Halpern, Rick. "Organized Labour, Black Workers and the Twentieth-Century South: The Emerging Revision." *Social History* 19 (October 1994): 359–83.

Halpern, Rick, and Melvyn Stokes, eds. *Race and Class in the American South since 1860*. Oxford: Berg, 1994.

Hardman, J. B. S. *The Amalgamated: Today and Tomorrow; the Accomplishments, the Policies and the Aims of the Organized Clothing Workers of the Nation*. New York: Amalgamated Clothing Workers of America, 1939.

Heckman, James J., and Brook S. Payner. "Determining the Impact of Federal Antidiscrimination Policy on the Economic Status of Blacks: A Study of South Carolina." *American Economic Review* 79 (March 1989): 138–77.

Helmbold, Lois Rita. "Downward Occupational Mobility during the Great Depression: Urban Black and White Working Women." *Labor History* 29 (Spring 1988): 135–72.

Hill, Herbert. "The ILGWU Today: The Decay of a Labor Union." *New Politics* 1:4 (1962): 6–17.

———. "Lichtenstein's Fictions: Meany, Reuther, and The 1964 Civil Rights Act." *New Politics*, n.s., 7:1 (Summer 1998): 82–107.

———. "Lichtenstein's Fictions Revisited: Race and the New Labor History." *New Politics*, n.s., 7:2 (Winter 1999): 148–63.

———. "Myth-Making as Labor History: Herbert Gutman and the United Mine Workers of America." *New Politics* 2 (1988): 132–41.

———. "Race, Ethnicity, and Organized Labor: The Opposition to Affirmative Action." *New Politics* 1 (1987): 31–77.

———. "The Racial Practices of Organized Labor: The Contemporary Record." In *The Negro and the American Labor Movement*, edited by Julius Jacobson, 186–357. New York: Anchor Books, 1968.

———. "A Reply to Gus Tyler: The ILGWU, Fact and Fiction." *New Politics* 2:2 (1963): 17–27.

Hill, Patricia Evridge. "Dallas Garment Workers' Strike." *Handbook of Texas Online*, accessed July 22, 2012, http://www.tshaonline.org/handbook/online/articles/oedfb.

———. "Real Women and True Womanhood: Grassroots Organizing among Dallas Dressmakers in 1935." *Labor's Heritage* 5 (Spring 1994): 4–17.

Hirsch, Barry T., David A. Macpherson, and Wayne G. Vroman. "Estimates of Union Density by State." *Monthly Labor Review* 124:7 (July 2001): 51–55.

Hodges, James A. *New Deal Labor Policy and the Southern Cotton Textile Industry, 1933–1941*. Knoxville: University of Tennessee Press, 1986.

Honey, Michael K. "Operation Dixie: Labor and Civil Rights in the Postwar South." *Mississippi Quarterly* 45:4 (Fall 1992): 443–50.

———. *Southern Labor and Black Civil Rights: Organizing Memphis Workers*. Urbana: University of Illinois Press, 1993.

Honig, Emily. "Women at Farah Revisited: Political Mobilization and Its After-
    math among Chicana Workers in El Paso, Texas, 1972–1992." *Feminist Studies*
    22 (Summer 1996): 425–52.
Hunter, Tera. *"To 'joy My Freedom": Southern Black Women's Lives and Labors after
    the Civil War.* Cambridge, Mass.: Harvard University Press, 1997.
Ingalls, Robert P. "The Wagner Act on Trial: Vigilante Violence and the Struggle to
    Organize Textile Workers in Fitzgerald, Georgia, 1937–1940." *Georgia Historical
    Quarterly* 80 (Summer 1997): 370–94.
Irons, Janet Christine. *Testing the New Deal: The General Textile Strike of 1934 in the
    American South.* Chicago: University of Illinois Press, 2000.
Janiewski, Dolores E. *Sisterhood Denied: Race, Gender, and Class in a New South
    Community.* Philadelphia: Temple University Press, 1985.
Jensen, Joan M., and Sue Davidson, eds. *A Needle, a Bobbin, a Strike: Women Nee-
    dleworkers in America.* Philadelphia: Temple University Press, 1984.
Kerber, Linda. *Women of the Republic: Intellect and Ideology in Revolutionary
    America.* 1980. Repr., New York: W.W. Norton, 1986.
Kessler-Harris, Alice. *Out to Work: A History of Wage-Earning Women in the United
    States.* Oxford: Oxford University Press, 1982.
King, Martin Luther Jr. *"All Labor Has Dignity."* Edited by Michael K. Honey. Bos-
    ton: Beacon Press, 2011.
Kleiner, Lydia. *Oral History Interview with Evelyn Dubrow, International Ladies'
    Garment Workers' Union.* The 20th-Century Trade Union Woman: Vehicle for
    Social Change Oral History Project. Ann Arbor: University of Michigan, 1978.
Kluger, Richard. *Simple Justice: The History of* Brown v. Board of Education *and
    Black America's Struggle for Equality.* 1975. Repr., New York: Vintage Books, 1977.
Korstad, Robert. "Daybreak of Freedom: Tobacco Workers and the CIO, Winston-
    Salem, North Carolina, 1943–1950." PhD diss., University of North Carolina at
    Chapel Hill, 1987.
Korstad, Robert, and Nelson Lichtenstein, "Opportunities Found and Lost: Labor,
    Radicals, and the Early Civil Rights Movement." *Journal of American History* 75
    (December 1988): 786–811.
Lahne, Herbert J. *The Cotton Mill Worker.* New York: Farrah and Rinehart, 1944.
Lapides, Kenny. *The Battle of the Boycott: Free Speech for Labor.* New York: Center
    for United Labor Action, 1974.
Leiter, Jeffrey, Michael D. Shulman, and Rhonda Zingraff, eds. *Hanging By a
    Thread: Social Change in the Southern Textiles.* Ithaca, N.Y.: ILR Press, 1991.
Lepawsky, Albert. *State Planning and Economic Development in the South.* King-
    sport, Tenn.: Kingsport Press, 1949.
Letwin, Daniel. *The Challenge of Interracial Unionism: Alabama Coal Miners, 1878–
    1921.* Chapel Hill: University of North Carolina Press, 1998.
Levine, Louis. *The Women's Garment Workers: A History of the International Ladies'*

Garment Workers' Union. New York: B.W. Huebsch, 1924. Repr., New York: Arno and the *New York Times*, 1969.

Lichtenstein, Nelson. *The Most Dangerous Man in Detroit: Walter Reuther and the State of American Labor*. New York: Basic Books, 1995.

———. "Walter Reuther in Black and White: A Rejoinder to Herbert Hill." *New Politics*, n.s. 7:2 (Winter 1999): 133–42.

Lim, Linda. "Women's Work in Export Factories: The Politics of a Cause." In *Persistent Inequalities: Women and World Development*, edited by Irene Tinker, 101–22. New York: Oxford University Press, 1990.

MacLean, Nancy. "Postwar Women's History: The 'Second Wave' or the End of the Family Wage?" In *A Companion to Post-1945 America*, edited by Jean-Christophe Agnew and Roy Rosenzweig, 235–59. 2002. Repr., Malden, Mass.: Blackwell Publishing, 2006.

Marshall, F. Ray. *Employment of Blacks in the South: A Perspective on the 1960s*. Austin: University of Texas Press, 1978.

———. *Labor in the South*. Cambridge, Mass.: Harvard University Press, 1967.

———. *The Negro and Organized Labor*. New York: John Wiley & Sons, 1965.

Massey, Doreen. *Spatial Divisions of Labor*. 2nd ed. New York: Routledge, 1995.

McArthur, Judith N., and Harold L. Smith. *Texas through Women's Eyes: The Twentieth-Century Experience*. Austin: University of Texas Press, 2010.

McCreesh, Carolyn Daniel. *Women in the Campaign to Organize Garment Workers, 1880–1917*. New York: Garland, 1985.

McGill, Ralph. *The South and the Southerner*. Boston: Little, Brown and Company, 1963. Repr., Athens: University of Georgia Press, 1992.

McLaurin, Melton A. *Paternalism and Protest: Southern Cotton Mill Workers and Organized Labor, 1875–1905*. Westport, Conn.: Greenwood, 1971.

McLemore, Richard Aubrey, ed. *A History of Mississippi*. Vol. 2. Hattiesburg: University and College Press of Mississippi, 1973.

McLendon, Paula. "Time and Time Again: The Women, the Union and the Vanity Factory." *Southern Changes* 6 (October/November 1984): 8–17.

McMillen, Neil. *The Citizens' Council: Organized Resistance to the South's Second Reconstruction, 1954–1964*. Urbana: University of Illinois Press, 1971.

Milkman, Ruth. *Gender at Work: The Dynamics of Job Segregation by Sex during World War II*. Urbana: University of Illinois Press, 1987.

———, ed. *Women, Work, and Protest: A Century of Women' Labor History*. Boston: Routledge & Kegan Paul, 1985.

Minchin, Timothy J. "'Color Means Something': Black Pioneers, White Resistance, and Interracial Unionism in the Southern Textile Industry, 1957–1980." *Labor History* 39 (May 1998): 109–33.

———. *"Don't Sleep with Stevens!" The J. P. Stevens Campaign and the Struggle to Organize the South, 1963–80*. Gainesville: University Press of Florida, 2005.

———. *Hiring the Black Worker: The Racial Integration of the Southern Textile Industry, 1960–1980*. Chapel Hill: University of North Carolina Press, 1999.

———. *"What Do We Need a Union For?": The TWUA in the South, 1945–1955*. Chapel Hill: University of North Carolina Press, 1997.

Mitchell, Broadus Mitchell. *The Rise of Cotton Mills in the South*. 1921. Repr., Gloucester, Mass.: P. Smith, 1966.

Montgomery, David. "The Struggle for Unions in the South." In *Perspectives on the American South: Annual Review of Society and Politics and Culture*, vol. 1, edited by John Shelton Reed and Merle Black, 35–47. New York: Gordon and Breach, 1981.

Nelson, Bruce. *Divided We Stand: American Workers and the Struggle for Black Equality*. Princeton, N.J.: Princeton University Press, 2001.

Newby, I. A. *Plain Folk in the New South: Social Change and Cultural Persistence, 1880–1915*. Baton Rouge: Louisiana State University Press, 1989.

Norrell, Robert J. "Caste in Steel: Jim Crow Careers in Birmingham Alabama." *Journal of American History* 75 (1988): 786–811.

Northrup, Herbert R., and Richard L. Rowan. *Negro Employment in Southern Industry*. Philadelphia: Industrial Research Unit, Wharton School of Finance and Commerce, University of Pennsylvania, 1970.

O'Farrell, Brigid, and Joyce L. Kornbluh. *Rocking the Boat: Union Women's Voices, 1915–1975*. New Brunswick, N.J.: Rutgers University Press, 1996.

Page, Erin Mackenzie. "The Intersectoral Incidence of the National Industrial Recovery Act: Did the Blue Eagle Play Favorites?" PhD diss., Harvard University, 1993.

Patton, Randall J. "'A World of Opportunity . . . within the Tufting Empire?' Labor Relations in North Georgia's Carpet Industry, 1960–1975." *Georgia Historical Quarterly* 80 (Summer 1997): 426–51.

Peña, Devon Gerardo. "Las Maquiladoras: Mexican Women and Class Struggle in the Border Industries." *Aztlan* 11 (Fall 1982): 159–229.

Pratt, Robert A. *We Shall Not Be Moved: The Desegregation of the University of Georgia*. Athens: University of Georgia Press, 2002.

Reich, Michael, David M. Gordon, and Richard Edwards. "A Theory of Labor Market Segmentation." *American Economic Review* 63:2 (May 1973): 359–65.

Rodengen, Jeffrey L. *The Legend of VF Corporation*. Ft. Lauderdale: Write Stuff Syndicate, 1998.

Roediger, David. *Towards the Abolition of Whiteness: Essays on Race, Politics, and Working-Class History*. London: Verso, 1994.

Roediger, David R., and Elizabeth D. Esch. *The Production of Difference: Race and the Management of Labor in U.S. History*. Oxford: Oxford University Press, 2012.

Rosen, Ellen Israel. *Making Sweatshops: The Globalization of the U.S. Apparel Industry*. Berkeley: University of California Press, 2002.

Salmond, John A. *The General Textile Strike of 1934: From Maine to Alabama.* Columbia: University of Missouri Press, 2002.

Schulman, Bruce J. *From Cotton Belt to Sunbelt: Federal Policy, Economic Development, & the Transformation of the South, 1938–1980.* Durham, N.C.: Duke University Press, 1994.

Scott, Anne Firor. *The Southern Lady: From Pedestal to Politics, 1830–1930.* 1970. Repr., Charlottesville: University Press of Virginia, 1995.

Simon, Bryant. "Rethinking Why There Are So Few Unions in the South." *Georgia Historical Quarterly* 80 (Summer 1997): 465–84.

Spedden, Ernest R. *The Trade Union Label.* Baltimore, Md.: Johns Hopkins Press, 1910.

Spero, Sterling D., and Abram L. Harris. *The Black Worker.* New York: Columbia University Press, 1931.

Steedman, Mercedes. *Angels of the Workplace: Women and the Construction of Gender Relations in the Canadian Clothing Industry, 1890–1940.* Toronto: Oxford University Press, 1997.

Stein, Leon. *Out of the Sweatshop: The Struggle for Industrial Democracy.* New York: Quadrangle/The New York Times Book Co., 1977.

Stevens, Evelyn P. "*Marianismo*: The Other Face of *Machismo.*" In *Confronting Change, Challenging Tradition: Women in Latin American History*, edited by Gertrude M. Yeager, 3–17. Wilmington, Del.: Scholarly Resources, 1994.

Stoney, George, Judith Helfand, and Susanne Rostock. *The Uprising of '34.* Directed by George Stoney and Judith Helfand. New York: First Run/Icarus Films, 1995. VHS.

Terrill, Tom. "No Union for Me." In *The Meaning of South Carolina History: Essays in Honor of George C. Rogers, Jr.*, edited by David R. Chesnutt and Clyde N. Wilson, 202–13. Columbia: University of South Carolina Press, 1991.

Thomas, Mary Martha. *Riveting and Rationing in Dixie: Alabama Women and the Second World War.* Tuscaloosa: University of Alabama Press, 1988.

Tiano, Susan B. "Export Processing, Women's Work, and the Employment Problem in Developing Countries: The Case of the *Maquiladora* Program in Northern Mexico." *Western Sociological Review* 15:1 (1986): 53–78.

———. *Patriarchy on the Line: Labor, Gender, and Ideology in the Mexican Maquila Industry.* Philadelphia: Temple University Press, 1994.

Tindall, George Brown. *The Emergence of the New South: 1913–1945.* Baton Rouge: Louisiana State University Press, 1967.

Tomlins, Christopher L., and Andrew J. King , eds. *Labor Law in America: Historical and Critical Essays.* Baltimore: Johns Hopkins University Press, 1992.

Tullos, Allen. *Habits of Industry: White Culture and the Transformation of the Carolina Piedmont.* Chapel Hill: University of North Carolina Press, 1989.

Tyler, Gus. "Contemporary Labor's Attitude toward the Negro." In *The Negro and the American Labor Movement,* edited by Julius Jacobson, 358–79. New York: Anchor Books, 1968.

———. *Look for the Union Label: A History of the International Ladies' Garment Workers' Union.* Armonk, N.Y.: M.E. Sharpe, 1995.

———. "The Truth about the ILGWU." *New Politics* 2 (1962): 1–12.

Van Liemt, Gijsbert, ed. *Industry on the Move: Causes and Consequences of International Relocation in the Manufacturing Industry.* Geneva: International Labour Office, 1992.

Woodward, C. Vann. *Origins of the New South, 1877–1913.* 1951. Repr., Baton Rouge: Louisiana State University Press, 1971.

———. *The Strange Career of Jim Crow.* 3rd ed. New York: Oxford University Press, 1974.

Wrong, Elaine Gale. *The Negro in the Apparel Industry.* The Racial Policies of American Industry Series, no. 31. Philadelphia: Industrial Research Unit, the Wharton School, University of Pennsylvania, 1974.

Wyatt-Brown, Bertram. *Southern Honor: Ethics and Behavior in the Old South.* New York: Oxford University Press, 1982.

Yeager, Gertrude M. *Confronting Change, Challenging Tradition: Women in Latin American History.* Wilmington, Del.: Scholarly Resources, 1994.

Zieger, Robert H. *American Workers, American Unions, 1920–1985.* Baltimore: Johns Hopkins University Press, 1986.

———. *The CIO: 1935–1955.* Chapel Hill: University of North Carolina Press, 1995.

———. *Organized Labor in the Twentieth-Century South.* Knoxville: University of Tennessee Press, 1991.

———. *Southern Labor in Transition, 1940–1995.* Knoxville: University of Tennessee Press, 1997.

Index